The Sociology of the Body

D1595521

The Sociology of the Body

Mapping the Abstraction of Embodiment

Kate Cregan

⑤ SAGE Publications

London ● Thousand Oaks ● New Delhi

First published 2006

SAGE Publications Ltd
1 Oliver's Yard
55 City Road
London EC1Y 1SP

SAGE Publications Inc.
2455 Teller Road
Thousand Oaks, California 91320

SAGE Publications India Pvt Ltd
B-42, Panchsheel Enclave
Post Box 4109
New Delhi 110 017

British Library Cataloguing in Publication data

A catalogue record for this book is available
from the British Library

ISBN-10 0 7619 4023 5   ISBN-13 978 0 7619 4023 4
ISBN-10 0 7619 4024 3 (pbk)   ISBN-13 978 0 7619 4024 1

Library of Congress control number 2005928001

Typeset by C&M Digitals (P) Ltd., Chennai, India
Printed on paper from sustainable resources
Printed and bound in Great Britain by Athenaeum Press, Gateshead

For friendship

Contents

Author Details

Dr Kate Cregan is an Australian Research Council postdoctoral research fellow in the Globalism Institute, RMIT University. She has also been an Honorary Research Associate of the Department of Politics, Monash University during the writing of this book.

She is currently completing a three-year research project on the social impact – from the local to the global – of embryonic stem cell technology at the Globalism Institute. All her research is concerned with social ethics and embodiment, most particularly in relation to the history and philosophy of medicine. Her writing ranges from studies of anatomy and criminality in seventeenth-century London, to the bio-medical trade in human tissues, to the commemoration of non-combatants killed in violent conflict. She is particularly interested in the variation in understandings of embodiment across time, space and culture.

Acknowledgements

First I would like to acknowledge and thank Chris Rojek, both for commissioning this book and for his ongoing support of its publication. I would also like to thank Sage assistant editors, Kay Bridger and Mila Steele, and assistant rights manager Huw Alexander, whose efficiency and helpfulness have been greatly appreciated, and the anonymous reader whose kind words and expert criticism I accept with gratitude.

Next I should like to express my gratitude for the institutional support I received. I must thank Monash University, where I was working on a postdoctoral fellowship when I began writing this book. In particular I would like to thank Dennis Woodward of the Department of Politics, for his thorough-going decency and generosity of spirit, and Denise Cuthbert, for her encouragement and friendship over many years. Second, my thanks must go to the Australian Research Council for granting me the research fellowship during which most of this book was written. More importantly, I would like to thank my friends and colleagues at the Globalism Institute – Damian Grenfell, Paul James, Martin Mulligan, Yaso Nadarajah, Tom Nairn, Peter Phipps, Leanne Reinke, Chris Scanlon and Christopher Ziguras – for creating the most collegially supportive and intellectually stimulating working environment I have known. I thank them particularly for their support in the difficult final stages of writing this book. I also extend my sincere thanks to Helen Hickey and Anna Trembath for providing invaluable administrative support and expert research assistance as the final manuscript took shape.

At a more personal level, I would like to thank Christopher Scanlon for his irrepressible sense of humour and for proofing the final manuscript at short notice. I also thank Alan Roberts for his moral support and a kindly ear on many a dog-walk. I am always thankful for my son, Camille Robinson, but in this case I thank him most of all for his appreciation of the fine line between tragedy and farce, and his keen sense of the absurd. During the writing of this book I turned on my computer one morning ... and it didn't. Forty thousand words of this book and as many again of other writing were lost. And we laughed.

Finally, my sincerest thanks go to Paul James, Stephanie Trigg and Joel Trigg for their kindness, their generosity, their love of music, and for lending me a quiet space when I needed it most. My deepest thanks go to Paul, without whose sustained friendship and support this book would not have been written.

Introduction

It has become commonplace that there is a tension within classical social theory, in particular between Marx, Weber and Durkheim. This has played out across modern sociology and the way it tends to treat the body as an object of study. Marxist-influenced sociology has emphasised the social relations of groups and classes. Liberal sociology has tended to concentrate on either the work of the mind or the interactions of (embodied) individuals rather than on the question of embodiment itself. It has concentrated on how either materially resonant artefacts of the mind or 'social facts' – opinions, beliefs, responses, and group, socio-economic or cultural identifications – can be experienced between individuals and collectively acted upon. In this sense it has been much easier to account for the differentiated (individuated) body, and to argue for its 'ownership' and rights within theories reliant on liberal individualism than in theories based in ideas of collectivity or group interaction. Nevertheless, in both trajectories the body has until recently been largely taken for granted. Over the past two decades this has changed. The body and embodiment have become objects of direct critical reflection.

Anthropology on the other hand, especially when it has been – or perhaps because it has been – concerned with societies that interact more immediately through embodied relations, has given a more prominent place to bodily matters. Tribal peoples' interactions are likely to be more face-to-face, more immediate and embodied, than the relations between technologically mediated, modern/postmodern individuals. But even in dealing with embodied relations, anthropologists on the whole have historically also paid far more attention to the verbal and symbolic meaning of those interactions than to the intrinsic corporeality of that ontology. This too has changed.

In sociology, the change has been thanks in part to the publication of such books as Bryan Turner's *The Body and Society* (1984) and

Featherstone, Hepworth and Turner's *The Body: Social Process and Cultural Theory* (1991), which helped lay the groundwork for the emergence of the sociology of the body. They were reacting to a shift that was already occurring in other disciplines, much of which was influenced by the work of Michel Foucault. Further, the journals *Theory, Culture & Society* (1982 to the present) and *Body & Society* (1995 to the present) have been central to the promulgation of this area of sociological theorisation, providing a vital forum for those conducting research on the body. They have published work from some of the most influential writers in, and those on the cutting edge of, the field.

In the second edition of *The Body and Society* (1996) Bryan Turner remarks that, up until the first edition of his book in 1984, sociology had largely been blind to the body. Turner is right in the sense that the body was often taken to be merely an interface at which social interaction took place, and that that interface was often unthinkingly treated or read through an undifferentiated norm (the body as white, heterosexual, able-bodied, adult, male). In this sense, all academic disciplines had been body-blind until at least the early 1970s. Chris Shilling (1993) is also right, however, that the body was always 'there' in sociological or anthropological theories: it was just not explicitly accounted for. For example, in Mauss's work one of the most potent gifts exchanged between social groups is the human body, in the form of wives or children, and yet this is explained in terms of its symbolic or social rather than its material, gendered, embodied content. Indeed, in his all too brief but highly suggestive work on 'body techniques' in the early 1930s, Mauss prefigured much of the work on the sociology and anthropology of the body (Mauss 1979). In sociology, Simmel's discussion of 'the stranger' similarly gestures towards and yet elides the delineation of that stranger on the basis of physical, embodied difference. He focuses instead on cultural displacement. Overall we can say that embodiment as a grounding condition of social existence was, like other ontological categories such as time and space, implicit but unrecognised.

Noting the absence of a theorisation of social embodiment was an enormously important first move. It is just as important, however, to move on and to look at how this incorporation of embodiment into sociological and anthropological theory has proceeded from what, with the benefit of 20–20 hindsight, has become blindingly obvious: bodies are socially integrated and socially important phenomena.

Shilling's *The Body and Social Theory* (1993) offered future directions for the sociology of the body and he has recently returned to his theme, in *The Body in Culture, Technology and Society* (2005). *The Sociology of the*

Body has a related project though with a different, but complementary, emphasis. Shilling's command of sociological approaches to the body is comprehensive and acute, as is Bryan Turner's; this allows each of them to identify the kernel of a writer's thought, to set it within the context of other writers, and to cover a field within the flow of their respective arguments. *The Sociology of the Body* instead takes key theorists who are representative of a trend in the study of the body and treats core texts from each of those writers in detail. It does so by showing how their approaches were formed over time, offering an analysis of their arguments, and giving examples of either those who have followed in a given writer's footsteps or those who write in a cognate field. *The Sociology of the Body* does this while framing its trajectories within a broader theory of bodily abstraction.

Arguing from Abstraction

Embodiment – the physical and mental experience of existence – is the condition of possibility for our relating to other people and to the world. Fully able or seriously disabled, it is through our physicality that we function as social beings, whether in face-to-face communications, through hand-written letters, printed missives, or by keying disembodied electronic symbols into a computer to 'stay in touch' with someone half a world away. Embodied social relations exist both as the context (the prior circumstances) and as an outcome (a consequence) of given social formations, given systems through which we create and gain social meaning.

The ways in which different societies constitute social practice affect how that meaning is shaped, presented or represented. And both within and across societies those meanings can change. Rules of bodily probity, for example, vary enormously across cultures. Blowing one's nose directly into one's hand and quickly discarding the product is proper in one culture; blowing into a piece of cloth and keeping that cloth about one's person, proper in another – each finds the alternative equally distasteful. People living in tribal or traditional societies have a fundamentally different sense of their bodies and their embodied relations with their community. These differences also occur across time within a given culture. The dead body of someone you knew – possibly your neighbour – was an unremarkable sight in medieval Europe, particularly during the plagues, even if it was never normalised as a moment emptied of emotions. The physicality of death was relatively open, public and ritually managed. In more recent times, the publication of such images as the assassinated Dutch politician Pym Fortuyn lying in a

Netherlands street, a man whom many people felt they 'knew' through the promulgation of his physical image in the media during his life, is considered shocking not just because of the violence that led to the fact. In contemporary Western culture even the photographic representation of death – unless it is in some safely 'anonymous' war zone or natural disaster – is now seen as a deeply private matter, unspeakable and to be resisted. The naked, floating dead damming the waterways of Bandah Aceh are fit fare for the nightly news, but the returned bodies of US soldiers killed in Iraq are not.

Within a society or culture, the slow and uneven shifts from the dominance of tribal and traditional to modern and postmodern social formations, are characterised by a shift in the dominant understanding of embodiment.[1] Those shifts have involved an increasing abstraction, a lifting away from and re-presentation or reconstituting reinterpretation, of embodiment. More concrete social interaction – such as face-to-face communication – is reconstituted at one remove: technological interventions such as writing or print culture are examples of vehicles of this abstraction. Which is not to say that those prior forms are obliterated, they are not: but they are fundamentally altered by the cumulative layers – the social accretions – that like a palimpsest build upon and remake earlier forms. Nor, it must be stressed, are dominant forms of embodiment entirely successful in succeeding those prior forms. Life is never that tidy. Nor is a 'prior' form in any sense less sophisticated or complex than what succeeds it. Prior forms exist alongside – often in tension – with later forms. It should also be stressed that, while there are often historical precedents by which to gauge them, these are not simply shifts of epoch (history), but shifts in ontology (meaningful existence as practised).

> Embodiment is lived across all forms of community as a deeply-embedded social-relational category. It is an ontological category constituted as both the context and the outcome of patterns of social practice and meaning ... Different social formations are framed in terms of fundamentally different dominant senses of embodiment ... Across history, more abstract modes of living our bodies have become layered across more concrete ways of doing so, reconstituting rather than replacing those 'prior' forms. That is, across world-time and world-space, bodies are constituted in differently intersecting levels of abstraction ... This reconstitution of embodiment has political consequences intimately connected to the abstraction of time and space. As the dominant ways in which we live have become more abstract, our bodies have become more open to processes of rationalization, objectification, commodification and political-cultural management. (James 2006)[2]

The turn to theorising the body, from the late-twentieth century into the present, is a particular moment in this reconstitution of the body through abstraction – both in terms of how our bodies are lived (ontology) and how they are known (epistemology). In other words, both the practice and the theory have, at one level, been changing in relation to each other.

4

Over the past two or three decades the body has become an object of theoretical reflection: rationalised, abstracted and reconstituted as a socio-logical object. Simultaneously, the experience of embodiment has been subject to an intensification of the extension, abstraction and reconstitution of the individual's body via technological and bio-technological means. Not only has the turning to the body as an object of theoretical reflection marked the moments of intensification, but it has also participated in and shaped that intensification. Feminist Donna Haraway's techno-fantasy of the cyborg body (discussed in Chapter 6) is a case in point. It is a body that can be reimagined beyond the limitations of physical embodiment: part corporeal matter, part techno-machine.

As James argues, there are political consequences in the constitution of embodiment in these fundamentally different, imbricated social forma-tions. Different relations to and understandings of time and space are fundamental to the processes of abstraction, as can be seen in the example already cited of the shift from the dominance of oral communication to that of writing, print and electronic communication. People in societies predominantly dependent on oral communication relate in the moment, in the presence of the person with whom they are communicating. The social framing of that moment links people to others across time and space, but it remains held together by modalities of presence. An email is increasingly perceived as an immediate and on occasion deeply personal communica-tion, and yet its immediacy is framed by techniques and technologies of systematic mediation over (sometimes) vast distances that do not depend on embodied relations. It is an intensely abstracted immediacy. The more that new layers of abstracted relations and understandings come to medi-ate one's relation to one's own body and to others, the more one tends to rely on re-presenting oneself through the use of technological means. This ranges, for example, from simple technologies such as the bathroom scales to massive reconsiderations of the human body such as therapeutic cloning and the human genome project. In the process it becomes easier, and more naturally 'appropriate', to objectify, rationalise, quantify, package, process and market the self, and the other.

To reiterate, the argument from abstraction can be summarised into these steps:

1 We relate to each other as social beings through our embodied being, and the fact of our social interrelationships shapes the way we constitute our embodied being.

2 Different societies, different cultures, constitute embodiment in fundamentally different ways.

3 As social formations change over time, the settings in which bodies are lived layer more abstract disembodied relations over more immediately experienced embodied relations. Importantly,

however, that does not mean that prior understandings of embodiment disappear: different 'embodiments' can and do co-exist, albeit in tension.

4   Those shifts, and the intensification of the processes of abstraction, are related to wider shifts in interpretations of the physical world and our relation to it, which in turn lead to an intensification of the rationalisation (the body as particularised, divisible object) and commodification (the body as property) of embodiment.

Each of these facets underpins the writing encompassed by this book. It needs to be said, however, that the theorists and subject matter of this book are based in Eurocentred 'body theory'. Even if a theory has come out of the ethnographic observation of African, Papuan or Polynesian cultures, it has largely been through the work of Western academics. Because this is a book on what is most influential in current academic social theory, and it is Western social theory that has 'found' the body, that is almost inevitable. Further, modern forms of embodiment are increasingly the dominant forms of embodiment across cultures: with the intensification of globalisation, they are infiltrating and reshaping other traditions of embodied being. Media communications, political incursions, a multiplicity of United Nations, World Trade Organization, and World Health Organization initiatives disseminate a dominant form of embodiment in film, television, internet, commercial products, medical regimes, work patterns, monetary 'reform' and educational programmes, amongst many influences. Even if different places have taken hold of the waves of modernisation and postmodernisation in varying ways, practices of embodiment across the globe have had to come to terms with the effects of European expansion. Western 'progress', or 'civilisation', continues to make incursions into and foster the reconstitution of the cultural forms it encounters, just as it has broken down and re-formed earlier forms of embodiment and society within Western culture.

The advantage of approaching theorisations of embodiment through the idea of bodily abstraction is that it gives a means of addressing the historical and cultural variation that arises in and across each of the sections. Modes of abstraction are observable across and between cultural and/or historical forms. For instance, the conceptions of embodiment that Mary Douglas, Norbert Elias or Donna Haraway write about are fundamentally different in ways that are related to the qualities of the abstraction which they exhibit, which in turn are related to the social forms on which those writers focus – tribal, traditional, modern or postmodern – as well as those they inhabit.

To expand, Douglas deals largely with tribal societies and their customs as they have survived into the twentieth century. Elias traces the shift in manners related to bodily functions in Europe from the Middle Ages through to the early-twentieth century, covering a movement from traditional to modern social forms and the complementary understandings of acceptable bodily behaviour that obtained in each. Haraway writes of late-twentieth-century, modern, Western, industrialised societies and of fragmented, postmodern, technoscientific futures. To put it very simplistically, in a tribal society embodiment is more concretely lived and experienced than in a traditional, modern or postmodern society. Shifts in technological forms, techniques of ontological abstraction that range from the stethoscope to X-rays to MRIs, are implicated in shifts in self-understanding or self-representation which exhibit corresponding levels of abstraction from, and reintegration of, the embodied self. These shifts are observable through historical comparison within a culture or society, or across different, contemporaneous social or cultural forms.

It is important to recognise these differences, to be aware of the context from which these theories are garnered: for one, translation of a given sense of embodiment from one social setting to another can lead to anachronistic appropriation. As I have just acknowledged, for all the inclusion of issues of difference in the sociology of the body, at base most of the theories from which the discipline springs are based in Eurocentric notions of embodiment. Indeed, arguing from the position I am advocating allows one *to see* anachronistic appropriations inherent in some of the theories that are covered. There is always a danger in generalising theories that historical or cultural difference will become flattened out. There are also problems inherent in appropriating theories based in textual studies to the study of lived experience. Arguing from constitutive abstraction effects precisely the opposite: it accounts for and encourages the recognition of interleaving, contradictory forms of embodiment. The approach is a universalising, but not a flattening or teleological approach.

Object, Abject, Subject

The themes of object, abject and subject, which are used to structure this book, neatly encompass the uneven nature and shifts in the dominant theoretical approaches. These three themes refer to ways in which the body has been framed. The body as object is a body that is being shaped to conformity to external rules and regimes. The body as abject is a body that is socially ambivalent – sanctified and reviled – and that exceeds bodily boundaries and borders. The body as subject is a body that is very much invested in the individual and in individual experience within a wider social complex. In broad terms, theories that treat the body as a social object come out of studies of societies in which the body is less abstracted than the studies that deal with the social subject: the individual in society. The abject body falls between the two – sometimes tribal, sometimes French cosmopolitan. In the conclusion we will see how these approaches inform and cut across understandings of embodiment as they function in different social formations.

To expand, the theories that are dealt with under the theme of 'object' are based in studies across time within a culture, or across a culture within a specific timeframe: in each the body is treated as an entity that comes into being out of collective understandings. In the theories in which the body is treated as a social subject, the basis of bodily understanding tends to come out of individual experience, individual concerns or cultural groupings that, for all they may be committed to broad social ideals, rely heavily on appealing to neo-liberal individualistic rights. The abject body tends to come out of theories that – whether spiritual or psychoanalytic, contemporary or historic, based in studies of tribal or postmodern cultures – centre on the individually situated mental control of bodily acts and processes. This may be because most of them come out of theories that try to find universals – specifically cognitive universals – across cultures. For example, we will see in Chapter 4 how psychoanalytic theorist Julia Kristeva uses some of anthropologist Mary Douglas's explanations of tribal mores to explain psychological traits of modern and postmodern cultures, specifically feelings of attraction to and repulsion from bodily excretions. There is an implicit assumption that psychic traits are cross-cultural and pan-historical. As the reader may already see, arguing from abstraction places more emphasis on social and historical context, implicitly arguing against any such assumption.

Each of our three themes – the body as object, abject and subject – characterises a first move towards including the body as a specific sociological concern. The work of each of the writers addressed across these themes has been germinal for subsequent developments in theorisations of the body. The three themes of object, abject and subject also provide an entry into some of the most fecund areas of sociological and anthropological research into the body, while also allowing us to venture beyond these disciplines. The sociology of the body is the outcome of interdisciplinary research. Therefore, the writers who appear in this book are not all sociologists or anthropologists – critical theory, literary theory, cultural studies, women's studies, history and critical science studies have all been influential on the integration of the body into sociological and anthropological analysis.

Indeed there are numerous writers who have contributed in other fields to the critique of late-twentieth-century embodiment, whose work intersects with the concerns of this book even though they cannot be dealt with here. They have supported and extended historical scholarship on the body. For example, there has been important and influential work done on the place of the body in the history of Western religious thought that has been appealed to and deployed in contemporary debates on the ritual body in anthropology (Bynum Walker). Other historical and cultural studies have followed Foucault's example to trace the construction of the medicalised subject from the early-modern period to the end of the twentieth century (Barker, Jordanova, Gallagher, Laqueur). Feher's broad-ranging volumes contain numerous 'fragments', as he says, on cultural evidence for a history of the human body. There have also been successive critics of science and scientific methodology (Harding, Gatens) who took part in an opening of the way for a general reinterpretation of sex, sexuality and gender (Weeks, Synnott, Sontag). Some have also suggested thoughtful metaphors for questioning the supposed solidity of embodiment. Liz Grosz, for example, has asserted the body can be seen as voluntary, fluid, malleable and eternally undecided, like a möebius strip: worked and reworked into existence, resisting stable classification.

Nor should one forget that there are important, acknowledged precedents in sociology and anthropology that have recognised the centrality of the body in social relations. We will see in Chapter 1 how Norbert Elias's work addresses the power of social control through norms of bodily deportment or comportment, the function of the body as social object. Mary Douglas (Chapter 4) opened the way for discussions on corporeality in ritual and spirituality, and the interpretation of the body and/or its products as abject. And the plethora of feminist writers who brought to the forefront the social construction of sex and gender distinctions, have served as an impetus to the division of the body into many degrees of subjective difference (Chapters 6 and 7).

Part I: Object – the Regulated Body

Given how persistent the privileging of the mind over the body has become in the three-and-a-half centuries since Descartes dozed off in front of that mind-altering fire, it is not surprising that the recuperation of the body into social theory should have begun in terms of its status as an objectified entity. Each of the theorists in Part I of the book, while working hard to recuperate embodied being, does so (to varying degrees) by dealing with the body in its material, objectified state. Controlling, shaping and regulating behaviour is effected through the 'training up' of bodily motion or bodily habits. In doing so, even while there is an implicit credence or value accorded to physical being, the bifurcation between mind and body remains. The mind takes control of that in which it lives, even if it is seen as a slightly more symbiotic relationship than a ghost controlling a machine.

The study of the training up of the body, whether through manners (Elias), taste, or through the demarcation of life stages (Ariès), implicitly takes the body as an entity under the control of some other force (Chapter 1). That force may seem to be external, in court-ratified modes of behaviour, high-culinary tastes or socially ratified life-stages, but in each case they are in fact behavioural modifications that require the 'object' to internalise systems of control. As a social entity, a body is a social object insofar as attempts are made to subject it to social controls. Those social controls can be exerted in a range of ways. Customary controls, the regulation of social habits, socially acceptable behaviours, are exerted through the regulation of bodily habits. Any (Western) child knows that picking one's nose is not considered socially acceptable in public: they are constantly reminded that this is the case. They also gain great pleasure from subverting attempts to enforce that control, and are delighted when an adult is caught out at the traffic lights committing the same act in the supposed anonymity of their car. There are also bounds of what is acceptable in public and in private, as that same driver knows: it is just that he or she has mistaken the public privacy of the car cabin for an unobserved privacy, forgetting the transparency of the windows that surround the consolingly intimate space.

Institutional authorities – whether legal, medical or religious (Foucault – Chapter 2) – patrol the social body. The most wretched expression of this can be seen in recent cases of people with psychiatric diagnoses failing to adhere to socially acceptable norms of behaviour, coming under the purview of another institutional authority (the police) and being imprisoned or, in several tragic instances, shot dead. Foucault's contribution to the mechanisms of control of the body through social institutions – prisons, schools, hospitals, sexual mores – has had the most profound effect on the place of the body in all spheres of academic endeavour. While there are disputes about the way he has characterised embodiment and history, there can be no dispute that he changed the way people approach questions of embodiment. In each of these three examples – of customary, spatial and institutional controls – we see the body being taken as and treated like an object.

A similar dynamic is at work in the regulation of place and space (Bourdieu – Chapter 3). Individuals, family units or whole social sub-groups are corralled and routed into and out of specific social spaces (Sennett). There are means of policing private and public space, in the construction of cities, homes or shopping centres, through urban planning and the regulation of amenities like public transport. These facilities regulate us as a mass and as individuals. The breaking of those bounds can lead to public prosecution, even the pathologisation and detention of the individual if a given behaviour is characterised as a gross breach of social norms.

The three chapters in the first part of *The Sociology of the Body* look at theoretical streams of thought within sociology and anthropology that encompass the regulation of the objectified social body. They deal with the socially regulated body, in theorisations of social control through behavioural norms such as manners and eating habits on the micro level, and (institutional) religious, legal and political mechanisms on the macro level. They cover the ways in which the body has been constituted or modified through external and internalised power relations. There is also a historical turn in these chapters, with most of the authors investigating shifting social forms over time: the shifting nature of social norms makes clear both the historical contingency of ideas of embodiment and their differentiation along class lines.

Part II: Abject – the Bounded Body

Just as the objectified body approaches the reintegration of the body into social theory through a recuperation of Descartes's 'machine', the abjected body recuperates the body from the point of view of the individual 'ghost': the cogito's perceptions and conformations of the body through concerted attempts to control its excrescences, patrol its boundaries or refigure it entirely. The abject, or abjected, body is the product of the power of spiritual and/or psychological systems to make and unmake the corporeal world. Each of the theorists dealt with in Part II of the book appeals more to psychic than to social controls – the belief systems or cosmologies – that shape the interpretation of bodily being. This has variously led to a concentration on the perception of bodily parts or excretions, attempts to reshape bodily matter through the power of the mind, and, ultimately, to the attempt at a total remaking of that matter through a complete renovation of perception.

The abject body, while it is within the tradition that privileges a controlling mind over the material form of a person, exceeds the status of an objectified entity: it is the focus of a love–hate relationship. The abject body is at once a site of attraction *and* revulsion. The two chapters of this section look at that paradoxical relationship as it plays out in theories that are highly influenced by cosmologies, both religious and secular.

The study of the body as a site of spiritual and ritual significance (Douglas), or as the producer of reviled products (Kristeva), whether in sub-Saharan Africa or contemporary Western culture, implicitly recreates the body as an abstracted, abjected form (Chapter 4). In ritual and in daily culture, bodily excretions or by-products are the focus of both fascinated attraction and repulsion. Across cultures and across time, those fascinations and attractions differ: menstrual blood may be alternately sacred or putrid waste, powerful or disempowering, depending on the context. The same can be said, with some modification, of semen. These excretions are, however, significant whatever the context. Like the mannered body, spiritual or ritual codes are aimed at regulating and controlling the body within society. The abject body is similarly at the mercy of a wider set of rules, which are inculcated into the individual as a means of other-regulation through self-regulation. They are more rigidly set and obviously stated, however, not as diffuse or mutable as the control exerted by codes of manners, and where manners are socially value-laden but generally spiritually neutral, the codes that regulate the abject body are spiritually, emotionally and morally value-laden. Our traffic-light nose-picker may be considered 'common' or unsanitary, but he is unlikely to be thought of either as in danger of eternal damnation or imbued with miraculous powers for his bodily habits.

A related dynamic is at work in the psychoanalytic theorisation of the body. Based in a pseudo-scientific, rather than a spiritual, belief system, the abjected body of psychoanalysis comes a poor second to the power of the mind. In psychoanalytic theories the bodily form is generally taken to be either under the unconscious influence or the direct control of the mental processes at work within individuals. It is also implicit that what can happen in an individual mind can be extrapolated across many minds, and across social or cultural belief systems. In the work of some feminist psychoanalytic theorists, this has culminated in a theorisation that embodiment, or at least the presentation and perception of the body in the world, is an individual act of self-construction (Butler – Chapter 5): we bring ourselves into being, perform ourselves, through our bodies.

Part II therefore looks in the first instance at anthropological precedents for the fascination with the gory and/or scatological turn in the anthropology and sociology of body and the importance of rites, religion and rituals. These are linked to both historical works on the Western body and influential psychoanalytic theories. The theories covered in the two chapters of this second part are aiming at the imbalance between mind and body in social theory from the perspective of beliefs, ritual practices, and the power of the mind to shape and reshape perceptions of embodiment. This part covers texts that are weighted towards theorising how mental artefacts shape the social reception of the body and its products. There is both a historical and a cross-cultural element in most of the works in this part of the book, which, despite the intention of the authors, reinforces the cultural contingency of notions of embodiment. The comparison of the writings covered yet again lays bare the tensions between the different levels of abstraction at work.

Chapter 5, devoted to the practical power of the mind over the body, is placed so as to provide a thematic segue into the concerns of Part III. The chronological development of the preceding theorisations is intended to lay bare my contention that, as we come closer to theorisations of contemporary (postmodern) social formations, the body becomes an increasingly subjectivised, individualised project. It is the increasingly abstracted project of 'autonomous subjects' as they try to reclaim what has been problematised for them by a changing world.

Part III: Subject – the Body of Difference

Of all the natural sciences which Shilling identifies at the close of his book (1993) as sociology's primary rival in the interpretation and study of the body, it is medicine that takes the human body most directly as its subject. As a consequence, directly or indirectly – in studies of disability, sexuality, gender, race, reproductive and other body technologies, body modification, beauty, ageing – the sociology of medicine has had a disproportionate and dominant influence on the field. Biological and medical interpretations of the human body are part of a complex of abstracting mechanisms that shape the way we perceive and experience our bodies. The theorists in the third part of *The Sociology of the Body* are in one way or another building on or reacting to theorisations of the medicalised body; they are renegotiating medical ideas of normalcy or normativity, and they all work towards the individualised contingency of embodiment.

There is a tension here. While, on the one hand, we are looking at theories that aim to encompass the social subject, on the other hand that subject is increasingly individualised. In looking at how broad categories of subjectivity have been created in the past, and how they have obliterated the subtleties and complexities of individual being, the focus has moved firmly towards the complexity of the individual and focused on that individual's body: often at the expense of the complexity of the social. But then medical science, while it has proved invaluable in improving the physical health of societies, has no obligation or commitment to the social sphere outside of public health measures. At a deeper level, medical science comes into being alongside and helps to create the liberal individual's body. Scientific abstraction requires a lifting away from the distractions of social engagement: it demands a clear and 'objective' eye. Is it any wonder then that medico-social approaches to embodiment should devolve onto the body as an increasingly sophisticated set of components in an individualised form? This is the body as machine, *in toto*. At its most extreme, medical and scientific theorisations of embodiment see social life as an artefact, a biologically advantageous means of furthering the species: even thought, the mind, is a biochemical illusion that can be reproduced outside an embodied form. We are only matter, and we can transcend ourselves bio-technologically. Ironically, however, in being so determinedly corporeal in an individualised project, it cannot help but be the case that it is in fact the mind – mental theorisations, mental control – that again take the upper hand.

I begin this part of the book with Donna Haraway's early arguments around the separation of sex and gender and their importance to differentiation and distinction in the theorisation of embodiment (Chapter 6). The influence of a range of feminisms is central to the recognition and proliferation of difference, and by extension on the sociology of the body. The theories analysed here take the body as an individual subject, most of them implicitly attempting to overcome the imbalance between mind and body in social theory altogether, in some instances by treating the body as a DIY project, and in others by rejecting the body, leaving it behind, at least in any normative form.

This takes the ideas of Chapter 5 a step further into the theoretical, self-construction of individual embodiment. As such, Butler's work on material bodies implicitly extends into this. But the key theorist here, Haraway, writes in a way that has implications for eluding the natural bounds of material embodiment. Her work is symptomatic of a move towards arguments around the body in which, while talked about obsessively, notions of physicality fade away even as its narrators concentrate on medically influenced studies of the body. Many of these writers are heirs to Foucault's discussion of the discursively constructed, bio-medically contained body, but take a distinctly postmodern turn in the way that body is understood. Despite the avowed intent to reclaim embodiment for the new millennium, at heart Haraway idealises radical disembodiment (1997). Chapter 6 deals with the future fantasies of un-bodies, the rejection of embodiment, and the embracing of cyborg or techno-bodies. The cyborg body represents the post-modern experience of embodied abstraction whereby the materially embod-ied subject is, on the one hand, romantically fused with technological apparatuses, and on the other hand, distanced and devalued by the reinter-pretation of the body through bio-technological means. Haraway's work has been most notably deployed in sociological and anthropological studies of reproductive procedures (Franklin, Shildrick).

Chapter 7, 'The Social Subject: Life-Experiences, Lifestyles and Life-Stages' reflects on the preponderance of work that is related to the explo-sion of categories of bodily difference and the sociological studies devoted to them. Amongst the range of embodied differences, apart from gender and sexuality, that have been the subject of sociological investigation are factors such as: disability, age, aesthetics, size and shape. In this chapter I take the writing of Susan Bordo as emblematic of a strain of writing that gives full weight to the social, historical, cultural and contextual threads that inform embodiment. Here I shall also look at issues of embodiment in which difference is rarely a matter of choice but is nonetheless cen-tral, beginning with the general idea of the socially constructed body, disability (Seymour) and beauty (Gilman).

In the concluding chapter, I offer a view towards the future, and the possible directions for the theorisation and the living of the body. In it I give my own interpretation of embodiment as it is recast and reconsti-tuted through bio-technological visions of the human body in current work on embryonic stem cell technology. In this technology, and other allied technological interventions that reflect upon and refract through corporeality, we can see how the abstraction of the body is understood within modern/postmodern culture.

The overall structure of *The Sociology of the Body* can be stated thus: it begins with theories that are predominantly concerned with recuperating the body; leads into theories that have the contrary approach whereby the body is incorporated but the mind is uppermost; and closes with the-ories that attempt to reintegrate the mind and the body in what are increasingly individualised projects of self-creation or self-construction.

Notes

1 The terms 'tribal, traditional, modern and postmodern' are used in a commonsense way here. For fuller analytical definitions of these terms, see Paul James (2001) and cited below. Broadly speaking, tribal social formations are based in kinship relations; traditional social formations are based in patrimonial bureaucratic

relations and/or kingship; modern social formations in the abstracted bureaucracy of the nation-state; and postmodern social formations in the globalising bureaucratic abstraction of postnationalism.

2 Paul James (2006) Chapter 8. The analytical approach of this book is deeply indebted to the work of Paul James, a social theorist whose refinements upon the theory of constitutive abstraction (Sharp 1985) come out of the collaborative work of the group of writers and theorists associated with *Arena* (Melbourne). Thanks to his intellectual and personal generosity, I have mobilised and adapted his work on constitutive abstraction throughout this book.

Part I

Object – the Regulated Body

ONE 'Manners Maketh the Man'

Social Norms and Customary Control

The two theorists covered in this chapter are concerned with social and cultural change across the second millennium CE, the final century of which much of their careers bridged. This common thread in their work, and the fact that they concentrate particularly on cultural shifts in Western Europe, is one of the reasons that I have paired them together. Norbert Elias (1897–1990) was a sociologist with a bent for history. Philippe Ariès (1914–82) was a social historian. It is significant that although Elias was writing the primary work that features here in the 1930s and therefore predates Ariès's by twenty years, it was not well known until four decades later. Even where it was known, it was not particularly influential in Anglophone sociology until it was translated into English in two volumes (1978, 1982). At that time Ariès was undoubtedly the better known of the two writers and the more influential on historical understandings of social forms, his *Centuries of Childhood* (1960) having first appeared in English in 1962. Not only have they both written on the same period of Western European history, they also cover common themes. But for all their similarities, they are not all of a piece: Elias has had good cause to criticise Ariès on several grounds. They also come out of different intellectual traditions.

After serving in the German army in World War I and subsequently completing a medical degree, Norbert Elias turned to sociology. In the early 1930s he was briefly on the periphery of the Frankfurt School before fleeing Nazi Germany in 1933 – like many Jewish intellectuals – and eventually settling in England just prior to World War II. There he had a long, productive but quiet scholarly career that saw him associated with the LSE, Cambridge and finally the University of Leicester. It was not until his 'retirement' and the translation of his major writings into English that Elias rose to academic prominence (Goudsblom and Mennell 1998). Ariès trained as a historical demographer and like Elias came relatively late to scholarly fame, not publishing his groundbreaking historical contextualisation of childhood until 1960, when he was in his mid-forties. Ariès was one of the *Annales* 'School' in Paris, and a direct inheritor of that school's emphasis on tracing the history of structures and social trends, its attention to the social sciences: in short, social history (Burke 1990: 67–70). Elias's early work, while largely unknown and unpublished at the time, was written as the *Annales* first gained notoriety and runs parallel to some of its movements. Inheritors of the *Annales* School and Elias also have in common an abiding interest in mentalities, in social psychology. But in a sense it is unremarkable that a participant in a historical school that began with attending to Durkheimian sociology should have much in common with a sociologist who had studied with Alfred Weber and Karl Mannheim, and had a great interest in the history of societies.

Elias

While Norbert Elias was writing *The Civilizing Process* in the 1930s, notions of 'civilisation' and 'nationhood' were taking a particularly programmatic turn in his homeland, under the influence of national socialism.[1] This remarkable book traces the evolution of manners and state formation in Western Europe from the Middle Ages until the twentieth century. In the first instance it does so by looking at bodily habits and their increasing regulation. Although Elias does not spell out specifically that he is dealing with the body in society, it is clearly the focus of his discussion, particularly in Volume I: *Changes in the Behaviour of the Secular Upper Classes in the West* ([1936] 1978). Volume II: *State Formation and Civilization* ([1936] 1982), as its title implies, deals with the evolution of political systems. While these two volumes are intended to be read together, it is the first volume that is most intimately involved with shaping human bodies, and therefore is the focus here.

The Civilizing Process

Elias opens his discussion of civilisation and culture by implicitly trying to distance himself from positivist notions of civilisation. He makes clear that he is talking about a historical moment in European – particularly German – notions of culture and civilisation, and that conceptions of culture vary from nation to nation, from culture to culture.

According to Elias, the German concept of *Zivilisation* 'describes a *process*, or at least the result of a process. It refers to something that is constantly in motion, constantly moving "forward"' (Elias 2000: 6). This is specifically identified as being allied with or an outcome of political and economic structures. The German concept of *Kultur* in use when he was writing, 'has a different relation to motion. It refers to human products, which are there like "flowers of the field", to works of art, books, religious or philosophical systems, in which the *individuality of a people*[2] expresses itself. The concept of *Kultur* delimits. To a certain extent, the concept of civilisation plays down the national differences between peoples; it emphasises what is common to all human beings or – in the view of its bearers – should be.' *Kultur*, on the other hand, consists of 'accomplishments' that form the basis of national sentiments, of differentiation (6–7).[3] It is simultaneously a means of unification (for the self/selves) and differentiation (from the other/s).

Elias differentiates these German notions from the French and English usage of civilisation, which he claims carry connotations of both political and economic advancement and what the Germans think of as the more rarified accomplishments of *Kultur*. He links this to differences between French and German national 'character' or identity. The German notion of *Kultur* came from an eighteenth-century bourgeoisie that remained demarcated from court manners and mores: they each spoke 'different languages'. The courtly state remained aloof from the non-nobility and vice versa. The French bourgeoisie, on the other hand, mixed with and (in both senses) affected the manners, habits and standards of the court. The advent of the Revolution made the dissemination of bourgeois characteristics and their welding to the 'national character' a natural progression:

> Stylistic conventions, the forms of social intercourse, affect-moulding, the high regard for courtesy, the importance of good speech and conversation, articulateness of language and much else – all this was first formed in France within court society, then slowly changed, in a continuous diffusion from a social into a national character. (32)

In Germany bourgeois *Kultur* remained separate from court culture and therefore, when it became the dominant cultural form, it had a different aspect to that which took hold in France (and England).

Thereafter, Elias offers an archaeology of manners – bodily customs, habits, courtesy and civility – in Western Europe in general since the Middle Ages, using Germany, France and England as his major models with some examples from Italy.[4] Using textual evidence – specifically, literary sources and courtesy manuals – he looks to court society for his examples, and argues that the progress of manners and the taking up of the concept of *civilité* are expressions of the progress of European ideas of civilisation. Civility is described in much the same terms as those he uses for national identity. It was the rallying point by which court society came to self-recognition, and the development of recognisable characteristics: a 'self-image' (47).

Erasmus's 1530 publication, *De civilitate morum puerilium* [On Civility in Boys], is a turning point in the dissemination of those mores:

> Erasmus's book is about something very simple: the behaviour of people in society – above all, but not solely, 'outward bodily propriety' ... Bodily carriage, gestures, dress, facial expressions – this 'outward' behaviour with which the treatise concerns itself is the expression of the inner, the whole person. (48–9)

It marks a point between earlier, more didactic models and more appealing ways of inflicting behaviour modification on people in the 'transitional period after the loosening of the medieval social hierarchy and before the stabilizing of the modern one' (63). Erasmus was one of a new class of man, in the peculiar position of not being of the courtly classes himself and yet able to comment upon and shape courtly manners. 'He saw very exactly that the real nurseries of what was regarded as good manners in his time were the princely courts' (63). He could be 'detached' from the court, because of his own position, and yet lend credence to and disseminate its mores, helping make middle-class what was at court. Most importantly, '[a]ccordingly, Erasmus did not see his precepts as intended for a particular class. He placed no particular emphasis on social distinctions, if we disregard occasional criticism of peasants and small tradesmen' (65–6).

Erasmus definitely shifted the rhetorical strategy, moving from direct command to examples couched in personal observation or anecdote, which implies a far greater degree of the internalisation of the importance of the opinions of others – how one seems to an observer, in public. Elias links this to medieval traditions, to the revivification of mores from antiquity with the Renaissance rediscovery of the ancients, and to the increase in literacy: 'reading has sharpened seeing, and seeing has enriched reading and writing' (67). This internalisation of the importance of the gaze of the other extends to one's individual outward appearance, through dress, which is 'the body of the body' (67): clothing, gesture and bodily deportment are signs of inner life that are explicitly linked to mental states.

The new stage of courtesy and its representation, summed up in the concept of *civilité*, was very closely bound up with this manner of seeing, and gradually became more so. In order to be really 'courteous' by the standards of *civilité*, one was to some extent obliged to observe, to look about oneself and pay attention to people and their motives. In this, too, a new relationship of person to person, a new form of integration is announced. (67)

The longer-term outcome was a gradual pressure to conceal, cover, hide or suppress what was increasingly seen as improper.[5] This imperative to conceal becomes more and more successful over time, to the point where what Erasmus could once speak of directly – farting, belching, guzzling, slurping, dribbling, pissing, shitting – if in far more restrained tones than his predecessors, eventually became unspeakable. In turn, *civilité* was superseded, or lost its strength, with the social elites it had originally been copied from: the term became so current it also became bourgeois and beneath them. So there was another shift in the rhetoric, as well as the mores, from the seventeenth century onwards (87).

Elias supports these claims by giving a series of selected examples – predating and postdating Erasmus – from courtesy manuals and other literary sources from the thirteenth through to the eighteenth centuries, specifically drawing out dictates related to table manners in the first instance: how to eat in public without really (being) trying. The fork, in particular, is shown to be an implement that marks one of those turning points in eating habits. At a time when soup was drunk out of communal bowls and all one required was a platter (or a stout slab of bread) and a knife to cut off your choice of meat from the roasted carcass, forks were initially thought affected. Forks enabled one to lift food from a communal eating pot, and eventually from individually served plates, without dirtying one's fingers. Or, as was the case with a spoon, having your spittle mix with everyone else's. 'The fork is nothing other than the embodiment of a specific standard of emotions and a specific level of revulsion ... a change in the economy of drives and emotions' (107). Coming into too close contact with the bodily effluxions of others, bar the closest of family members, became a matter of increasing disgust. And eating utensils distanced people from each other in more ways than one. When they were luxury items they did so hierarchically, and as they became more common, they contributed to an increasing distance between individuals of all social strata.

This pattern of argument is followed through a variety of other bodily behavioural controls, including the curbing of speech. Again, we have the problem of the shift in styles, making social divisions more obvious and acting as an exclusionary measure: courteous language, if too formal or archaic, made clear one's social position, identified one as a try-hard. But,

Elias argues, despite this the spread of the civilising influence flattened out social difference. 'Here, too, as with manners, there was a kind of double movement: a courtization of bourgeois people and a bourgeoisification of courtly people. Or, to put it more precisely: bourgeois people were influenced by the behaviour of courtly people and vice versa' (93–4).

Similarly, there are shifts in the eating and serving of meat, from proud traditions of carving whole beasts to the obfuscation of meat beneath sauces until their animal origin is totally obscured; the shift in the use of knives from personal weapons as well as implements, to the point where it is considered utterly improper to bring a knife to one's mouth. The same pattern is repeated in his treatment of 'Natural Functions' – the title of which is a neat example of 1930s manners in itself – in the retreat of acts of bodily evacuation from the courtyard or the street to specific enclosed spaces. In the process of marking out what is proper and improper, 'it is quite clear that this treatise had precisely the function of cultivating feelings of shame' (114). And where in Erasmus's writing it was thoroughly recommended to release wind in either direction, by the eighteenth century even the mention of holding in wind, which was by then required, has become a matter of delicacy.

> The situation was similar with the exposure of the body. First it became a distasteful offence to show oneself exposed in any way before those of higher or equal rank; with inferiors it could even be a sign of good will. Then, as all become socially more equal, it slowly became a general offence. The social determination and embarrassment-feelings receded more and more from consciousness. (118)

Further,

> Society was gradually beginning to suppress the positive pleasure component in certain functions more and more strongly by the arousal of anxiety. Or more exactly, it was beginning to 'privatize' them, to force them into the 'inside' of individuals, into 'secrecy', and to allow the negatively-charged affects – displeasure, revulsion and repugnance – to be the only socially allowed feelings that are developed through socialization. But precisely by this increased social proscription of many impulses, by their 'repression' from the surface both of social life and of consciousness, the distance between the personality structure and behaviour of adults and children was necessarily increased. (121)

Here we see clearly Elias's debt to Freud.[6] But, he rightly goes on to emphasise, we cannot deduce from the increasing unacceptability of behaviours such as spitting and sharing food that there was any consciousness of public health involved: that simply was not an issue until the nineteenth century. These proscriptions are about social boundaries, 'changes in the way people live together, in the structure of society' (135). These changes also extended to the bedroom, where 'the emotional barrier erected by conditioning between one body and another, had grown continuously. To share a bed with people outside the family circle, with strangers, is made more and more embarrassing' (142).

While his point that 'a fundamental change in interpersonal relationships and behaviour is expressed in our manner of living' (142) is compelling, it is strange for a contemporary reader to find that when he extends his discussion to bed habits, Elias separates out the sharing beds from sexual conduct, which is left to his treatment of the relations between men and women.[7] This is particularly so when Elias also notes the easy inclusion of sexual relationships in Erasmus's book.

To close, I believe it is worth quoting at length a passage that from the point of view of the argument from abstraction,[8] is the turning point of the book.

> The affect-structure of human beings is a whole. We may call particular drives by different names according to their different directions and functions. We may speak of hunger and the need to spit, of the sexual drive and of aggressive impulses, but in life these different drives are no more separable than the heart from the stomach or the blood from the brain from the blood in the genitalia. They complement and in part supersede each other, transform themselves within certain limits and compensate for each other; a disturbance here manifests itself there. In short, they form a kind of circuit in the human being, a partial unit within the total unity of the organism. Their structure is still opaque in many respects, but their socially imprinted form is of decisive importance for the functioning of a society as of the individuals within it. (161)

Throughout *The Civilizing Process* Elias traces the increasing abstraction of the human body, its distancing from self and other, as effected within the evolution of regulatory regimes that characterise traditional and early modern societies, where the body is made up of parts that function as a whole. This is the end product of what Shilling has rightly identified as the triple process of 'individualisation', 'rationalisation' and 'socialisation' underpinning Elias's theories. At the beginning of the third millennium CE the affect-structure of human beings is no longer so easily taken as a 'whole'. As we shall see in relation to later writers like Donna Haraway, and in the conclusion, bodily organs are increasingly seen as capable of functioning autonomously, or at least as replaceable, interchangeable items.

The Loneliness of the Dying

By the time Elias came to write *The Loneliness of the Dying* (1985) he understood this. While the body is still not openly discussed, it is clearly implicit in Elias's speaking of the physicality of dying, death and decay. He is interested in the sociality of death in the 'repression' of death from social consciousness: the receding from public/attended deaths and a movement towards contemporary habits of private/hidden, and at times extraordinarily lonely, death. He contrasts this with the open physicality of death of former times, using as examples the open celebration of breasts and lips in death, of worms and corruption. It is true, Donne or Marvell could, and frequently did, link death and sexual delights in ways that have only recently regained currency.[9] But then, when Marvell or Donne wrote of rotting flesh, they had first-hand experience of it, thanks in no small part to the plague. They were warning their audience to enjoy the warmth of life while it is available: death and Judgment Day will come soon enough.

This repression of the social function of death and dying extends to the care of the deceased and their resting places. The care of graves, and of bodies, is now the province of specialists rather than family members. With this particularisation and professionalisation of death processes, combined with longer life spans, death has become more remote both for the individual and for society. Elias openly brings the themes of his masterwork into the discussion of mortality:

> If we speak of the civilizing process in whose course dying and death are moved more firmly behind the scenes of social life and fenced in by relatively intense feelings of embarrassment and relatively strict verbal taboos, we must qualify this by adding that experiences of the two great European wars, and perhaps far more of the concentration camps, show the fragility of the conscience that prohibits killing and then insists on the isolation of dying and dead people, as far as possible, from normal social life. The mechanisms of self-constraint that are involved in the repression of death in our societies clearly disintegrate relatively quickly once the external mechanism of self-constraint imposed by the state - or by sects or combat groups - basing itself on authoritative collective doctrines and beliefs, violently changes course and orders the killing of people. In the two world wars the sensitivity towards killing, towards dying people and death clearly evaporated quite quickly in the majority of people. (Elias 1985: 50-1)

Again we see the process by which people have become increasingly individualised, alienated and abstracted from each other over the centuries. And Elias is deeply critical of the alienating effects of individualisation. It is through our relations with others that meaning comes into being:

> [T]he concept of meaning cannot be understood by reference to an isolated human being or to a universal derived from it. What we call 'meaning' is constituted by people in groups who are dependent on each other in this or that way and can communicate with each other. 'Meaning' is a social category; the subject corresponding to it is a plurality of inter-connected people. (54)

This argument has great intuitive appeal. While Elias relies on other examples, it is clear that even a profoundly deaf, mute and blind infant, unless reared in circumstances even less stimulating than a Skinner Box, relies on interaction outside his or her own bodily bounds to form meaning. Helen Keller, prior to learning sign language, could be dressed and fed: she must have had some level of interaction and understanding – some meaning – even with the restrictions to her sensory world.

As a result of this individualisation, and the hiding away of even the approach of death, ageing bodies are treated differently within society, are not valued or understood. Ageing bodies have gradually shifted from being cared for within village life/family groups, to industrialised, specialised, institutionalised 'care' facilities for the ageing and dying – which 'means not only the final severing of old affective ties, but also means living together with people with whom the individual has no positive affective relationships' (74).

Elias closes this brief but important book with the observation that our increasing concentration on the fragmented body is at the cost of the whole person:

> The problems I have raised here are, as you may see, problems of medical sociology. Present-day medical measures relate mainly to individual aspects of the physiological functioning of a person – the heart, the bladder, the arteries and so on – and as far as these are concerned medical technique in preserving and prolonging life is undoubtedly more advanced than ever before. But to concentrate on medically correcting single organs, or areas of organs that are functioning more and more badly, is really worthwhile only for the sake of the person within whom all these part-processes are integrated. And if the problems of the individual part-processes cause us to forget those of the integrating person, we really devalue what we are doing for these part-processes themselves ... It is perhaps not yet quite superfluous to say that care for people sometimes lags behind the care for their organs. (89–91)

This is the very process of bodily abstraction, a process that we will see recurring throughout this book and to which I shall return in the Conclusion. For now, however, we will turn to the criticisms that have been levelled at Elias's ideas.

Analysis

For all Elias's attempts to avoid the most obvious criticism of his work – that it is an extension of nineteenth-century positivist histories – and despite Shilling's defence of him on this count, it is not at all clear that it has been successfully refuted. Despite his stated intentions, there are certain assumptions built into Elias's trajectories of manners that deserve comment and require caution in its application. It is, clearly, openly and consciously Eurocentric. It is classist. Elias concentrates heavily on

Erasmus, who chose physical training as his main subject matter and who differentiated his imperatives on manners along class lines. Erasmus frequently frames his advice in a way that presses: 'Don't behave in a particular way, that's the way someone of a lower class would behave' The narrative of courtesy or civility is a story of upward social mobility, and there are other instances in courtesy manuals that point out the dangers of trying too hard: civility cannot be learned simply by rote, courtliness is also somehow inherent (read noble) and the false show of it will be detectable to a truly courtly and civilised person.[10] But as a result, when Elias speaks of society in *The Civilising Process*, he is really speaking of the courtly level of society, or those who aspired to it, even if he argues that there was a mutual exchange of behaviour modification.

Simply because of the terms of his study, there is an immediate setting-up of an opposition between 'civilised' and 'uncivilised' ways of being – between primitivism and progress. Certain passages do nothing to dispel this: 'Was European society really, under the watchword of *civilité*, slowly moving towards that kind of refined behaviour, that standard of conduct, habits and affect formation, which is characteristic in our minds of "civilized" society, of Western "civilization"?' (Elias 2000: 71). Whilst Elias is not unaware of the consequence of such an opposition it does, unfortunately, open the way for value judgements about the worth of certain behaviours over others. Aggressive 'uncivilised' behaviour is not applauded – a 'culture' can be seen from the outside as being less worthy or even absent, just as peoples can be seen as being 'uncivilised'. There is also a sense in his description of *Kultur* that it is somehow 'natural', whereas, clearly, it is just as constructed as civilising norms. This, in turn, is presented within an oddly value-laden introduction to what follows, no doubt at some level influenced by centuries of national rivalry between Germany and France. Finally, while in Volume II and his later work he expanded upon and refined his views, his assertion that aggression has been 'subdued', 'confined' and 'tamed' (161) is also culturally specific. While it may not have been Elias's intention, it can be seen to be playing into prejudices around 'primitive' and 'civilised' beings, as if 'those people who still indulge in open aggressiveness are primitives, uncivilised'. Despite these difficulties, many of which Elias redressed in his later writing, overall Elias's work is some of the most useful and influential for understanding the human body as a socialised, rationalised, individualised object.[11] The following comments are more by way of expanding on Elias's work than criticising it.

To return to the centrality of Erasmus, Elias's implication that Erasmus was addressing everyone, not just a specific social class, needs to be treated with caution. I don't believe for a moment that Erasmus thought his book, even with the increasingly openness of schooling when he was writing, would appeal to a labourer. Few people could read in the sixteenth century, and even fewer could read Latin. And though it quickly appeared in vernacular printings, books were expensive commodities and would have been accessible primarily to the (male) middle-class and above.[12] Further, the barely implicit point of the asides about the inadvisability of leaving snot hanging from the nose is precisely to differentiate and exclude people who did – that is people of lower rank – from his audience. Erasmus does not need to make a major point of criticising 'peasants and small tradesmen' because it is taken as read they are not part of his intended audience. Finally, Erasmus is most particularly addressing boys: women are not the objects of his regimes of civility, except insofar as a man interacts with them. This is a major, if for its time understandable, omission from Elias's thesis. Women – Miss Manners – increasingly became the custodians, arbiters and enforcers of many of the manners he addresses. And even in their time the handkerchiefs employed to retain the aforementioned snot were no uncomplicated markers of class and probity, as Shakespeare made clear in *Othello* when he allowed Desdemona's richly embroidered handkerchief to be stolen and copied for a whore.

All that Elias looks at, all his examples – because he has chosen pedagogical printed forms – are didactically aimed at shaping and changing behaviour. He, along with Ariès, either ignores or elides the possibility that while they were highly successful at one level, they were not necessarily, and were certainly never uniformly, successful. There is a point to concentrating on 'civilising' structures, insofar as they have become a dominant political form and tool, through colonial expansion. And yet, civilising structures are as much social delineators as racial or national ones: they leave so much of society out. These are the mores and rules most dear to the middle classes and above. These are not the uniform mores of everyone in a society. Codes of conduct are constantly broken, whether overtly or covertly. Even today, when spitting is considered in most Western cultures to be at least a public health hazard and more generally simply to be unpleasant, watch any code of football and see how many sporting gods (repeatedly) gob on field, in full view of the spectators and the cameras: this is not acceptable behaviour off the field, but it *is* considered manly. And when it is broadcast to a worldwide audience of over a billion, as is the case with the World Cup, what does that say?

And compare the increasing 'delicacy' over farting with toilet humour, the repression of sex with pornography. Foucault's discussion of the 'repressive hypothesis', which will be dealt with in Chapter 2, has ramifications not just for Freud but also for Elias in his following of Freud. Repression, in some instances, led to the incessant talking about that which was supposed to be repressed. The fact that this happened mostly in a medicalised, pathologised manner is pertinent for Elias's late writings on the dying.

In relation to Elias's work on the dying, while it is reassuring to see him withdrawing from too rosy a view of the supposed civility and decrease in aggressiveness of the affect-structure in the twentieth century that marked his discussion of aggression in *The Civilizing Process*, I think his assertions around 'the fragility of the conscience that prohibits killing' need some qualification. It has the same flaw as his example of early modern cat massacres being a form of aggressiveness that 'we' have outgrown. It is obvious that there was a long popular association between cats and witches, and that they were contemporaneously burned at the stake. These acts of animal cruelty clearly had another logic than the simple pleasure in the pain of a defenceless creature, as Robert Darnton has since shown.[13] Similarly, it was possible for those wholeheartedly killing in the concentration camps not to (negatively) 'feel' the death of their victims because they did not consider those being murdered to be 'people'. The same people's grief at the death of their comrades and families would not necessarily have been any less. Further, shellshock, battle fatigue or Post-Traumatic Stress Disorder would not exist if people could discard their horror of violence and carnage so easily. Returned servicemen from both world wars had nightmares, some for the rest of extremely long lives, and many have and will go to their graves refusing to talk about their experiences. In my own experience of speaking to elderly women who were on the home-front in England during World War II – one woman and her two small sons were strafed in the middle of the day in their village street – those memories were extremely vivid and disturbing for them to revisit even sixty years later.

However, Elias's work on the civilisation of social beings through the regulation of the body is essential for much of the work that has been done in disability and ageing studies. The notion of a contingent civility, or of civilisation as an ongoing process, makes clear the constructed nature of 'good', healthy bodies. The fact that people feel so ashamed of incontinence, uncontrolled flatulence, and any of the other infirmities of ageing or disability, is a direct product of the internalisation of just the civilising standards that Elias outlines. These things are not acceptable in a 'healthy' adult and incontinence even becomes pathologised in children over the age of two. This kind of dictum ignores the wide variability of bodily development, and leads to the pathologisation of what are essentially natural bodily functions. Incontinence, impotence and even pregnancy thereby become medical conditions to be treated and contained.[14] As Elias says, the organs receive more care and attention than the integrated social being. Witness mental disability and the shooting and strangling of paranoid schizophrenics at the hands of the police; the revulsion at (obvious) street people, who are bussed out to the outer reaches in cities like Paris; and seeing only dust and dirt in remote Aboriginal communities, ignoring the close family ties and desire for self-determination. In the latter example this has led to proposals that ongoing government funding of communities be made dependent on proof that the faces of children are washed twice daily. From a public health perspective this is motivated by a desire to minimise the risk of trachoma, but as policy it is clearly framed in punitive terms and based on a perception of socially unacceptable behaviour. So, while Elias may think manners have seemingly loosened up in certain ways since he first wrote *The Civilizing Process* – the sexual revolution, various forms of bohemianism and revolt – in other ways they have not. In his terms, they have simply continued to process, with new forms of approved and disapproved behaviours emerging. Manners, unlike custom, are an inherently socially exclusionary tool. They are hierarchical. Custom, by contrast, is inclusive.

There is much to value in Elias's work and I think Shilling's three-point précis still stands as the best encapsulation of his method. Manners work as a means of *socialisation*, bringing us into society. Manners foster the process of *rationalisation*, leading us to rationalise ourselves, our behaviour, to quantify and commercially value our actions and behaviours. Manners instil *individualisation* by which we internalise order and become self-regulating individuals.

Ariès

To a similar degree, social historian Philippe Ariès, in turn, has influenced thinking about the fundamentally embodied, everyday and (seemingly) ahistorical human life-categories – family, childhood and dying – so much so that they are no longer taken as simple givens. Although, like Elias, he does not do so through directly addressing embodied issues, his rethinking of the above-mentioned categories is based in embodied change, in the recognition of the contingency of physical stages.

Centuries of Childhood

Ariès's basic argument on childhood is that it is a construct of bourgeois sentimentality or affectivity. Childhood and the differentiation we would understand between infant, child, adolescent, youth, adult and aged infirmity only came into being in the seventeenth and eighteenth centuries. Seven was considered the age of reason – Ignatius Loyola's dictum 'Give me the child until he is seven and I will give you the man' is still well known – and thereafter the young were considered to have the ability to take all that life offered or required of them. Ariès argues that this evolution of childhood is observable through shifts in the positioning of games, clothing and education in relation to age and social strata. These are all effected through bodily techniques.

Popular concepts of the stages, or ages, of life have their origin in Ionian philosophy, according to Ariès (1962: 19). Using medieval and early modern illustrations in support of his thesis, he argues that the major physical differentiations of those ages are between the cradle and the neo-adult, and the aged and the bed-ridden (imbecilic) infirm who have returned to an infant-like state. The illustrations he provides track life-stages but do not include a period that is recognisable as 'childhood'. First came infancy, then a remarkably extended youth, and eventually old age. The idea of adolescence – a period in which one became a social being – did not exist. Rather, '[t]he idea of childhood was bound up with the idea of dependence: the words "sons", "varlets" and "boys" were also words in the vocabulary of feudal subordination' (26). So, conversely, a 'lad' or 'boy' could be in his twenties.

Children in medieval art are uniformly depicted as small adults and Ariès links this back to Roman non-specification of children (33–4), explaining the manifold stiff, odd-looking baby-Jesuses prior to the Renaissance. Small children, he argues, were considered unimportant because they were likely to die: recognition only came with the likelihood of survival. The shift towards the invention of a sentimentalised childhood is evident in the inclusion of infants in funerary monuments and family portraiture in the seventeenth century (46–47). Further, clothing became an important marker in the creation of this differentiation, for

> the Middle Ages dressed every age indiscriminately, taking care only to maintain the visible vestiary signs of the differences in the social hierarchy. Nothing in medieval dress distinguished the child from the adult. In the seventeenth century, however, the child, or at least the child of quality, whether noble or middle-class, ceased to be dressed like the grown-up. (50)

That is, if the child was a boy. There was no differentiation in female dress in any class after infancy (swaddling) except in terms of expense of fabric and intricacy of construction. Girls and boys were uniformly dressed in skirts up to the point when boys were 'breeched', usually around the age of seven. These ubiquitous skirts have their origin in the uniform and unisex long-coats of the Middle Ages, which only bore small details that denoted masculinity and femininity. 'The evidence provided by dress bears out the other indications furnished by the history of manners: boys were the first specialized children' (58). This was particularly evident amongst the upper classes: children of artisans and those of lower classes continued to wear the same kinds of clothes as their parents.

In a similar way, games, music and dancing gradually became differentiated. Where adults of the Middle Ages happily sported at leapfrog, various games gradually became associated specifically with childhood. Conversely, everyone took part in games of chance but by the eighteenth century, under the influence of the introduction of ideas of 'childhood innocence', children were discouraged from gambling. Similarly, sophisticated dancing and music became adult preoccupations as they became more intimately connected to rituals of courting. 'Healthy' pursuits, like gymnastics, on the other hand, were specifically recommended for boys. Another effect of the invention of 'innocence' was that sexualised behaviours – arousal, sexually explicit and implicit play – became confined to adults.

All this changed as the rise of an effectively controlling 'pedagogic literature for children as distinct from books for adults made its appearance' (119). Communion became an important marker between childhood and the next stage: you had to be rational to appreciate the gravity of the act. And by the eighteenth century, the physical upward training of the immature body became a major pedagogical preoccupation, as did personal hygiene.

> Care of the body was not ignored by seventeenth-century moralists and pedagogues. People nursed the sick devotedly (at the same time taking every precaution to unmask malingerers), but any interest shown in healthy bodies had a moral purpose behind it: a delicate body encouraged luxury, sloth, concupiscence – all the vices in fact! (133)

If the newly invented child was 'innocent', he or she was also 'weak', and if not cared for effectively, would fall into vice. Ariès elucidates this argument through an extraordinarily long disquisition on the French educational system from the Middle Ages through to the twentieth century, but here it is only necessary to note the main points that are of relevance to our discussion. First and foremost girls, by and large, were not *formally* educated in subjects that were and are of enormous cultural capital. I stress formally because Ariès only deals with institutional education and there were clearly practical forms of learning that girls acquired in the home; they were simply not valued in the same way as a boy's intellectual education.

The early scholastic education was in Latin, aimed at church life, and confined to boys and men. Ages and subjects were mixed. Universities existed, but devolved colleges gradually arose out of what had originally been boarding houses run by masters, which over time started to take on the character of teaching institutions. The kind of teaching offered eventually shifted towards a system of classes (around the time of Erasmus) where subjects were differentiated and arranged in progressive stages, although ages could still be well and truly mixed. Eventually colleges and schools attained special premises. The ability to attend any of these institutions depended on wealth and family situation, and this also governed the starting age to some degree: families would wait until they could afford to send a son to a college, even if this meant small boys learned alongside adults. By the seventeenth century this becomes more regularised. And as was the case up to the nineteenth and even into the twentieth century, the very rich could have their children tutored at home until they were ready to go to a college or university. This mixing of ages fits in with the idea of there being no real differentiation after infancy: if one had attained rationality, one could be schooled.

The progressive gradation of schooling concretised the differentiation in the ages of adolescence, youth and adulthood as marking bodily stages. These differences also became increasingly connected to the differentiation between social classes, with the restricted availability of education. This would go some way to explaining why child labour 'retained this characteristic of medieval society: the precocity of the entry into adult life ... There is accordingly, a remarkable synchronism between the modern age group and the social group: both originated at the same time, in the late eighteenth century, and in the same milieu – the middle class' (336). With education came control, constraint and corporal punishment, supporting the idea of delicate bodies being vice-prone bodies. In the eighteenth century discipline in schools became more militarised. The shift to boarding schools – the removal of children from their homes – or 'little schools', and the consequent further differentiation of levels and places of education, split life stages and the classes even more markedly. School defined all the stages between the leaving of skirts and the entering into adult life/employment. This, in turn, effected a shift in the perception, reconstruction and representation of the 'family'. Families appear as *the* subject of portraiture and everyday life, overtaking earlier depictions of wider societies, or social scenes, that one finds in paintings by people such as Breughel, or in many of the earlier biblical tales. The portrait became secularised and bourgeois as the concept of 'the family' solidified (353). Although '[t]he concept is new but not the family ... the family existed in silence: it did not awaken feelings strong enough to inspire poet or artist' (363–4). Of course, families existed, but just as children were perceived differently, so too were family groupings. We move from a society in which nobody is left alone, to a confined social space, the bourgeois family, where children and childhood were propagated: 'this family has advanced in proportion as sociability has retreated ... it reinforced private life at the expense of neighbourly relationships, friendships, and traditional contacts' (406). In the final line of his book Ariès goes even further, implicitly damning the nuclear family: 'The concept of the family, the concept of class, and perhaps elsewhere the concept of race, appear as manifestations of the same intolerance towards variety, the same insistence on uniformity' (415).

The Hour of Our Death

In the more than 600 pages of his subsequent major work on the history of death and dying, *The Hour of Our Death* (1981), Ariès appeals to the same basic argument, namely that our relationship to death is a construct of bourgeois society, the rise of the individual, and Enlightenment ethics. He claims that in the Middle Ages people met death gladly, that it was an open and present concept. Unlike our comfortable contemporary developed-world expectations, it was accepted that everyone was considered capable of dying at any moment. In the sense that they were aware of the strong possibility that it would happen, people were prepared to lose their children. Ariès concludes from this that children therefore meant less to, and were loved less intensely by, their parents.

In setting out his history of death and dying over the second millennium CE, he demarcates the shifting attitudes towards death into five epochal stages: 'the tame death, the death of the self, remote and imminent death, the death of the other, and the invisible death'. He argues that these stages are characterised by 'variations' in people's adherence to the four psychological themes that he deploys throughout his thesis: *'awareness of the individual ... the defense of society against untamed nature, belief in an afterlife, and belief in the existence of evil'* (1981: 603). These stages represent an evolution, much as he described childhood through a process of evolution, and the historical phases he describes are roughly equivalent to those he sees in the differentiation of the child from the infant and the adult.

The first and earliest stage, 'tame death', was dominant in the Middle Ages. He argues that people were, by and large, sure in the fact that there was some form of life after death. Death was a socially accepted reality, it was not a fearful prospect, and for some it was a positively welcome release into a better life. People lived and died 'in the sure and everlasting hope of eternal life, and the resurrection'.

> Death is not a purely individual act, any more than life is. Like every great milestone in life, death is celebrated by a ceremony that is always more or less solemn and whose purpose is to express the individual's solidarity with his family and community. The three most important moments of this ceremony are the dying man's acceptance of his active role, the scene of the farewells, and the scene of mourning. (603)

The dying prepare for and actively embrace the rites and processes of their deaths. After death, the body was openly displayed prior to burial, and in such funerary monuments as existed, the figure represented is unmistakeably dead.

The second epochal model of mortality takes hold in the Renaissance, and is characterised as the 'death of the self', which 'is obtained quite simply by a shift of the sense of destiny toward the individual' (605). This consciousness of one's own position, separate from the masses, had appeared earlier but only amongst the highly placed individuals of the later Middle Ages, who hankered for a more prominent and active afterlife. Royalty, nobles and bishops

> split into two parts: a body that experiences pleasure or pain and an immortal soul that was released by death. The body disappeared, pending a resurrection that was accepted as a dogma but never really assimilated at the popular level ... This fully conscious soul was no longer content to sleep the sleep of expectation like the *homo totus* of old - or like the poor. Its immortal existence, or rather its immortal activity, expressed the individual's desire to assert his creative identity in this world and the next, his refusal to let it dissolve into some biological or social anonymity. (606)

Ariès cites the change in funerary monuments – where corrupt bodies may be shown but they are overlain with the resurrected, eternally wakeful self – as evidence of this. As far as the process of dying is concerned, where the acts at the deathbed had been paramount in the Middle Ages, by the eighteenth century the formal, ecclesiastical ceremonies that took place between death and burial are far more important (607). Added to this abstraction through ceremonial representation, is the fact that after the fourteenth century the body was progressively concealed, under the material accoutrements of interment: pall, shroud, coffin, sarcophagus and carved monument: 'the material covering of the deceased became a theatrical monument such as was erected for the décor of the mystery plays or for grand entrances' (607). The further one moved away from the open veneration of the dead body – the more it was hidden from view – the more fearful a prospect it became.

Ariès characterises the third succeeding epochal mode of death, as a 'savage', 'remote and imminent death', in direct contrast to the 'tame' death of the Middle Ages.

> Where death had once been immediate, familiar, and tame, it gradually began to be surreptitious, violent, and savage ... At first sight it may seem surprising that this period of returning savagery was also characterized by the rise of rationalism, the rise of science and technology, and by faith in progress and its triumph over nature. (608)

Death, which once had been a natural process, increasingly came to be seen as the end-point of a pathological condition. Illness, diagnosed and treated, could lead to death or cure. Death was savage in the sense that it was increasingly taken out of the hands of the person who was dying. Illness was no longer something one diagnosed for oneself, however, it had become the purview of experts who didn't just confirm one's own beliefs (see Duden 1991) but told you what your body was undergoing. The boundaries between life and death became less clear, and conversely much more imminent. If death was no longer the outcome of a process, it was increasingly understood as the act of a 'moment': this is a notion that is still familiar today.

The fourth mode is what Ariès calls the 'death of the other', that is the romanticisation and veneration of the death of a family member or dear friend: the near other, not the 'other' other.

> Privacy is distinguished both from individualism and from the sense of community, and expresses a mode of relating to others that is quite specific and original. Under these conditions, the death of the self had lost its meaning. The fear of death, born of the fantasies of the seventeenth and eighteenth centuries, was transferred from the self to the other, the loved one. (609-10)

So, while people may have been concerned with their own end and still suffered from fear of a savage death brought on by scientific 'progress', when one looks to the ways in which bodies are interred, the monuments to and representations of the dead, one finds memorials that concretise the loss of the living far more than they mark the lives of the dead.

The fifth and final model, which Ariès ascribes to relatively current attitudes to the dead, is one of near total suppression. In this he has much in common with Elias. He argues that death in the late-twentieth century bears with it much of the affective sentimentality and insistence on privacy of death as in the nineteenth century, but '[a]ctually, the intimacy of these final exchanges had already been poisoned, first by the ugliness of disease, and later by the transfer to the hospital. Death became dirty, and then it became medicalized' (611–12). So it is also an extension of the 'savage' scientific death.

> Either way, the result is the same: Neither the individual nor the community is strong enough to recognize the existence of death. And yet this attitude has not annihilated death or the fear of death. On the contrary, it has allowed the old savagery to creep back under the mask of medical technology. The death of the patient in the hospital, covered with tubes, is becoming a popular image, more terrifying than the *transi* or skeleton of macabre rhetoric. (614)

And, to extend Ariès's work into the absolute present, thanks to this medicalised suppression of death, it becomes possible for impossible dreams of permanently avoiding death to take hold. The fantasy of the post-human cyborg (see Chapter 6), whose infinitely replaceable organs and cells are beyond mortality, is the logical extension of that self-important individual of the Middle Ages.

Analysis

When Ariès published his work on childhood, Elias, understandably, criticised him on several counts – primarily for flattening out individual experiences and for overly romanticising the life of the young in medieval France (Goudsblom and Mennell 1998: 196–8). Further, he questioned whether people at that time were quite as happy and resigned to death as Ariès makes out, and rightly so (Elias 1985: 12–13). There are a multitude of images of horrible hells and tormented deaths. There was, after all, supposed to be some threat in retribution in the prospect of Judgment Day and the afterlife. Not everyone was going to go to Heaven: there were also the damned. Further, the examples Ariès cites are written for an audience who are supposed to be learning the art of a 'good death', and which it has to be acknowledged were intended to be propaganda as much as anything else. But while Elias may have (repeatedly) called Ariès a romantic in his descriptions of the past, he agreed that death was certainly more open, acknowledged and spoken of in earlier times.

It is also difficult to accept the assertion that because infants were more likely to succumb to death, their parents were therefore less attached to them. While on the periodisation Ariès uses it may be possible to include early modern English poet Ben Jonson (1572–1637) within the era of 'death of the self', and therefore a more affective attitude to the dead, his poetry on the death of his children asserts a clear attachment to an infant daughter as well as to a boy of seven.[15] In this Jonson is taking part in a revival of the use of classical conventions – consolation – which leads me to a related point. While he does mention the connection to classical precepts, Ariès does not give sufficient weight to the possibility that the Renaissance reverence for and revival of Greek and Roman conventions and the depiction of children as small adults may just indicate a convention for depiction rather than an actual 'seeing' of children in that manner: it is impossible to know what people 'saw' when they looked at an infant without other evidence.

And again, understandably for the time in which he was writing Ariès, like Elias, does not go into any depth on the schooling of girls – they are essentially dismissed in a couple of sentences – nor that while boys were being exhorted to exercise, girls were increasingly restricted in their physical pursuits. Girls became delicate creatures, unless they were of a lower class and had to work to earn their keep. Nor is there any suggestion of the very obvious gendering of death. But the greatest and most persistent criticism of Ariès's description of the historical contingency of childhood – and also the shift in attitudes to death – is that they are based almost exclusively on French examples. Many aspects of his arguments have been shown to be culturally specific.

Inheritors

The intellectual trajectories to which these two writers gave impetus have influenced academic debate across the disciplines for decades, and have spawned both imitation and refutation.

Doing for England what Ariès did for France, Lawrence Stone's *The Family, Sex and Marriage in England: 1500–1800* (1979) has become one of the touchstones of British social history. Like Ariès, Stone has followed through detailed records to trace shifts in family formation over three centuries. He explicitly follows Ariès's thesis on the construction of childhood and the importance of bourgeois affectivity in the shift in relations from a supposedly emotionally detached Middle Ages to a sentimental nineteenth century. While Stone's book, in some measure, redresses criticisms of Ariès's cultural specificity, it is also possible to criticise Stone on the grounds that he begins by too easily accepting Ariès's hypothesis and repeats some of his 'mistakes', such as flattening out the experiences of individuals or groups within the larger social whole. Even so, neither Ariès nor Stone can be ignored.

Carmen Luke (1989) writes on the pedagogic literature of sixteenth-century Germany, but explicitly rejects aspects of Ariès's work, taking his subject matter and period from the theoretical standpoint of Foucauldian discourse analysis. Like Elias, she looks to the writing of Erasmus but even more to the writings of Luther on the upward training of children and how the technology of print influenced 'how the child came to be a focus of study' (ix). Such an approach addresses and redresses that very flattening out of historical and regional difference that can be subsumed within a generalising approach, while at the same time supporting the notion that broad shifts in social practice were taking place. It also problematises and nuances those wider shifts.

In relation to understandings of death, there have been several key studies but one of those most frequently appealed to in relation to early modern British history is Clare Gittings's *Death, Burial and the Individual in Early Modern England* (1984). Gittings makes clear her debt to Ariès but extends beyond his assertions on people's relation to their own death or the abstract concept of death to the very real relation of people to the deaths of those around them. She does this by examining the ways in which they ritually attended to the remains. In fact, Gittings specifically distances herself from any psychological approach to her subject matter. Her work on the social history of death sensitively plots shifts in the understanding and celebration of death at the micro-level.

As a final example I include Stephen Mennell (1996), not least because he is an enthusiastic adherent and editor of Elias. However, unlike the aforementioned authors who approach the same subject matter but adapt the method to a different locale – or reappraise the same locale from a different theoretical standpoint – Mennell takes Elias's methodology and applies it to a subject that is only contingently related. Mennell explicitly uses Elias's work as a template for a study of the changes in 'taste' in relation to food from the Middle Ages to the present in both England and France. But from the outset there is a problem with the use of the word 'taste', and in his reliance on the evidence of cookbooks – texts with totally different functions to manners manuals.

In relying almost exclusively on the evidence of cookbooks – printed texts, and really only the one form of printed text, supporting the thesis he draws from them with secondary sources – Mennell implicitly assumes that cookbooks were followed. Even courtly manners books, which are didactic and pedagogic texts, clearly were not uniformly successful in their messages or they would not have required the repetition of certain directions for so very long. Cookbooks are not about teaching cooking. They are more like a pharmacopoeia, a list of receipts or formulae that function within an accepted and understood framework of practice. Cooking is learned by observation and practice. It is largely handed down from parent to child, or from master to servant, or from senior servant to junior servant. It is the outcome of an apprenticeship. You can learn to cook from a book or from a TV show, but this is not, historically, the most common or indeed the most effective way. And even if a given cookbook is didactic, cooks are not. Cooking is ruled by available produce: ingredients will be substituted either for reasons of availability or taste preference. There is precious little link between the 'gourmet' cooking he describes and day-to-day eating for the majority of the population. And the most recent shifts in the 'taste' in food that he is trying to describe have come from a colonisation of world foods, which are largely taken from traditional regional dishes, not from professional or expert canons of taste. Food in a traditional culture, as an anthropologist knows even if a sociologist doesn't, can hold far more meaning than the simple act of requiting hunger.

Mennell uses 'taste' in a way that implies some kind of increasing civility of food habits, in deference to Elias. But if you are talking about food and you use the word 'taste', you are appealing to its physicality, its reception and ingestion into the human body. On the second point, Mennell's book is curiously lacking. Strangely, for a book on 'taste', it is not until he comes to what people *don't* like to eat, that he takes into account or mentions what food tastes like, feels like, or even consists of. In a book of over 400 pages, he gives perhaps two recipes (from a Depression era hotel trade magazine) and only then to ridicule them because they are made of leftovers: pure snobbery. He is clearly unaware how delectable some meals made from leftovers can be – pirozhki for one. In other words, what is most remarkable about this book is the absence of the body, of embodied eating, in stark contrast to Elias's description of the shaping of the body through manners.

That said, both Elias and Ariès do give us a trajectory of the abstraction of the human body as it gradually shifts and intensifies across time and across borders. We can see clear evidence of shifts from traditional to modern modes of embodied being. They each do so through clear exhortations to the young, or more precisely, young males. I want now to turn to a writer on the body who was less interested in stated rules and regulations than in the general ways in which knowledge(s) gained authority and believability within dominant social formations. Michel Foucault also touches upon the power of educational institutions to affect embodiment within a similar timeframe and covering a similar geographical area. But he also sees in the general acceptance of education and other social institutions a legitimation of those institutions' ability to pronounce on the 'truth' of their field of knowledge. This results, he agues, in a much more subtle and diffuse power by which we internalise regimes of control and learn to self-regulate ourselves, through the regulation of our bodies.

Notes

1 He was fortunate enough to avoid first-hand experience of the atrocities that followed but the combined volume is dedicated to his parents, both of whom died under Hitler's Reich: his father in their home town of Breslau in 1940, his mother shortly after in Auschwitz. (Elias 2000: ii; Goudsblom and Mennell 1998: 77).

2 My emphasis. There is something delightfully absurd in this phrase, but at the same time it epitomises the outcome of the process he is describing: progressive individualisation.

3 This idea of culture can be found in various discourses of 'multiculturalism'.

4 Spain is a rather surprising omission in this list, given the cultural centrality of courtesy across Spanish cultures – but then perhaps it is too confronting because of the mixture of cultures and nationalities within its shifting borders, and its long occupation by a non-Western culture: the Moors.

5 There is a tension in this attitude: this was also an age in which falsehood – seeming and show – were social preoccupations, particularly in relation to women and their capacity to deceive.

6 The connection to Freudian typologies will prove important to the later discussion of Kristeva in Chapter 4.

7 As more recent scholarship has shown (Orgel, Bray, etc.) there is no reason to assume that because people shared beds regularly that sexual relations of all sorts did not occur. Clearly, what we now think of as homosexual, lesbian and pederast acts did happen in more socially open, shared beds, although while not necessarily approved of they were understood in quite different terms.

8 See Geoff Sharp (1985).

9 Although this has been largely in cultural forms whose relation to these metaphors seems far more detached, prurient, and ethically vacant, I am thinking particularly of artists like Damian Hirst.

10 See Anna Bryson (1990).

11 These are Shilling's terms (1993: 164–6).

12 See Carmen Luke (1989). She discusses the influence of Protestant pedagogical primers for the upward training of children (boys) in sixteenth-century German grammar schools.

13 This was a widespread early modern carnivalesque ceremony in which cats were hanged and immolated in public. See Darnton (1984).

14 My thanks to Patricia McGarrity (RN) for this point.

15 See *On My First Daughter* (c.1596) and *On My First Son* (1603) in G. Parfitt (1988: 41, 48).

TWO Regimes and Institutions

Authority and Delimited Control

Where Elias and Ariès were both relatively late-bloomers – and in Elias's case his influence is still gaining in appreciation – Michel Foucault (1926–84) rose comparatively swiftly to intellectual prominence and blazed bright on the international intellectual circuit before an untimely death. He was in the thick of the intellectual debates around structuralism, postructuralism and postmodernism, and frequently clashed with his more politically programmatic contemporaries – most notably Habermas. Influenced and informed by 'his theoretical forefathers – Marx, Nietzsche, Freud, Sartre' (Foucault 1988b) and taught by Althusser, he came to reject ideology and general political projects, instead moving on to form his own method to explain subjectivity and power, one that critiqued institutions and their effects on the individual.

Foucault was born in Poitiers into a 'petit bourgeois, provincial milieu', was educated in philosophy at the École Normale Supérieure, and in the early 1950s he also studied psychology while working at the Hôpital Ste. Anne. He was four years older and therefore several years ahead of Derrida and Bourdieu. Those years were sufficient to make Bourdieu – whom he lectured – feel as if they belonged to different academic generations.[1] He was a prominent and popular public intellectual, photographed in street demonstrations, frequently published in newspapers and magazines. The success and influence of his publications were mirrored in his academic positions. He was director of the Institut Français, Hamburg and at the Institut de Philosophie at the Faculté des Lettres at the University of Clermont-Ferrand. At the time of his death he held a chair at the prestigious Collège de France. In a bitter irony, the author of books deeply concerned with the control and containment of the human body through medical means fell victim to AIDS, the containment and treatment of which epitomise his observations on medical science.

Unlike Elias and Bourdieu, Foucault's writings were translated into English relatively quickly and his ideas were both argued about and adopted much more rapidly than those of most of his similarly intellectually prominent countrymen. Like Ariès, Foucault was trained in history – though the philosophy of history rather than demography. He was a protégé of the famous French historian of medicine, Georges Canguilhem. And like Ariès, his work was influential upon the *Annales* writers, though largely because it was hotly contested. In the Introduction I said his historical scholarship has been questioned – largely because he is frugal in citing documentary sources to support his (often) sweeping and epochal conclusions. What cannot be contested is the breadth and depth of his influence. As one would expect from its title, this chapter deals with Foucault's descriptions of the body as constituted or formed through the practices of social institutions – educational, medical, religious and judicial. Foucault's work on destabilising the taken-for-granted authority of institutional frameworks that have been in place from the seventeenth century to the present has been responsible in turn for the reconception of many academic disciplines, including sociology and anthropology.

Foucault

Michel Foucault was neither a sociologist nor an anthropologist, nor even a social historian as such, and has no clear 'theories'. However, the influence of his ideas and his writings has been felt across most disciplines in the humanities, particularly in relation to understandings of the body in society. He liked to think of himself as an archaeologist of the present. Because he wrote extensively on issues that are integral to contemporary Western social being and society – power as it is exercised in medical apparatuses, legal systems, through sexual mores – the influence of his ideas has been particularly powerful in comparative sociology. It has to be said that his work has been the impetus for a good deal of what has become known as the sociology of the body, and underpins much of the work discussed in Parts II and III of this book.

While it may sound dismissive to say that Foucault has no theories, it is not inaccurate, at least in the sense that Bourdieu and Elias each have a world-view that permeates and is developed progressively throughout their work. We saw this in the previous chapter in relation to Elias's recognition of the importance of the body as an object of social control. In the following chapter I will deal with Bourdieu, an anthropologist who brought the body's function in social space into focus. They have each provided social and theoretical approaches that have had considerable influence outside their own specific fields. Foucault is more eclectic. He has persistent ideas, but they are never formulated as clearly nor as boldly stated as one finds in standard social theory. This has led many people to dismiss his work as amorphous and unhelpful. While I acknowledge there is much that is unresolved in Foucault's work, and there is a persistent inattention to gender issues – though the same has to be said of Elias and Bourdieu – without his demystifying of systems of thought (medical, psychological, penal, sexual), it is difficult to see how many areas of sociological inquiry would have progressed (medicine, psychology, criminology) or in some instances begun (queer studies, disability studies). Further, some of that indeterminacy or analytic evasiveness is also inevitable when what he was most interested in is the hardest of all phenomena to capture, particularly in historical terms: thought. What is harder to ameliorate is that while demystification is undoubtedly important and interesting in itself, there is little in his work that offers a positive political or social outcome. This is a point to which I shall return later. What he does have in common with Elias and Ariès is a deep interest in the shifts that have occurred in social behaviour across time and a concomitant concern with the importance of the shaping and control of the body, as they are effected through 'mentalities'.

Foucault is interested in tracing antecedents to present conditions, in mapping progressions across time. Over the course of his various 'histories of the present' his own ideas shifted and evolved – for instance, he left behind the notion of 'archaeology' as a way of describing his approach to history in favour of 'genealogy'. Archaeology implies the collection of objects as traces from which events and lives of a period are reconstituted, whereas a genealogy implies a tracing of links between people or events across time, up to the present moment. Neither of these terms is pressingly important here – I offer this contrast merely as an example of the ways in which Foucault's own thought shifted. What is important, and what lies behind all the terms I shall discuss below as central in the sociohistory of the body found in Foucault's writings – 'gaze', 'discourse', 'authority', 'panopticon', 'power', 'the repressive hypothesis' – is the idea of the 'episteme' and 'epistemic shifts'.

Epistemology is the science or philosophy of knowledge. An 'episteme' is a body of knowledge or a system of meaning. For Foucault, an episteme is fundamentally associated with a socially recognised institution that has the power and authority to define the parameters of that knowledge, and its language or 'discourse'. For example, medicine has or is an episteme, in that it has its own authoritative discourse. An 'epistemic shift' then, as the term implies, refers to a shift in meaning. These shifts are not confined to just a word, or a group of words. A 'discourse' is the sum of an area of knowledge in a given historical period that constitutes a world-view. World-views do, and will continue to, change. It is then that epistemes, epistemologies, 'shift'. And it is through those discourses, those shifting epistemologies, that Foucault's notion of a diffuse power is enabled. It is not a power that resides in any one person's hands, rather it is the sum total of the power of discourses to influence, shape and control, *from below*. And, most importantly for our purposes, they are enacted on and through the body. To give a well-known example, up until the late-nineteenth century homosexuality did not exist. While that may sound absurd – clearly homoerotic encounters and relationships have occurred throughout history – the idea of a medically and legally defined 'condition' known as homosexuality did not exist before that time. Always there but understood and named in different ways, homosexuality became known in a medico-legal way within particular knowledge systems that thereafter have controlled its meaning.

Just when these shifts happen is important too. Foucault situates the most important epistemic shifts for his histories of the present in the social changes that have occurred in post-Renaissance Europe: Western culture since the seventeenth century. Indeed, in Foucault's terms, what Ariès describes as the invention of childhood is the product of an epistemic shift in education – Elias's evolution of manners is describing epistemic shifts in courtesy. These ideas recur throughout his work and will be drawn out more fully in the following explorations of the works that are the most immediately concerned with, and most influential upon, the sociology of the body.

Madness and Civilization

Foucault's description of the medicalised body that is fully explored in *The Birth of the Clinic* (1975) is closely related to this earlier work on a cognate field: mental illness. In the Middle Ages, people whom we would now think of as mentally ill were seen as spiritually blessed or afflicted. Foucault describes a process whereby distracted minds became the subject of medical treatment. He makes the case that with the general shift away from the notion of health and illness as defined in humoral theories – which occurred from the seventeenth century onwards – came a shift in the understanding of mental states. In the theory of the humours, four fluids or humours circulated around the body. If one looks at contemporary sources, such as Montaigne, one can see that each of these humours was deemed to have a characteristic effect on the mind and body; each was associated with a particular part of the body and each humour was constitutionally moist or dry, hot or cold. Black choler (cold and dry) leads to melancholy; yellow choler (hot and dry) promotes anger; blood (hot and moist) denotes a sanguine nature; and phlegm (cold and moist) is characteristic of those with a phlegmatic nature. In harmony and balance, you have a rounded personality, rude health and a happy mind. A preponderance of any particular humour leads to imbalance and ill-health: to cite a well-known literary example, Hamlet is a classic melancholic, suffering from an excess of black choler.

Foucault argues that when 'madness' was humoral, it involved a mind *and* body complex, and the two were dealt with as such. While neither directly attributable to nor immediately in response to Descartes's writings, his work was pivotal in this epistemic shift. After Descartes pondered upon the separation of the mind and the body – the idea of the body as a machine inhabited by a thinking 'ghost' – and these notions began to circulate, it set the groundwork for humoral theory to be superseded. Mechanistic bodies had *nervous* complaints that could be treated by addressing a mechanical structure, the nervous system. The emphasis shifted from holistic rebalancing of the mind and body to treatment of the malfunctioning machine. The disordered body was 'punished' to treat mental states, to shock the mind out of its torpor. The nervous explanation took on the construction of the body as a conduit for impulses distinct from and yet influential upon the workings of the mind. Concomitant with this came a gradual shift in the practical treatment and detention of the mentally ill, from one where the 'madmen were running the asylum' to a system dominated by the trained keeper and attendant, who 'intervenes, without weapons, without instruments of constraint, with observation and language only; he advances upon madness, deprived of all that could protect him or make him seem threatening, risking an immediate confrontation without recourse' (Foucault 1988a: 251). This is much like the shift in imprisonment we see described in *Discipline and Punish*, where gaolers moved from being alternately torturers and hoteliers, to a system of warders and watchers.

The first major innovation in the handling of the mentally ill that Foucault describes is the practice of detention. The housing of the 'mad' in specific institutions across the centuries – hospitals, 'Bedlams', asylums, sanitaria – simultaneously hid away and drew attention to the fact of their state. The Age of Reason was thoroughly discomfited by what it defined as unruly and dangerous unreason.

> Confinement hid away unreason, and betrayed the shame it aroused; but it explicitly drew attention to madness, pointed to it. If, in the case of unreason, the chief intention was to avoid scandal, in the case of madness that intention was to organize it. A strange contradiction: the classical age enveloped madness in a total experience of unreason; it reabsorbed its particular forms, which the Middle Ages and the Renaissance had clearly individualized into a general apprehension in which madness consorted indiscriminately with all the forms of unreason. But at the same time it assigned to this same madness a special sign: not that of sickness, but that of glorified scandal. (70)

Where passion, divine madness, irrational ecstasy, can be a recognised and accepted state of 'grace' brought on or supported by humoral imbalance, unreason is the shameful and scandalous outcome of a malfunctioning body which poisons the beauty and reason of the mind. Unreasonable, animalistic bodies betray the light of pure reason in the mind because they are passionate objects.

As the episteme shifts, it is the meeting of the animalistic, passionate and active body with the rational but essentially passive mind that leads to mental disorder. These are two entities that work in tandem but not in harmony, unlike earlier understandings of medicalised embodiment. 'The medicine of humours sees this unity primarily as a reciprocal interaction' (86).

> Madness, then, was not merely one of the possibilities afforded by the union of soul and body; it was not just one of the consequences of passion. Instituted by the unity of soul and body, madness turned against that unity and once again put it in question. Madness, made possible by passion, threatened by a movement proper to itself what had made passion itself possible. Madness was one of those unities in which laws were compromised, perverted, distorted – thereby manifesting such unity as evident and established, but also as fragile and already doomed to destruction. (89)

This led to the reconception of all sorts of maladies. Any kind of distraction of the mind, if it could not be understood as a predominantly physical/mechanical syndrome, was in danger of being classified as a form of madness.

> As long as vapors were convulsions or strange sympathetic communications through the body, even when they led to fainting and loss of consciousness, they were not madness. But once the mind becomes blind through the very excess of sensibility – then madness appears. (158)

We do not really need to go into the ways and means by which those classified as mad were increasingly incarcerated – and physically abused – from the seventeenth century onwards. What is important here is Foucault's honing in on the moment of the Cartesian dualism – the mind–body split – in terms of an epistemic shift. Foucault unpicks a largely unquestioned assumption that Descartes had got it 'right' and humoral theory is an outmoded and nonsensical world-view. He recasts the epistemic shift in the understanding of 'madness' in terms of a shifting of mentalities around mentality and embodiment: in short, the conditions of possibility for psychology to emerge in the nineteenth century.

> It was no longer the presence of truth that determined the cure, but a functional norm. In this reinterpretation of the old method, the organism was no longer related to anything but itself and its own nature, while in the initial version, what was to be restored was its relation with the world, its essential link with being and with truth: if we add that the rotatory machine was soon used as a threat and a punishment, we see the impoverishment of the meanings which had richly sustained the therapeutic methods throughout the entire classical period. Medicine was now content to regulate and to punish, with means which had once served to exorcise sin, to dissipate error in the restoration of madness to the world's obvious truth. (177)

The mad need to be (rudely) awakened from their slumber of (immoral) unreason: 'A purely psychological medicine was made possible only when madness was alienated in guilt' (182–3). And until they awaken they need to be restrained, either by institutionalisation or through medical therapies that contain and control their symptoms in one form or another. Historically contextualising mental illness in this way simultaneously uncovers and calls into question current carceral tendencies in the treatment of the mentally ill, and the power-plays at work in the medication of the mentally ill to rein them in to an acceptable 'norm'. It offers other ways of looking at different mental states, whether within or across cultures. And it lays bare how a fundamental but taken-for-granted reconception of the body is at the centre of how the dominant medical treatments of mental illness have become enshrined.

The Birth of the Clinic

In *The Birth of the Clinic* (1975) Foucault rewrites the history of medicine, undoing the 'enlightened march of progress' narrative that medical science holds dear to itself. He moves away from the positivist notion that science has increasingly got things 'right', that superseded medical systems were based on ignorance or 'bad science'. Foucault instead looks to the shifts in the systems of meaning that have supported the different medical beliefs that have culminated in modern Western medicine. He implicitly accords equal weight to each of the medical epistemologies, showing that each relied on an internally coherent world-view that mutated along with the mutation in social forms in which they functioned.

The effect that these epistemic shifts in medical theories had was particularly important for the understanding of the human body; for, in Western cultures at least, medicine or biology (the science or study of life) has become the primary means of approaching and interpreting the body. There are a number of ways in which the nature or culture of medical science shifted. The core features of the epistemic shifts that Foucault describes here are the medical 'gaze' – medical perception – and the importance of the gaze for the abstraction of the body. The closer doctors came to the body in the ways in which diseases were diagnosed – from feeling the pulse to biopsy – the further away they were drawn from the embodied patient. It is important here to be careful and note that while Foucault uses the word 'abstract', it is in the general sense of that term, not in the analytical sense of arguing 'from abstraction'. However, in the terms of the overall argument from abstraction of this book, the process did involve a material abstraction (James 2006) carried by the practices within the field of medicine. At the same time, we can say that the further the medical gaze penetrated into the body using increasingly technoscientific means – from anatomy to the MRI – the more *abstract* have its representation and its understanding become.

Foucault claims that with the coming of the clinic – the medical establishment that superseded the lazar house and the infirmary in the seventeenth century – earlier surface diagnostics were also superseded:

> Not only the names of diseases, not only the grouping of systems were not the same; but the fundamental perceptual codes that were applied to patients' bodies, the field of objects to which observation addressed itself, the surfaces and depths traversed by the doctor's gaze, the whole system of orientation of this gaze also varied. (Foucault 1975: 54)

Physic, the scholarly medicine learned in universities as opposed to the practical apprenticeship of surgery, was based in theories that expressly avoided contact with the body. Surgeons were mechanicals who set bones, cut for the stone and applied external treatments. Physicians were scholars who diagnosed by symptoms and administered internal medications. Physicians ran the 'clinics' or hospitals.

> But in a few years, the last years of the [eighteenth] century, the clinic was to undergo a sudden, radical restructuring: detached from the theoretical context in which it was born, it was to be given a field of application that was no longer confined to that in which knowledge was *said*, but which was co-extensive with that in which it was born, put to the test, and fulfilled itself: it was to be identified with the *whole* of medical experience. For this, it had to be armed with new powers, detached from

the language on the basis of which it had been offered as a lesson, and freed for the movement of discovery. (62)

That theoretical context was Linnaean taxonomies. Medicine became observational and 'experimental' – that is empiricist, identified and classified by genus, taught theoretically instead of by an insistence on an unquestioning scholastic reverence for texts: 'Once one defined a practical experiment carried out on the patient himself, one insisted on the need to relate particular knowledge to an encyclopaedic whole' (71). Combined with this, medical healing (very) gradually moved out of the home and into the hospital, which had once been the site of treatment only for society's poorest and most feared.

Hospitals were increasingly funded by rich benefactors and therefore continued to be charitable institutions, as they had been under the aegis of the various religious orders that had initially set up the lazar houses and hospices in the Middle Ages. However, there was a different tenor to the arrangement once capital entered into the picture. The rich gave the funds but the poor repaid in kind.

In a regime of economic freedom, the hospital had found a way of interesting the rich; the clinic constitutes the progressive reversal, of the other contractual part; it is the *interest* paid by the poor on the capital that the rich have consented to invest in the hospital; an interest that must be understood in its heavy surcharge, since it is a compensation that is of the order of *objective interest* for science and of *vital interest* for the rich. The hospital became viable for private initiative from the moment that sickness, which had come to seek a cure, was turned into spectacle. Helping ended up by paying, thanks to the virtues of the clinical gaze. (85)

To extend Foucault's example, this is the beginning of the experimental scientific medicine that we live with to this day, where teaching hospitals – historically, by their nature public hospitals – are used for experimental procedures on those who have least choice in life. The disempowered, and predominantly the poor under duress, end up benefiting the rich. While Foucault does not go into specifics, it is a simple fact that plastic surgery techniques (nose, jaw and cheek 'jobs') have become possible because of what has been learned from both the emergency treatments applied to burns victims, and through the reconstructive surgery on trauma victims and those with cranio-facial anomalies. Standard orthopaedic surgery (hip and knee replacement) has learned much of its 'art' from battlefield surgery or the treatment of road-trauma victims. Embryonic stem cell technology would not exist without IVF.

Foucault argues that what the medical 'gaze' did was to render visible and understandable surface symptoms, but it also led to the visualisation of internal structures, symptoms and pathologies. The doctor's visual attention, rather than his theoretical learning, brought the truth of illness to the surface. What the sufferer felt or believed came to mean less and less: it was the physician's observations that lent coherence to disease processes. The medical gaze structured them, much as 'natural history' structured and classified the natural world (89). But observation alone was not sufficient, it had then to be interpreted through an authoritative language.

> In this regular alternation of speech and gaze, the disease gradually declares its truth, a truth that it offers to the eye and ear, whose theme, although possessing only one *sense*, can be restored, in its indubitable totality, only by two *senses*: that which sees and that which listens. (112)

Vision is rendered into discourse. The body came into a new kind of existence through the abstracted visualisation and auralisation of its symptoms, its boundaries, its depths and cavities. What we would now call a 'clinical history' as a means of diagnosis is an outcome of this process. In the general sense of the word, that visual cognition and its consequent discourse *abstract* embodied disease experiences into the hands, eyes, ears and mouth of the physician (119). And in the analytical sense, the symptoms and the experience of disease are abstracted away from the body in which it is housed. It becomes an entity in itself under the gaze of the physician, over which he has the power of bringing into being. But, most importantly:

> The access of the medical gaze into the sick body was not the continuation of a movement of approach that had been developing in a more or less regular fashion since the day when the first doctor cast his somewhat unskilled gaze from afar on the body of the first patient; it was the result of a recasting at the level of epistemic knowledge [*savoir*] itself, and not at the level of accumulated, refined, deepened, adjusted knowledge [*connaissances*] ... It is not a matter of the same game, somewhat improved, but of a quite different game. (137)

Ultimately, disease has a topography in the corpse that can be 'mapped' and, as a result, the focus on anatomy as a means to pathology became increasingly important, rather than just a means to identify and learn bodily structures as it had been from the time of sixteenth-century Italian anatomist Andreas Vesalius.

> From the point of view of death, disease has a land, a mappable territory, a subterranean, but secure place where its kinships and its consequences are formed; local values define its forms. Paradoxically, the presence of the corpse enables us to perceive it living – living with a life that is no longer that of either old sympathies or the combinative laws of complications, but one that has its own roles and its own laws. (149)

And so death ends up defining life. Up to the late-nineteenth century the normative subject of anatomy was the criminal body: what is otherwise reviled became the template for the healthy body (Cregan 1999). The problem being, of course, that in relying on anatomical investigation as a guide to life, certain processes implicated in death do not allow a direct translation to the function of disease in the living body – something that did not become fully apparent until the successful use of anaesthesia. Basing the idea of living on death had odd consequences on the meaning of what it was to be within one's body, what a body meant at all: 'the idea of a disease attacking life must be replaced by the much denser notion of *pathological life*' (Foucault 1975: 153).

Paradoxically, the whole notion of the ailing body shifted from diagnosing from symptoms or external evidence and verbal inquiry – whereby, the patient had the power over what ailed him or her[2] – to a surrendering of that power to a doctor. And it was the doctor who at once projected beyond the surfaces of the body, laying on hands and ears, intruding with a penetrating gaze, while at the same time rendering the body more abstract and more distanced both from the patient, and from himself.

> Sounding by percussion is not justified if the disease is composed only of a web of symptoms; it becomes necessary if the patient is hardly more than an injected corpse, a half-filled barrel. To establish these signs, artificial or natural, is to project upon the living body a whole network of anatomo-pathological mappings: to draw the dotted outline of the future autopsy. The problem, then, is to bring to the surface that which is layered in depth; semiology will no longer be a *reading*, but the set of techniques that make it possible to constitute a *projective pathological anatomy*. The clinician's gaze was directed upon a succession and upon an area of pathological events; it had to be both synchronic and diachronic, but in any case it was placed under temporal obedience; it *analysed a series*. The anatomo-clinician's gaze has *to map a volume*; it deals with the complexity of spatial data which for the first time in medicine are three-dimensional. Whereas clinical experience implied the constitution of *a mixed web of the visible and the readable*, the new semiology requires a sort of *sensorial triangulation* in which various atlases, hitherto excluded from medical techniques, must collaborate: the ear and touch are added to sight. (162-3)

This is the description of the 'before' and 'after' moments of a major shift in the medical episteme.

Though these are not Foucault's terms – nor particularly in sympathy with them – it also identifies a moment in the intensification of the abstraction of the human body that is at the heart of the medical way of understanding being that is dominant in the contemporary world: technoscientific medicine. Foucault identifies the instrumental means of representing bodily processes that were the first step in the on-going process of the analytical abstraction of embodiment: the body as read and interpreted by ultrasound, X-ray, ECG, EEG, by CT, MRI and PET scans.

He rightly notes that something as simple as the 'stethoscope, solidified distance, transmits profound and invisible events along a semi-tactile, semi-auditory axis' (164). It sets up a physical and moral distance between the doctor and the patient. The physician's senses become a means of triangulating and unmasking invisible diseases: 'A gaze that touches, hears, and, moreover, not by essence or necessity, sees' (164). While putting it in a far more ideological form than Foucault would be comfortable with, this is the necessary grounding for contemporary experiences of constitutive abstraction (Sharp 1985) to obtain.

> Conceived in relation to nature, disease was the non-assignable negative of which the causes, forms, and manifestations were offered only indirectly and against an ever-receding background; seen in relation to death, disease becomes exhaustively legible, open without remainder to the sovereign dissection of language and of the gaze. It is when death became the concrete a priori of medical experience that death could detach itself from counter-nature and become *embodied* in the *living bodies* of individuals. (Foucault 1975: 196)

So, in essence, the 'modern' body is patterned on, modelled on, interpreted through, the corpse. Ironically, as we saw in studies of death and dying in the work of both Elias and Ariès, this eventuates in a medical science that is determinedly at war with death. This is a battle that some science fictionalised accounts of embodiment see as pyrrhically, and even potentially literally, winnable. We will return to this in Chapter 6 in discussions of the work of theorists like Donna Haraway. But for Foucault, the modern medical body brought into being through the 'gaze' is an abstracted body – not dead, but seen through a glass darkly.

The Archaeology of Knowledge

What is not stated outright, but is implicit in both *Madness and Civilisation* and *The Birth of the Clinic*, is how these epistemic shifts that result in the reconception of the body take hold. In *The Archaeology of Knowledge* (1994) Foucault gives his most ordered attempt at a theorisation of how this happens. I have already introduced the episteme – a body of knowledge that encompasses a world-view that is fundamentally associated with a socially recognised institution. That institution has the power and authority to define the parameters of that knowledge, and its language or 'discourse'. That authority may or may not be granted in the first instance by a state body – it may have been conveyed by much more amorphous means and in Foucault's terms, in either case, it maintains its authority by a diffuse, nebulous power.

The 'authorities of delimitation' within these institutions – that is experts in the field – are vested with the authority of the language or discourse of that field. In the preceding two examples, the most obvious 'authorities' are the doctors who have the power of knowing more about what is going on inside an individual than the individual experiencing the disease or the mental illness. They 'own' the 'discourse' of medicine and medical psychology. An epistemic shift takes place when the meanings within their discourse shift: from a holistic embodiment to a mind–body dualism; and from an opaque and self-knowing sufferer to a compliant patient under the watchful diagnostic 'gaze' of a physician. But that shift is at no time at the will of the 'authorities of delimitation': they are just as much enmeshed in the diffuse power of discourse as those who do not have access to that authority. They merely enact and are vested with the authority of what becomes taken for granted over time.

Discipline and Punish

Having uncovered the archaeology of psychology and medicine, Foucault moved on to combine the concerns of each of them in a study of judicial authority, *Discipline and Punish* (1991). In approaching the bodily control and demarcation of the criminal, Foucault's work both draws together the concerns of the clinic and the asylum and is a logical extension of that work, dwelling as it does on the pathologisation and the incarceration of aberrant individuals. Indeed, he writes:

> This book is intended as a correlative history of the modern soul and of a new power to judge; a genealogy of the present scientifico-legal complex from which the power to punish derives its bases, justifications and rules, from which it extends its effects and by which it masks its exorbitant singularity. (Foucault 1991: 23)

In the Middle Ages and the Renaissance, at a time when the mind and the body were holistically intertwined, punishment was far more visceral and physical. Where the mad were tolerated for their flights from the truth of the world, criminals who knowingly abused the sovereign's and – in a time when the sovereign ruled with divine authority – by logical extension God's law, had their bodies mortified. As Foucault lovingly describes in the opening pages of this book, the sovereign's divinely sanctioned will was quite literally written into the flesh of one as wicked as an attempted regicide. If the soul or mind was dispersed throughout, or at least indissociable from, the corporeal form then inflicting physical punishment makes absolute sense. 'Treatment' and rehabilitation, which

55

became fashionable in the nineteenth century, only makes sense in a world in which the mind is separable from the actions of the body. Applying a medical or psychological solution to the 'wicked' or 'sinful' would have seemed absurd in the Middle Ages except in the case of possession, and even then exorcism was often effected via physical means.

In the case of the social means of dealing with criminal acts, the epistemic shift comes with a move away from punishing the body to supposedly retraining – or punishing – the mind. Up to the eighteenth century, prison was a place in which one languished while awaiting punishment, or in which your physical punishment was meted out. Foucault is interested in the 'new tactics of power' (23) that are characteristic of modern Western culture:

> [T]he systems of punishment are to be situated in a certain 'political economy' of the body: even if they do not make use of violent or bloody punishment, even when they use 'lenient' methods involving confinement or correction, it is always the body that is at issue - the body and its forces, their utility and their docility, their distribution and their submission. (25)

> Replacing the adversary of the sovereign, the social enemy was transformed into a deviant, who brought with him the multiple danger of disorder, crime and madness. The carceral nework linked, through innumerable relations, the two long, multiple series of the punitive and the abnormal. (299–300)

So, the twinned effects of the medicalisation of aberrance and the abstraction under the medical 'gaze' meet in the prison. The phenomenon that Foucault identifies as the exemplary institution of this conjunction is the 'panopticon'. Literally, the panopticon is a building, or rather exists in a structural plan for a prison devised by a nineteenth-century Englishman, liberal and social reformer – Jeremy Bentham. The design consists of separate cells for each criminal – in which they are constantly visible through a grilled front. The cells are arranged in a circular array facing towards a central tower. Prison guards, who are not visible, watch the prisoners from this tower. The power of the panopticon lies in self-regulation. The 'penitent' cannot see the warders – never knows for certain if the warder is actually watching or even in the tower – but under the unseen but all-seeing eye regulates his or her behaviour *as if* s/he is under observation. God, the sovereign, or 'The Man' is always watching. While Bentham's design was never carried out to the letter, the theoretical approach behind it is clearly recognisable in contemporary prison design and management, and indeed in all contemporary social surveillance techniques.

What in comparison to flaying and torture at first appears to be a 'lenient' and 'redemptive' system of rehabilitation actually relies on absolute authority. Foucault uses the term 'panopticon', like 'the gaze', to describe the full political outcome of the absorption into oneself of self-regulatory behaviour that stems from the belief that one is always being watched. Here I am deliberately glossing over the stages in the shift from bodily to mental punishment, but the bases of it are recognisable from *Madness and Civilization*: the same dynamic that separates the soul of the madman out for attention as a means to the body is revisited here in the case of the criminal.

> A 'soul' inhabits him and brings him to existence, which is itself a factor in the mastery that power exercises over the body. The soul is the effect and instrument of a political anatomy; the soul is the prison of the body. (30)

This is an extension of the medical/psychiatric gaze, in a parallel epistemic shift. Only the impetus behind the panopticon is not merely diagnoses or treatment: it incorporates a mentality of training that goes beyond the carceral. This manifestation of power extends to a range of arenas in which docile bodies are trained into submission: for example, in military service, and in educational models, which according to Ariès in nineteenth-century France were based upon the techniques of military training. 'A glance at the new art of punishing clearly reveals the supersession of the punitive semio-technique by a new techniques of the body' (103).

The effect of the prison on criminal bodies is extended to the effect of power on and through the body in society. The carceral becomes a part of society in general, based in a new system of law, and a new system of general self- and other-control.

> The carceral network, in its compact or disseminated forms, with its systems of insertion, distribution, surveillance, observation, has been the greatest support, in modern society, of the normalizing power ... The carceral texture of society assures both the real capture of the body and its perpetual observation; it is, by its nature, the apparatus of punishment that conforms most completely to the new economy of power and the instrument for the formation of knowledge that this very economy needs. (304)

For Foucault, the deeper lesson to be learned is that the prison is not the only imprisoning object in society, it is 'linked to a whole series of "carceral" mechanisms which seem distinct enough – since they are intended to alleviate pain, to cure, to comfort – but which all tend, like the prison, to exercise a power of normalization' (308).

The History of Sexuality, Volume 1: an Introduction

If normalisation is the underlying motif of the area of prisons, sexual normalisation is the focus of the final book I discuss in relation to

Foucault's impact on the sociology and anthropology of the body. I will leave aside Volumes 2 and 3, which were works in progress when he died and were published posthumously, and confine myself to very briefly discussing Volume 1 of the *History of Sexuality* (1990). The nub of Foucault's thought in this final completed book to be published in his life-time is that there was an epistemic shift in Western societies's approach to sexual matters during the seventeenth century. He asserts that – where up to that time a great range of sexual activity was experienced, explored and openly spoken of – this period marks a shift that led to the 'closet-ing' and making shameful of all things sexual.

We can see in this a reflection of Elias's arguments on manners, that there are certain things that, by the nineteenth century, one no longer speaks of in polite company – and certainly not in front of children. Ariès also makes much of the inconsequence of sexual play involving the infant Dauphin at the French court in the sixteenth century and the increasing 'protection' of children from sexual knowledge up until relatively recently. Foucault goes beyond this by arguing that what in fact happened was that while sex became a publicly indiscreet topic of conversation, in the confes-sional and on the psychoanalyst's couch it became the subject of uncon-tained chatter. Sex was not to be spoken of, and simultaneously to be spoken of in great detail. This conundrum is known as the 'repressive hypothesis'.

> I do not maintain that the prohibition of sex is a ruse; but it is a ruse to make prohibition into the basic and constitutive element from which one would be able to write the history of what has been said concerning sex starting from the modern epoch. All these negative elements – defenses, censor-ships, denials – which the repressive hypothesis groups together in one great central mechanism destined to say no, are doubtless only component parts that have a local and tactical role to play in a transformation into discourse, a technology of power, and a will to knowledge that are far from being reducible to the former. (Foucault 1990: 12)

Again, this comes out of the twinned effects of shifts in religious and med-ical epistemologies. The confessional is one site of this endless chatter, the other is the medico-psychological consulting room. Sex became a site of power and control on and through the body, within the descriptive and defining powers of religion and medicine.

> Discourse, therefore, had to trace the meeting line of the body and the soul, following all its meanderings: beneath the surface of the sins, it would lay bare the unbroken nervure of the flesh. Under the authority of language that had been carefully expurgated so that it was no longer directly named, sex was taken charge of, tracked down as it were, by a discourse that aimed to allow it no obscurity, no respite. (20)

That power was effected through self-regulation and self-control mecha-nisms, in much the same way as the body is trained under the carceral system. Diffuse mechanisms of power – under the authorities of delimitation in the Church, in the medical establishment, and in the courts – have led to the repression of sex through the paradoxically repressive 'discourse' *on* sex. It was a discourse that did 'not derive from morality alone but from rationality as well' (24). This, of course, had obvious effects on the way the body functions in society. If sex is a matter of guilt and endless verbal rehearsal, whole regimens of self-control and self-restraint around sexuality come into play. By the time he came to write the beginnings of the two subsequent volumes, Foucault's intention in uncovering the repression of sexual discourse was to demystify the guilt and shame associated with the endless silence and speaking about it, to recoup pleasure from the stranglehold of power.

There is much to take on board from this successive account of deep and diffuse power structures at work in recognised and established systems of thought. But was pleasure ever absent? Was Foucault a little too pessimistic and sceptical for his own (and our) good?

Analysis

Most of all, what Foucault has to say to us is that in the shift from traditional to early modern to modern and now postmodern embodiment, we have internalised the control mechanisms that are set in place by various authorities of delimitation and institutionally legitimated epistemologies. In essence, he is saying that we have 'bought the system'. This has great importance for sociology and anthropology, particularly as it pertains to just those authorities of delimitation: medicine, the law, religion, education systems, state systems, etc. It provides one means of demystifying how societies accept and absorb expertise or professional knowledges as truths. Unfortunately, in political terms, Foucault offers no way of returning the goods we have bought, except perhaps by ignoring them. There are certain perils contained in utterly dismissing modern 'establishments' – most notably the medical. In that respect at the very least, he minimises the content of epistemes too readily, for while in practice techno-medical regimes may repressively control and contain bodies, they also offer many useful means of curbing and treating the material effects of diseases on embodied, social beings.

With respect to the repressive hypothesis, one could almost say this was in direct reaction to Elias and the civilisation thesis: that is, Elias argued that as people become more civilised they became 'silent' on the grossest behaviours and stopped directly curbing them because they were understood as improper, except by the lowest of classes. Foucault is saying precisely the opposite in his description of the repressive hypothesis: people couldn't stop talking about their sexual behaviour. But at what level is this true? If one looks forward to the theorisations of Bourdieu, surely there is a huge differentiation to be made between the effectiveness of such mechanisms from social grouping to social grouping. We saw in relation to the criticism of Elias that he did not take into account that he was dealing only with the upper, courtly classes. A similar criticism can be levelled at Foucault. He is really only talking about the effects of these mechanisms on the middle classes.

Further, when it comes down to it, Foucault's discussions are invariably talking about 'mentalities', even when he is explicitly talking about bodily effects. There is no account of the difference there may be between the effects of his diffuse and amorphous power on the grounds of gender, class, race, culture, etc. Further, it is almost exclusively confined to Western thought. That in itself gives away too much, overempowers Western cultural history and makes it too hegemonic. There is no accommodation of cultural difference, the possibility that other ways of being survive and flourish beside the dominant modes of thinking and being he describes. It is true, however, that subsequent writers have certainly built upon his work to address these issues, for instance, Lois McNay's *Foucault and Feminism* (1992) attempts to find a place for the female body in his method, and Edward Said was influenced by Foucault in writing *Orientalism* (1978), even if he did so with qualifications.

Most damningly, however, Foucault's strategies offer no political alternative. His work is confined to the description of the material conditions of how things are and came to be from a particular perspective. As we shall see in the next chapter, like Bourdieu, Foucault does not seem to be able to offer any real explanation of agency, nor any hope of it, within such a diffuse power. But, while Foucault provides no means or real encouragement to go beyond this point to praxis, the demystifying tools within his work are an important first step and can offer a springboard to go beyond merely recognising the state of play.

Inheritors

One is faced with an embarrassment of riches when it comes to discussing the direct and indirect inheritors of Foucault. I shall confine myself to two influential writers who have used his work to great effect (Turner, Sennett) and to one example of the kind of static descriptive comparative sociology that it can lead to (Finkelstein).

Bryan Turner, along with Mike Featherstone, was one of the earliest sociologists to take up Foucault's preoccupation with the body and extend it into his sociological methodology. Turner has in his three key works – *The Body and Society* (1984/1996), *Medical Power and Social Knowledge* (1987/1995) and *Religion and Social Theory* (1983/1991) – literally built upon Foucault's three main concerns: the law, medicine and religion. He picks up where Foucault leaves off, extending into sociological histories, contemporary social interactions and the socio-political importance of the institutional power wielded in each of these spheres, on and through the human body. He has worked hard to pull out what unsystematic theorisation there is in Foucault's works and succeeded in opening up new ground on which much of the sociology of the body has been built. Religion, law and medicine have long been preoccupations of sociologists, but the intervention of Foucault's work into sociological theory through the aegis of writers like Turner has enabled a shift within sociology itself, whereby each of these areas has become a recognisable and named subdiscipline.

While not exactly a criticism, it should be noted that one of the outcomes of Foucault's extension by Turner – and in much of the other work that comes out of Foucault's rendering of the body – is that the body becomes fixated upon for its sexual or erotic potential. The body for Foucault and for those who follow him closely – whether in religion, the law, medicine or dietary regimes – is a sexualised body. And it is the sexualised body as constructed and shaped through mentalities, not as experienced in its sweaty and livid being. Whether Foucault is talking about prisons, madness or sexuality, he always comes back to the arch-fantasist Sade. In following Foucault's 'method' so closely, Turner tends to come across as agreeing that that is when the body becomes important.

Joanne Finkelstein's *The Fashioned Self* (1991) is, similarly, an extension of Foucault's approach into bodily self-regulation, but through cosmetic means – fashion, make-up and the face-lift. Like Stephen Mennell's homage to Elias, however, it is on the whole unconvincing. One of its weaknesses is that Finkelstein conflates and overstates the etymological link between fashion (clothing) and fashioning (constructing) with a material and political connection. While there are undoubtedly social pressures to conform to norms of beauty or taste in dress, the institutional power in which Foucault vests legitimating epistemic power is simply not there for clothing, the self-promotion of fashion houses aside. Even in the sixteenth and seventeenth centuries, when sumptuary laws were enacted and enforced, they were ineffective. Further, despite trying to draw a link between them, fashion is also unlike courtesy and manners, which Elias, Foucault and Ariès have each shown were promoted by pedagogic rule.

Nor does an attempt at bolstering these claims by stitching together a history of theories of medical aberrance or monstrosity lend sufficient support. Fashion is not a power base, and image is not self except to the exceedingly shallow, even when consciously shaped and self-fashioned.[3] To the contrary, there are ample tracts throughout history warning against vanity and the falsehood of outward show, including the very text she uses to argue that human appearance is easily accepted as a sign of human character, Oscar Wilde's *The Picture of Dorian Gray*. While it is easy (and banal) to agree that people commonly judge by appearances, it is also true that except in the face of ingrained bigotry, human interaction quickly disrupts and breaks down most preconceptions and prejudices. Reality television like *Extreme Makeover* aside, if that were not the case, the vast majority of us would be in serious trouble. The 'stars' of such pro- grammes undoubtedly find, soon enough, that the underlying conditions of their dissatisfaction remain despite a face-lift.

Richard Sennett was a friend of Foucault's, as his heartfelt dedication to *Flesh and Stone: The Body and the City in Western Civilization* (1994) makes clear, and was thoroughly sympathetic to Foucault's genealogical method. In this influential and beautifully written book, taking the best from Foucault and tempering it with insights from Jürgen Habermas (a keen critic of Foucault), Sennett covers the place of the body in space across a vast range of historical moments. Unlike Turner or Finkelstein, however, he does so not by drawing together examples from different eras but rather by taking intense historical snapshots of places and moments and drawing out links across time and space.

Flesh and Stone is divided into three parts: 'Powers of the Voice and Eye' (Classical – Ancient Greece and Rome); 'Movements of the Heart' (Medieval and Renaissance); and 'Arteries and Veins' (Early Modern into Enlightenment, Modern). Using disparate examples, he deftly traces a history of the human body as it relates to the history of cities. In doing so, he recognises successive epistemic shifts taking place both within and between the conceptualisation of the body and the concomitant civic and architectural formation. He offers alternative readings of the possibilities of the power relations at work within cities. He gives subtle readings of how cities and urban planning have functioned historically and continue to act as conduits for the control of human movement and embodied living. While Sennett does concentrate in detail on conceptions of the body (mentalities) and how these are carried over into physical construc- tions, it is his recognition and preoccupation with the movement of bodies within space that takes him beyond Foucault.

In this, we begin to see a shift towards the kind of writing and theorisations more associated with the author to whom we next turn, Pierre Bourdieu. Up to this point we have been dealing with writers who are concerned with history and change: change across time, across culture and across embodied ways of being. From this point onwards we will deal less with sweeping histories – macro-narratives – and much more with either writers who concentrate on serial studies of the minutiae of social processes around the body in a given place and time, or those who want to make all-encompassing claims about the future of embodiment. Bourdieu, the subject of the succeeding chapter, is a man whose work falls into the first camp. He writes in fastidious anthropological detail of specific snapshots of radically different social formations, the tribal and the modern. While there is little room to find a way to accommodate change or agency in his work, as we shall see, because he works across such disparate social forms, in its fullest context his writing across cultures provides extremely fruitful ground for understanding the variable nature of the abstraction of embodiment between social formations.

Notes

1 See Derek Robbins (2000) for a brief discussion of the early interactions of Foucault, Bourdieu and Derrida.

2 For an extended discussion of women's authority over the experience of pregnancy prior to the eighteenth century, see Barbara Duden (1991). See also Norman Jewson (1976) for the shift away from patient-centred knowledge.

3 Finkelstein would have profited from reading Stephen Greenblatt (1980) on the latter point.

THREE Place and Space

Habitus and Social Control

Pierre Bourdieu (1930–2002), like Michel Foucault, was born into that generation whose childhood was shaped by the Depression and who came to maturity witnessing World War II first-hand. He came from provincial origins – Béarn in the southwest of France – rising into the intellectual elite that dominated French culture through the 1960s and into the 1970s. At the same time, he always claimed and maintained a distance from that (Parisian) elite, preferring to situate himself as an outsider. He was a contemporary of Derrida at the École Normale Supérieure in the early 1950s, and one of a younger generation of highly influential academics during the student uprisings of 1968. Between his moving from one side of the academic 'fence' to the other, he served out his National Service in a war-torn Algeria, the place where he was shortly afterwards to conduct his first major enthnographic study, of the Kabyle. During his career he held highly prestigious positions, notably as Director of the Centre de Sociologie Européenne and Chair of Sociology at the Collège de France (see Robbins 2000). While his work was pointedly distanced from both structuralism and poststructuralism, it also became an integral part of an intellectual revolution in anthropology and sociology that came out of their clash. And theorising the social body only forms a part of his incredibly prolific intellectual output.

I closed the last chapter with Richard Sennett's writing on the effect of the city on the body and bodily requirements. His work on the spatiality of the city calls into question ideas of public and private, inside and outside, and the regimens imposed within and by civic living. The focus of this chapter on embodied space – social environments, material accoutrements and physical surroundings – and the ways in which the social body functions has obvious connections with Sennett's work. But Bourdieu approaches the body in social space from a different perspective, one far more informed by understandings of class. One's place in society is characterised by the spaces one inhabits and the places one frequents. Conversely, physical environments also shape one's embodied being. The differentiation of public and private life, and the regulation of urban life and urban space, is of great importance to any understanding of the social body. The influence of Bourdieu's notion of *habitus*, while it does include ideas analogous to Foucault's notions of diffuse power and 'authorised discourses', shifts the emphasis away from 'authorities of delimitation' and back to a subject's potential ability to affect or adapt that 'power' and those materialised 'discourses'. Whereas Foucault's work, even when explicitly focused on bodies and bodily actions, is really more concerned with mentalities, Bourdieu is interested in the materialities of daily life, and their implications for social control and sociological analysis of the bodily subject in society.

Bourdieu

In Chapter 1 we saw that history interpenetrates the sociology of Elias, and influences sociology through the social histories of Ariès, in his study of appropriate social behaviours. The theoretical approach of Pierre Bourdieu – as it relates particularly to the understanding of the body, its relation to social categories and its functioning within space across time – is interpenetrated with that most basic of Elias's concerns, manners or socialising behaviour. Elias worked with notions of the body as it was expected to adhere to shifting norms of social probity. Those norms were recorded in passing in poetry, plays and, increasingly from the Renaissance onwards, in pedagogic texts. Bourdieu's approach has a lot in common with Elias's model for tracing cultural formations. In *Distinction* (1979/1984) – unlike Elias who works with a vast historical survey focusing on a specific point of culture (i.e. civility) – Bourdieu conducts an immense and literal survey over a slice of time within and across a whole culture: France in the late 1960s. He does so through tracing the differential between appropriate social behaviours – including standards of courtesy – across that society. Shilling is quite right that in comparison with Elias, while 'synchronically dynamic, Bourdieu's work is diachronically underdeveloped' (Shilling 1993: 146). They are both, however, interested in the acquisition and formation of taste and acculturation, and their bodily ramifications.

65

Where Elias and Bourdieu differ most markedly, however, is that Bourdieu makes explicit what Elias leaves implicit. When the dominant high culture – or mode of civility – shifts, those who do not have access to the heightened form of culture retain earlier forms. Those earlier forms do not necessarily disappear. They co-exist with later forms, but the further they are from the latest fashion, the more predominantly are they associated with an incrementally lower cultural and social status. In a sense, Elias is much more optimistic about the civilising process, at least in his early work. He does not pay much attention to the stratifying process at work within the civilising process, the invention and intensification of class or cultural difference. Bourdieu does precisely that: he calls into question the means by which one identifies with one's association with certain cultural modes – the types of arts, education, media, politics one adheres to – and shows how they are a part of one's lived, bodily experience.

There are several key notions or 'tools' important to the theorisation of the body in Bourdieu's work. While they are central in much of Bourdieu's writing, their most explicit elaborations are to be found in *Distinction* (1979/1984), *Outline of a Theory of Practice* (1972/1977) and *The Logic of Practice* (1980/1990a). I initially wrote 'cogent elaborations', but for anyone coming to Bourdieu for the first time, that is a gravely misleading characterisation. It is worth stating at the outset that the theoretical work of Pierre Bourdieu is, by and large, some of the most impenetrably written social theory of the late-twentieth century – a bold assertion amongst such august company, but something even his most ardent admirers could not deny. It is, sadly, a trap into which many of his 'explicators' have also fallen. That said, Bourdieu's theorisations also provide some of the most useful demystifying tools of the socio-political realm – with relevance not only across all academic disciplines but also in everyday life. Once comprehended, they are remarkably simple tools at that.

What then makes up Bourdieu's toolbox for disassembling the taken-for-grantedness of the body in society? Two key implements in Bourdieu's work in relation to the body are *habitus*[1] and bodily hexis (or embodiment). I will shortly go into a detailed explanation of how Bourdieu deploys these terms, but in brief they function as follows. Our *habitus* is the social, cultural and physical environment that we as social beings inhabit, through which we know ourselves and others identify us. The factors that constitute a *habitus* are complex, detailed and interpenetrating. They are all the kinds of social connections, achievements, attainments and attachments one acquires from birth, whether by formal or informal means. These include, but are not limited to, the level of education one has reached, the kind of work one does, the sort of entertainments one enjoys, the places one goes, the cultural pursuits one takes part in or values, the class one identifies with, and so on. *Bodily hexis* or *embodiment*, is the political expression of all the factors that make up one's *habitus* – and embodied or embedded in our physical being. This occurs as they are played out in various fields of valued cultural knowledge or practice (education, sport, music, cooking, etc.). The possession of expertise in any such *field of practice*, Bourdieu has termed *cultural capital*. Put more simply, the sorts of sports one does or doesn't play, the kinds of food one eats, the clothes one wears, the distribution of muscles from manual labour or concerted exercise (or their absence) all play out one's *habitus* in and on one's body. We quite literally embody the social and political spaces we inhabit and/or identify with. The more 'expert' one is in a field of practice, the greater is one's cultural capital in that field, and the more cultural capital one has, the greater one's room to manoeuvre within or to manipulate that field.

To more fully elaborate the meaning of these and other terms, I shall begin with the more difficult, and more theoretical, *Outline of a Theory of Practice* before moving on to the more empirically elaborated and hence more pragmatically comprehensible *Distinction*. In *Distinction* the implications of these 'tools' are played out through the surveys of the kinds of access different groups of (French) people have to aspects of French culture. In *Outline of a Theory of Practice* they are discussed in relation to Bourdieu's fieldwork with the Kabyle, a Bedouin tribe of Algeria, and their ramifications are reiterated and expanded in *The Logic of Practice*.

Outline of a Theory of Practice

In the late 1950s and early 1960s, during an intense period of unrest between colonial France and an Algeria intent upon independence from colonial rule, Bourdieu undertook a detailed ethnographic study of the lives of a tribe of Algerian Bedouin. 'Algerian Bedouin' is a difficult concept in itself, for Bedouin do not live by such national boundaries. Through his work on the Kabyle, Bourdieu began to formulate his theory of social practice, to which he later submitted his own nation's culture. Bourdieu wanted to break from much of the anthropological and sociological work that preceded his own and to distinguish between recognised rules and rituals (structures), and the ways in which people deploy social behaviours in the moment. He did not agree with 'structuralist' arguments that people simply follow the rules laid down within their societies, he believed instead that there is a degree of manoeuvrability or *disposition* available to people. He argued that within fields of practice – that is, given areas of social and cultural capital as outlined above only in this case as they appear in a tribal culture – even when they consist of rigid cosmologies of rites or systems of appropriate behaviour, one can work within the bounds of that field and affect the flow or outcomes of a prescribed action. For example, in relation to the Kabyle, even when a specific response is demanded by a given action, there is a range within which that response can be modified. He gives the Kabyle's 'sense of honour' as an example.

The 'sense of honour' is a field of practice. It is constituted by a set of behaviours that the society recognises as the correct way to interact in a given social situation where the 'sense of honour' may be called into question. Upholding the sense of honour maintains cordial relations, whereas flouting it invariably leads to discord. The sense of honour is a part of the Kabyle's *habitus*, something they acquire as they grow up within their society. Individuals are variably expert in the rules and gradations of proper behaviour required to maintain their sense of honour and not offend another individual's or group's sense of honour. And for Bourdieu the sense of honour 'is nothing other than the cultivated disposition, inscribed in the body schema and in the schemes of thought, which enables each agent to engender all the practices consistent with the logic of challenge and riposte' (Bourdieu [1972] 1977: 15). However, it is not the case, argues Bourdieu, that rituals result in mere ritualised behaviour. There is room to manoeuvre.

> [E]ven the most strictly ritualised exchanges, in which all the moments of the action, and their unfolding, are rigorously foreseen, have room for strategies: the agents remain in command of the *interval* between the obligatory moments and can therefore act on their opponents by playing with the tempo of the exchange ... The skilled strategist can turn a capital of provocations received or conflicts suspended, with the potential ripostes, vengeances, or conflicts it contains, into an instrument of power, by reserving the capacity to reopen or cease hostilities in his own good time. (15)

And not only are strict rites malleable, the same actions or the same words – when performed by different agents who have different levels of cultural capital in a given field of practice – can carry different meanings, especially when the difference involved is gender.

> [T]he expression *err arrtal*, also used to express the taking of revenge, means the *returning of a gift*, an exchange, in the men's speech, whereas it means 'giving back a loan' when used by the women. Loan conduct is certainly more frequent and more natural among the women, who will borrow and lend anything for any purpose; it follows that the economic truth, held back in swapping, is closer to the surface in female exchanges in which there may be specific dates for repayment ('when my daughter gives birth') and precise calculation of the quantities lent. (62–3)

Men resist or avoid entering into loan transactions because borrowing lessens or weakens a man's status, his cultural capital. Men give and receive gifts instead. In the same field of practice, men's and women's actions embody different social and political consequences. Bourdieu's interpretation of the Kabyle's behaviour was a departure from and at odds with contemporaneous structuralist anthropology and sociology deeply influenced by and indebted to the work of linguist Ferdinand de Saussure. Bourdieu gave weight to the 'practical functions' of behaviour. These are, he maintains 'never reducible, as structuralism tacitly assumes, to functions of communication or knowledge' (24). *Err arrtal* is a case in point.

For Bourdieu the 'objective', 'scientific' anthropology and sociology that were dominant at the time he began writing need to be subjected to 'objective' scrutiny itself (72). He argues that while the postulation of overwhelming and determining structures is reasonable and their existence feasible – that they may even be impossible to escape – more importantly, they are not unremittingly deterministic of social life. How can he maintain this seemingly contradictory position? Because, he argues, one may adhere to rites and rituals, be subsumed within cultural practices, but as in his example of the sense of honour, there is always a degree of flexibility available. To bring this out and theorise how this happens, he wants instead to attempt a new objectivism that goes beyond structuralism and encompasses the complications inherent in *praxis*, lived actions in the moment. His aim is to create a social theory or methodology that is based on an objectivism that admits the subjectivism of the researcher and recognises the agency of the social actor within given fields of social action or interaction.

Habitus

This new 'theory of practice' gives rise to his idea of *habitus*, the complex mapping of the interpenetration of all the social, cultural and physical elements by which we know ourselves, and through which others recognise us in turn. In his own (and his translator's) obfuscating words, he aims 'to construct the theory of practice, or, more precisely, the theory of the mode of generation of practices, which is the precondition for establishing an experimental science of the *dialectic of internalization of externality and the externalization of internality*, or, more simply, of incorporation and objectification' (Bourdieu [1972] 1977: 72). The phrases in italics are sometimes termed the subject/object distinction. We absorb into our subjective lived experiences social behaviours – as Elias's examples of the acquisition of manners demonstrate. At the same time, in an ongoing synergistic movement, we re-present those behaviours in society as an object: 'me in the world'. The social theorist is not immune from this dynamic. Indeed the need to acknowledge the observer's own subjective experience is central to Bourdieu's theory of practice. The social behaviours and acquired knowledge that one absorbs are characteristic of a particular social environment – for Bourdieu this overwhelmingly means one's class. Individuals who inhabit different environments adhere to different 'fields of practice' or different levels of expertise in the same field. The sum total of the 'fields of practice' in a given environment

> produce *habitus*, systems of durable, transposable *dispositions*, structured structures predisposed to function as structuring structures, that is, as principles of the generation and structuring of practices and representations which can be objectively 'regulated' and 'regular' without in any way being the product of obedience to rules, objectively adapted to their goals without presupposing a conscious aiming at ends or an express mastery of the operations necessary to attain them and, being all this, collectively orchestrated without being the product of the orchestrating action of a conductor. (72)

Tortuously expressed as it is, this is the core of his argument on objectivism. A disposition is a tendency, a propensity, a likelihood to adhere to the structure incorporated in a field of practice. In other words, to adhere to a collective predisposition to a particular way of acting or knowing. An individual in a given *habitus* will display dispositions to behave in particular ways or to value a particular expertise or to possess cultural attainments that are characteristic of that *habitus*, without consciously following stated rules and without slavishly adhering to the unstated 'rules of behaviour' of that *habitus*. This is in turn linked to the judgement of taste, as will become clearer later in the discussion of *Distinction*. This is very like Elias's explicit pedagogic examples, wherein manners begin by being consciously adopted until, over generations, codes of behaviour become socially and individually internalised, so normalised they are no longer recognised as structured codes.

The earlier forms of (structuralist) objectivism from which Bourdieu is distancing himself presuppose a necessary sequence of actions in reaction to a given stimulus. For example, in Marcel Mauss's classic narratives of gift-giving, strict sequences of exchange or the circulation of objects are required to satisfactorily complete a gift exchange. There is no sense of any room to vary the pattern of an exchange and still achieve the desired outcome. Bourdieu disagrees with what he characterises as mechanistic or 'naïve' reductivism, arguing instead that 'habitus is the source of these series of moves which are objectively organized as strategies without being the product of a genuine strategic intention – which would presuppose at least that they are perceived as one strategy among other possible strategies'. (73). But neither are all actions and reactions the product of individual free will. These are complex interactions of the interconnection of unconscious, or at most semi-conscious, habits, 'thoughts, perceptions, expressions, actions – whose limits are set by the historically and socially situated conditions of its production' – that is, the *habitus*. '[T]he conditioned and conditional freedom it secures is as remote from a creation of unpredictable novelty as it is from a simple mechanical reproduction of the initial conditionings' (95).

It is through the proposition that people are able to manipulate – or at least work within – the structures of rules and rituals and thereby effect a degree of agency, that Bourdieu attempts to resist his theorisation of *habitus* becoming simply a static description of class or social or tribal boundaries.[2] Bourdieu's *habitus* encompasses both the broader cultural rules and rituals and the motility of those rules and rituals within the individual's enactment of them. He criticises 'sociology [that] treats as identical all the biological individuals who, being the product of the same objective conditions, are the supports of the same habitus' (85). His point is that neither the structure of 'class' or 'tribal society' nor the will of the individual are coterminous. People of a given social grouping are both the producers and products of the given *habitus* of that grouping. They share 'the system of dispositions (partially) common to all products of the same structures' (85).

These structures are not just restricted to ritual practices, they are integral to a person's relation to the space they inhabit and the relation of their physical bodies to – and the physical movement and placement thereof within – that space. It is through our bodies that we experience the world. Through them we learn to train, restrict, dispose and quarantine our bodily actions in ways that express and make material/political consequences. Through our bodies we make flesh the structures of a *habitus*, we embody the social and political effects of all the fields of practice in which we are involved. We embody our *habitus* through the way we walk; the way we conduct ourselves with others and in different spaces; our disposition to particular ways of dress; the places we do and don't go; the way we regulate our behaviour in certain areas of our homes and in different public spaces; the way we act depending on whether we are adults or children, male or female, young or old, etc. These are structures and behaviours we learn and reproduce from the moment we are born.

> [I]t is in the dialectical relationship between the body and a space structured according to the mythico-ritual oppositions that one finds the form par excellence of the structural apprenticeship which leads to the em-bodying of the structures of the world, that is, the appropriating by the world of a body thus enabled to appropriate the world. (89)

In a largely oral social formation, like the Kabyle, the kind of abstraction and objectification of cultural capital – the means of creating 'me in the world' – that enables the embodiment of the *habitus* is not passed on through the written word (formal education). It happens, rather, through the symbolic systems of the home and hearth which are more immediately related to one's body in space. One can see why Bourdieu resists psychoanalysis – 'the disenchanting product of the disenchantment of the world' (92). The psychoanalytic interpretation of embodiment leads to the reduction of actions to drives, all at base sexual: in other words, the reduction of the body's capacities, or embodied life to its erogenous or erotic potential. Psychoanalysis universalises social interaction by taking everything back to the individual – anathema to his method. He argues that it is naïve to read often mundane acts in sexualised terms, as 'naïve as it would be to reduce their strictly sexual dimension to countless acts of diffuse inculcation through which the body and the world tend to be set in order' (92).

Embodiment

In embodying the *habitus* in which we are steeped, we each in our way embody the political content of that space and its associations. As I mentioned briefly above, Bourdieu calls this materialisation within individuals of the *habitus* 'bodily hexis' or '*embodiment*'. 'Bodily hexis is political mythology realized, *em-bodied*, turned into a permanent disposition, a durable manner of standing, speaking, and thereby of *feeling* and *thinking.*' (1977: 93–4). Values and associations are '*made* body by the transubstantiation achieved by the hidden persuasion of an implicit pedagogy, capable of instilling a whole cosmology, an ethic, a metaphysic, a political philosophy, through injunctions as insignificant as "stand up straight" or "don't hold your knife in your left hand"' (94). These are just the sorts of inculcated training up we saw in Elias, the early pedagogic rules that gradually become so acculturated they don't need to be stated any more. They are implicit and tacitly understood, and they are deeply embodied. Far more so than Elias, however, Bourdieu pushes the point that the terms of civility are deeply political: 'concessions of *politeness* always contain *political* concessions' (95).

We can see here that Bourdieu's ethnographic observations of the Kabyle have the potential for far wider application. The complexities of *habitus* and bodily hexis or embodiment reinsert physicality into a philosophical tradition that has been dominated by mentalities since the mid-seventeenth century. Moving beyond Foucault's sense of social constructs, Bourdieu asserts that together with 'the Marx of the *Theses on Feuerbach*, the theory of practice as practice insists, against positivist materialism, that the objects of knowledge are *constructed*, and against idealist intellectualism, that the principle of this construction is practical activity oriented towards practical functions' (96). The sociology and anthropology that Bourdieu distances himself from have worked on those very bases, overlaying complex social interactions and social processes like seasonal and/or ritual calendars with a mapping that occludes the mobile and adaptive nature of the systems they seek to represent. The attempt to render coherent such complexity has frequently ended in reductive interpretations. In refutation, Bourdieu gives as an example a long, detailed and textured explanation of the flexibility of the Kabyle calendars for planting, recognising the seasons and their attendant rituals to illustrate his point convincingly. He shows that in their reactive flexibility to the lived conditions of agricultural realities, '[r]ites, more than any other type of practice, serve to underline the mistake of enclosing in concepts a logic made to dispense with concepts' (116). While undoubtedly guided by a mentally constituted series of prescribed acts, planting and all the rituals associated with it are inextricable from the physical acts that are required and conditions under which they are carried out. Further, rites and ritual are reliant on the semiotics of the human form.

> The language of the body, whether articulated in gestures or, *a fortiori*, in what psychosomatic medicine calls 'the language of the organs', is incomparably more ambiguous and more overdetermined than the most overdetermined uses of ordinary language. This is why ritual 'roots' are always broader and vaguer than linguistic roots, and why the gymnastics of ritual, like dreams, always seems richer than the verbal translations, at once unilateral and arbitrary, that may be given of it. Words, however charged with connotation, limit the range of choices and render difficult or impossible, and in any case explicit and therefore 'falsifiable', the relations which the language of the body suggests. (120)

The embodiment of *habitus*, with its political content and ramifications, is far more complex than any description of the structural relations of a society can be. Not that the language of the body is any more infinite than verbalised or written language, but it is more complex and amorphous than a system of words attached to gestures can convey. What Bourdieu does in this work is realise and redress the imbalance in sociology. It had privileged the mental structures that bind social groups over the bodies through which they are materialised and by which we interact with each other. He *explicitly* reinserts the body in society. As Bourdieu says,

> Every successfully socialized agent thus possesses, in their incorporated state, the instruments of an ordering of the world, a system of classifying schemes which organizes all practices, and of which the linguistic schemes ... are only one aspect ... [T]his principle is nothing other than the *socially informed body*, with its tastes and distastes, its compulsions and repulsions, with, in a word, all its *senses*. (123–4)

By senses, he means all the ways in which we perceive and materially interact in the world. And the illusion of objective truths that have been a part of the history of sociology and anthropology in fact create the systems of their own illusion. 'Scientific', 'objective' truth is always subjective:

> Rites and myths which were 'acted out' in the mode of belief and fulfilled a practical function as collective instruments of symbolic action on the natural world and above all on the group, receive from learned reflection a function which is not their own but that which they have for scholars. (156)

In other words, to misquote Wittgenstein, the problems of sociology and anthropology are anthropologists's and sociologists's problems.

Distinction

We have seen that the crux of the argument that underpins the theory of practice is that through the range of behaviours we adopt (our disposition) and by the ways in which we conduct our bodies in time and space (our hexis or embodiment), people live out their social and political milieu (habitus). In his mammoth work, Distinction (1979/1984), Bourdieu subjects French culture to this theorisation of social practice. How does it play out in a modern rather than a tribal culture where Bourdieu only (explicitly)[3] dealt with a single habitus? In Distinction we are faced with the differentiation between more than one habitus in the analysis of class divisions and an infinitely detailed analysis of the relative cultural capital held by those who inhabit different class positions. At first reading, the room for manoeuvre we saw in Outline appears more restricted in Distinction: a people seem more bound by their class in his eyes than a tribe are by their rites and rituals. The sort of flexibility we saw in the Kabyle's reactions to a potential breach of the sense of honour is harder to define in the descriptions he gives of cultural norms from within his own culture. For example, in relation to education, from the accounts in Distinction it is only the rare individual who is able to manipulate the possibilities available within the education to which they have access to move up and out of his or her class. Those rarities are the exception that prove the rule. But how different are these scenarios? I shall reserve judgement until we have seen how the theory of practice works in relation to modern French culture.

Defining 'Cultural Capital'

Habitus is both the progenitor and the product of the variable possession of what is probably Bourdieu's best-known theorisation, 'cultural capital'. Cultural capital is made up of the material possession of the aspects of culture that a society-as-a-whole values, and which in a 'modern' society different levels of society value unequally. These are the social acquisitions – like education, general knowledge, 'cultured' tastes, etc. – the possession or dispossession of which define one's place in society. Relative cultural 'wealth' is determined by the level of 'expertise' one has in a field of practice. The different levels of access to, and acquisition of, cultural capital is determined by the class and *habitus* to which one belongs. The working class operates within one *habitus*, the bourgeoisie another and the elite class another still. Each habitus is characterised by that class's disposition towards and relation to various aspects of French culture.

> In other words, what are grasped through indicators such as educational level or social origin or, more precisely, in the structure of the relationship between them, are *also* different modes of production of the cultivated habitus, which engender differences not only in the competences acquired but also in the manner of applying them. These differences in manner constitute a set of secondary properties, revealing different conditions of acquisition and predisposed to receive very different values in the various markets. (Bourdieu [1979] 1984: 65-6)

This is one point on which Bourdieu shows up a limitation or an under-developed aspect of Elias's work to which I have already alluded. Though in a sense Elias is more of an optimist, by concentrating on the uniting aspect of behaviour modification in *The Civilizing Process*, the way it brings together certain levels of people, shaping them within the bounds of what are the accepted set of social norms, the vast majority of people who are not 'upwardly socially mobile' are not addressed.[4] Bourdieu reminds us that manners are a mode of differentiating and stratifying society, not just of bringing a (certain level of) people together.

It does seem that even while Elias is uncovering an apparatus that has created the illusion of a natural sense of taste or of manners or of civility, his emphasis on the civilised outcome concentrates on the higher classes and their 'natural' taste. The obverse of this is that a lack of taste also becomes naturalised as appropriate to the lower classes. Elias does recognise that this is an illusion, a construction, but he spends precious little time on those who are left behind in that process: the less civilised, the uncivilised, the lower classes and the colonised. As I noted briefly in relation to the theorisation of disposition in *Outline of a Theory of Practice*, by linking disposition to the judgement of taste, this is exactly what Bourdieu does in *Distinction*.

> The ideology of natural taste owes its plausibility and its efficacy to the fact that, like all the ideological strategies generated in the everyday class struggle, it *naturalizes* real differences, converting differences in the mode of acquisition of culture into differences of nature; it only recognises as legitimate the relation to culture (or language) which least bears the visible marks of its genesis, which has nothing 'academic', 'scholastic', 'bookish', 'affected' or 'studied' about it, but manifests by its ease and naturalness that true culture is nature – a new mystery of immaculate conception. (68)

If you have acquired your taste by rote, as we saw has been the case as far back as Castiglione in the Renaissance, it will be seen to be unnaturally acquired and valued less. Manners and cultural capital define class, and vice versa.

> It is no accident that the opposition between 'scholastic' (or 'pedantic') and the *mondain* [everyday], the effortlessly elegant, is at the heart of debates over taste and culture in every age: behind two ways of producing or appreciating cultural works it very clearly designates two contrasting modes of acquisition, and, in the modern period at least, two different relationships to the educational system. (69)

That is, the difference between upper-class 'taste' which is 'natural' and a learned 'taste' that is devalued is that the latter is obviously acquired. The taste of a group, of a class, is transmitted across time. This is certainly the logic behind sovereignty, both personal and political, that the sovereign's values and constitution survive the individual's demise (72). Bourdieu thinks that class dispositions are passed on in this way too, although he cautions that more research would need to be done than he has completed in *Distinction* to support this assertion – an awesome thought indeed, given its already massive empirical basis. Yet, if you agree with class distinctions at all, it is intuitively appealing.

> The effect of mode of acquisition is most marked in the ordinary choices of everyday existence, such as furniture, clothing or cooking, which are particularly revealing of deep-rooted and long-standing dispositions because, lying outside the scope of the educational system, they have to be confronted, as it were, by naked taste, without any explicit prescription or proscription, other than from semi-legitimate legitimizing agencies such as women's weeklies or 'ideal home' magazines. (77)

So inherited taste and acquired taste show most obviously in these things, or rather the latter show most obviously in their departure from the 'long-standing dispositions' characteristic of a *habitus*.

Bourdieu looks at a range of cultural forms as the basis of his study, choosing certain examples which, he argues, are deeply, inherently embodied. Each is used within his massive questionnaire as a case study of the differentiation between different classes access to and disposition towards a mode of cultural capital, a field of practice. The examples he uses are food, art, music, decor, education and politics. He, like Elias, uses this as a critique of the acquisition or development of taste, but in the case of food – unlike Stephen Mennell discussed earlier in Chapter 1 – in both senses of that word. He recognises that the ingestion of food is indelibly a bodily experience. Bourdieu goes into details such as the importance of working-class plenitude, petit-bourgeois 'pot luck', and bourgeois formality in eating habits: 'it is probably in tastes in *food* that one would find the strongest and most indelible mark of infant learning, the lessons which longest withstand the distancing or collapse of the native world and most durably maintain nostalgia for it' (79). Food preference then, based in basic pleasures, is inextricably tied to *habitus*, which is in turn class driven. Similarly, art and music are something to which people, of whatever class, have a deeply embodied 'gut reaction'. To be trite, people may not 'know Art' or 'know Music' but they know what they like. Art is not exclusively an intellectual artefact to be decoded, it is

> by default, something that communicates, as it were, from body to body, like the rhythm of music or the flavour of colours, that is, falling short of words and concepts. Art is also a 'bodily thing', and music, the most 'pure' and 'spiritual' of the arts, is perhaps simply the most corporeal ... the least inadequate evocations of musical pleasure are those which can replicate the peculiar forms of an experience as deeply rooted in the body and in primitive bodily experiences as the tastes of food. (80)

Despite the latent romanticism embedded in these descriptions of culture, in essence Bourdieu is right in relation to the embodied experience and effects of food, art and music. They are basic cultural expressions, found in every social form you care to think of, which demand the attention and interaction of our embodied being. Indeed, Bourdieu asserts that, at least in relation to food, 'good taste' is inseparable from the literal sense of taste and culturally honed preferences.

> The abstraction which isolates dispositions towards legitimate culture leads to a further abstraction at the level of the system of explanatory factors, which, though always present and active, only offers itself for observation through those elements (cultural capital and trajectory in the case analysed below) which are the principles of its efficacy in the field in question. (99)

That is, unless one is born to the class *habitus* which is in possession or control of a field of practice of 'legitimate culture' – the rarer cultural capital, 'good taste' in art, appreciation of 'fine food' and 'good music' – one is unable to access them without succeeding in the near impossible task of being able to abstract and analyse one's own dispositions and *habitus* from within. Even if one is able to 'think outside the square' of all one's learned tastes and acquired behaviours, one then has to contend with the opacity of the rules of acquisition of the tastes and behaviours of the culturally endowed. One's knowledge and appreciation of art, the kind of art one finds attractive, define one in certain relations to the social group one belongs or aspires to:

> [T]hese 'cultural creations which we usually regard purely aesthetically, as variants of a particular style, were perceived by their contemporaries,' as Norbert Elias reminds us, referring to the society of the Grand Siècle, as 'the highly differentiated expression of certain social qualities.' (227)

77

Bourdieu identifies a paradox within this, however. Those who have no desire or ability to experience the 'higher' cultural forms – 'the culturally most deprived, the oldest, those furthest from Paris' – are often responsible for affirming their legitimacy (319).

Bourdieu is trying to maintain the complexity of social spheres and actions, recognising that analysis itself can obscure that complexity. As I have just shown in the discussion of *Outline of a Theory of Practice*, he wants to propose a new objectivism that recognises sociological and anthropological researchers's complicity in the suppression of that complexity, which he proposes can be rendered formulaically, thus:

$$[(habitus) (capital)] + field = practice \ (101)$$

This representation of his argument somewhat mysteriously concretises that, while we are bound by our *habitus* (the social conditions and space we inhabit and embody) and our access to cultural capital (expertise within a field of practice of socially valued attainments), there is a degree of room for manoeuvre within those bracketed boundaries. The interplay between our social origins and our cultural capacities when deployed within a given field (e.g. art, education, culinary habits, social power, etc.) leads to our actual practices, our competency within that field and the degree of cultural capital we have.

Education, or lack of it, is undeniably an extremely influential factor in the social position one will inhabit. Education is a field of practice that liberates or restricts opportunities to job markets, different types of education expose one to and equip one with different cultural capital. Education often – unrealistically – promises a way out of a given class *habitus* when it is not in practice possible for an individual or a class to truly access the means to do so. The rare individuals who do succeed help to maintain the illusion that it is possible, however. Bourdieu links this to adolescent rebelliousness, which comes out of the disillusionment brought on by the divide between what is promised and what is in fact the likely outcome (144). But one thing that education does effect is the legitimisation of cultural position and cultural capital in those who have access to it: it produces 'the need for and the rarity of their class culture' (153).

In the same way, that abstraction of dispositions also leads to the legitimation of 'experts' who tell us how to live and shape our bodies to meet with the standards of 'legitimate capital'.[5] In 'unconscious collusion' we buy the product they are selling, 'a new bodily hexis – the hexis which the new bourgeoisie of the sauna bath, the gymnasium and the ski slope has discovered for itself – produce the corresponding needs, expectations and dissatisfactions' (153). We see the same dynamic being played out more recently in the cultural commodification of the myriad means of bodily modification. As we saw above, hexis is the embodied political outcome of cultural capital in a field of practice. If a slim, athletic body is the sign of a cultured body, the means of attaining and maintaining that shape is taken on by those who desire it. They consciously reshape themselves in the pursuit of that cultural capital. And others are legitimated as those with the power to tell us how we should reshape and regulate ourselves. This is not programmatic politics, nor is it raw propaganda. It is inculcated within legitimated, 'rational' systems which have produced a new 'mode of domination, which, substituting seduction for repression, public relations for policing, advertising for authority, the velvet glove for the iron fist, pursues the symbolic integration of the dominated classes by imposing needs rather than inculcating norms' (154). These rational systems are a modern French cultural analogue of the regulatory systems of the seasonal rites and rituals of the Kabyle.

The pursuit and acquisition of cultural capital require one to become abstracted from one's basic dispositions, to retrain one's tastes and to recognise new 'needs'. The 'explanatory factors' that motivate the formulation of needs to suit the dominant cultural capital are not obvious, neither to those who seek nor those who proffer them: they too remain abstracted. The dominant class doesn't need to make visible, or be aware of, the specific rules that discriminate against those who don't have the necessary cultural capital. You don't need obvious rules or systems 'of selection, of inclusion and exclusion', it happens by default:

> In fact, the most select groups prefer to avoid the brutality of discriminatory measures and to combine the charms of the apparent absence of criteria, which allows the members the illusion of election on grounds of personal uniqueness, with the certainties of selection, which ensures maximum group homogeneity. (162)

As Elias showed in the case of *parvenus*, and as Bourdieu here makes clear, there is no way of winning against such inexplicit systems of social probity. This is so particularly when the 'vendors of goods and services ... exploit these lags, offering out-of-season (e.g., in the case of holidays), or when they are out of fashion (clothes, activities), things which have their full value only at the "right" time' (164). By attempting to attain the unattainable cultural capital, one legitimises the dominant form, forever putting it out of one's reach. It is only through methods, such as Bourdieu's new objectivism, that one is able to attempt to comprehend the complexity of the relations that foster, promote and support a given *habitus*.

79

> The habitus is both the generative principle of objectively classifiable judgements and the system of classification (*principium divisionis*) of these practices. It is in the relationship between the two capacities which define the habitus, the capacity to produce classifiable practices and works, and the capacity to differentiate and appreciate these practices and products (taste), that the represented social world, i.e., the space of life-styles, is constituted. (170)

In the culture analysed here, lifestyles are effected through and upon the body, in differing ways depending on the class *habitus* of the person involved:

> Taste is the practical operator of the transmutation of things into distinct and distinctive signs, of continuous distributions into discontinuous oppositions; it raises the differences inscribed in the physical order of bodies to the symbolic order of significant distinctions. (174–5)

All aspects of the use and dispositions of the body betray the *habitus* to which one belongs.

As we saw in Elias, certain ideas of bodily civility are indissociable from particular ways of disporting the body, from given modes of deportment. Bourdieu makes the same point in a more detailed observation of class groups (177). In relation to taste in food, this becomes expanded. Differentiation in what one eats, one's preoccupation (or lack of it) with the effect of food upon one's body shape, the sensitivity of one's palate – all these factors contribute to and are products of one's *habitus*. Their varied expression within and by individuals is the hexis of that *habitus*.

> Taste as class culture turned into nature, that is, *embodied*, helps to shape the class body ... It does this first in the seemingly most natural features of the body, the dimensions (volume, height, weight) and shapes (round or square, stiff or supple, straight or curved) of its visible forms, which express in countless ways a whole relation to the body, i.e., a way of treating it, caring for it, feeding it, maintaining it, which reveals the deepest dispositions of the habitus. (190)

Different classes will be more or less comfortable with and in their bodies on the grounds of different dispositions, but also in relation to 'the legitimate body and legitimate deportment' (207) and their ability to achieve it or not. Whether one agrees with Bourdieu's class analysis or not, it is undeniable that people of lower socio-economic status are less likely to have access to the bodily ideals of a society – and simple health – for a host of reasons. This is true both within first world cultures and between first and third world cultures. And the bodily realities, and deportment, of those who belong to a given *habitus* arm them better for the types of sports, pastimes and even speech to which they are disposed. A person embodies in their gestures their relation to the spaces they inhabit (218).[6]

Bourdieu argues that one is abstracted from oneself through the institutionalisation of the relations of a person to his or her body and, most particularly, the psychologisation of the relationship between the mind and the body. He is no fan of psychology, he sees it as a system in which the body is implicitly cast as an 'other' to the self of the mind (368). This is the effect of the individualisation of being. In this psychological structure, childhood and growing up also become related to a series of drives and principles based in bodily pleasures, at once acknowledged and suppressed. Each of these approaches devalues the social aspect of being in favour of the individualist's. In the case of Bourdieu's working-class, people who have little chance of accessing even basic goods and capital, let alone cultural capital, resign themselves to that state (372); that is a part of their *habitus*. To take a specific instance, 'a whole set of convergent indices tends to show that working-class women set less value on and have less interest in their bodies than women in other classes' (380). Bourdieu argues that they are less likely to use make-up or buy clothes that are anything but practical or spend time on slimming through diet or exercise, not just out of necessity but because they believe that is what is appropriate to their lives. They embody the lack of need or desire for those things.

Habitus is the sum of these dispositions. It is observable but not wholly definable. Nor can one simply take the markers of *habitus* as matters of mental choice – which Bourdieu dismisses as what are often called 'values' (466) – they are embedded in bodily being: embodied. Habitus produces and is a product of cultural capital, of bodily hexis, of embodiment. And this is not simply observable, the sociologist conducting the observation is embedded in the same structures which he or she observe. The sociologist's *habitus* frames his or her observations and conclusions (467). The 'objectivist' researcher simultaneously mystifies and de-legitimises the constitutive power of the *habitus*, deceiving both him- or herself and his or her audience. It is not that these are necessarily beyond comprehension, but that they are so 'taken for granted' that their recognition has to be effected consciously and with care.

The cognitive structures which social agents implement in their practical knowledge of the social world are internalized, 'embodied' social structures. The practical knowledge of the social world that is presupposed by 'reasonable' behaviour within it implements classificatory schemes (or 'forms of classification', 'mental structures' or 'symbolic forms' – apart from their connotations, these expressions are virtually interchangeable), historical schemes of perception and appreciation which are the product of the objective division into classes (age groups, genders, social classes) and which function below the level of consciousness and discourse. Being the product of the incorporation of the fundamental structures of a society, these principles of division are common to all the agents of the society and make possible the production of a common, meaningful world, a common-sense world. (468)

81

They are embedded in the consciousness, but far more deeply in the body. But just as the body and embodiment should not be undervalued, nor should physical attributes or actions be taken as simple measurable material properties. It is only through the theorisation of the *habitus* that full credit can be done to the complexity of social relations and the social importance of the body and bodily actions.

The Logic of Practice

Before attempting to give some kind of answer to the questions I posed at the beginning of my discussion of *Distinction* – just how different are the scenarios of that book from the studies of the Kabyle? – I want first to conclude this explication of Bourdieu's theory of practice in relation to the body by taking a small digression into the *The Logic of Practice* (1990). This will allow me to summarise some of the broader (meta) implications inherent in his theorisations. I made a passing reference to the subject/object distinction above and its centrality to Bourdieu's theoretical method. Object and subject, objective and subjective, objectivity and subjectivity, are all slippery terms the meanings of which shift depending upon the context in which they are deployed. Writing specifically about revisiting his own work in *Outline of a Theory of Practice* and *Distinction*, Bourdieu claims 'each doubling-back is another opportunity to objectify more completely one's objective and subjective relation to the object' (Bourdieu [1980] 1990a: 1). In this one half-line is a summary of what makes his theoretical method, and takes it beyond structuralism. The aim of the theory of practice is to stand back from and acknowledge (objectify) that in undertaking a sociological or anthropological study (the object), the 'observer' has already brought to the study his or her method (objective relation) and his or her *habitus* (subjective relation). This acknowledgement is not a single move. It is a practice that, to be effective, must be enacted repeatedly. The more one comes back to the object and one's relation to it, the more one sees not only in the object but also in one's own perception of it. In Bourdieu's words:

> In contrast to the personalist denial which refuses scientific objectification and can only construct a fantasized person, sociological analysis, particularly when it places itself in the anthropological tradition of exploration of forms of classification, makes a self-reappropriation possible, by objectifying the objectivity that runs through the supposed site of subjectivity, such as the social categories of thought, perception and appreciation which are the unthought principle of all representation of the 'objective' world. By forcing one to discover externality at the heart of internality, banality in the illusion of rarity, the common in the pursuit of the unique, sociology does more than denounce all the

impostures of egoistic narcissism; it offers perhaps the only means of contributing, if only through awareness of determinations, to the construction, otherwise abandoned to the forces of the world, of something like a subject. (20–1)

The theory of practice makes one 'externalise' one's own *habitus* (and all its attendant complexities), see the complexity in oneself and the ordinariness in what may have at first seemed exotic in another culture.

[Structuralist] [o]bjectivism, which sets out to establish objective regularities (structures, laws, systems of relationships, etc.) independent of individual consciousnesses and wills, introduces a radical discontinuity between theoretical knowledge and practical knowledge, rejecting the more or less explicit representations with which the latter arms itself as 'rationalizations', 'prenotions' or 'ideologies'. (26)

Bourdieu's approach turns this on its head, inserting a theoretical complexity into practical knowledge and unpicking the banality and subjectivity in theoretical knowledge. Put succinctly, if not elegantly, '[t]he unanalysed element in every theoretical analysis (whether subjectivist or objectivist) is the theorist's subjective relation to the social world and the object (social) relation presupposed by this subjective relation' (29).

With the last point in mind, to return to my earlier questions: how different are the implications of the theory of practice for the social situation under scrutiny in *Distinction* from the (limited) flexibility we saw amongst the rituals of the Kabyle? Bourdieu seems to be saying that the more one observes, the more complex the interpenetration of fields of practice, embodiment and *habitus* become. This is further complicated by the social scientist being subject to the same kinds of social artefacts. But there is no real room to manoeuvre when one is speaking of class – any suggestion of it is illusory. Can it really be the case that the only person who has room to manoeuvre in modern social formations is the social scientist who is using the theory of practice to uncover the complexities of the *habitus*? Is Bourdieu romanticising the Kabyle as 'natural' social theorists of a tribal social formation, who know how to employ the theory of practice to their own ends, and who could teach 'us' a thing or two about social interaction?

Analysis

Bourdieu's work is undoubtedly difficult to read because his concepts are difficult to grasp, but there is also no doubt that unlocking those concepts entails a high degree of concentration because of the way they are expressed, certainly as they have been rendered into English. This can complicate both one's understanding, and any criticism, of his work.

There are several serious criticisms that have been levelled at Bourdieu's method,[7] the most damning of which is that it is utterly static. In *Outline of a Theory of Practice* one finds the most definite statement in which there are firm grounds for criticising Bourdieu for theorising a system in which there is no 'real' agency. Here there is room for manoeuvre, but that room remains bounded by the given *habitus*.

> As an acquired system of generative schemes objectively adjusted to the particular conditions in which it is constituted, the habitus engenders all the thoughts, all the perceptions, and all the actions consistent with those conditions, *and no others* ... the habitus is an endless capacity to engender products - thoughts, perceptions, expressions, actions - whose limits are set by the historically and socially situated conditions of its production, the conditioned and conditional freedom it secures is as remote from a creation of unpredictable novelty as it is from a simple mechanical reproduction of the initial conditionings. (95: emphasis added)

This becomes even more problematic in his later work on his own culture, in relation to class *habitus*. There would seem to be no way of accounting for upward or downward social mobility. In his theorisations, it seems as if class is more rigid than rite and ritual, which is an odd – even counter-intuitive – circumstance.

The first problem one is struck by is that Bourdieu does not distinguish between cultures – implicitly, all fields of practice are equal or analogous. The possibility that fields are constituted differently in different cultures is simply not countenanced. Second, it seems from the description of French culture as described in *Distinction*, very much as if people in 'modern' societies don't know how to manipulate their fields of practice, their *habitus* or their hexis. Their class position renders them socially static. The Kabyle, by contrast, seem to be 'natural' observers of the rules of their cultures, who are able to take full advantage of what room for action exists within their society. That is as long as they are men, because even though he gestures towards the social differences inherent in gender (*err arrtal*), he does not give full weight to the fact that there is on his own account differential access to cultural capital amongst the Kabyle.

In his later works Bourdieu refuted criticisms that his theory is static by introducing the notion of 'interest'.[8] *Interest* is both the attachment one has for a field of practice and also implies the degree of expertise one has in that field. It is not quite in the sense of 'vested interest' – Bourdieu utterly rejects any idea that this notion of interest implies either conscious actions or a desire for personal gain (financial or otherwise). It is more in the sense of an unconscious allegiance, something that one cannot help but feel involved in because of one's *habitus* and hexis. When he characterises expertise or interest in a given field as having a 'feel for the game', he is appealing to unconscious aptitude, an ingrained understanding of how to do well that is influenced by the degree of cultural capital one has. Having a feel for and doing well at 'the game' can sometimes consist in doing 'poorly' – by conducting oneself in a way that to someone outside the game may appear 'disinterestedly' or generously. But the practical outcome of playing against the grain in such a way can end in advantage in the long term.

The notion of interest is supposed to flesh out the criticism of Bourdieu's work that it locks people into their classes (or fields, or *habitus*) by showing how individuals who have a 'feel for the game' can effect the kinds of change that we saw was possible for the Kabyle. It is hard to see, however, how this refutes the counter-claim that all actions are thereby being reduced to a more base form of self-interest. Acting unconsciously is not coterminous with acting unselfishly. Nor is it clear how this idea of interest really transcends the criticism that we are prisoners of our *habitus* and hexis. It just shows how some people are able to 'win' not how anyone gets away from, or outside of, the game.

Clearly, while Bourdieu is, like Elias, correct that *parvenus* and the *nouveaux riches* are social pariahs amongst the elites they aspire to, it is also true that over generations people do move between and become assimilated into higher or lower social groupings. Elias is less detailed but offers a diachronic answer. Between the two of them we have a fine way of explaining social structures and the shifting place and significance of the body within them. And while it is unclear to me whether it is precisely because he only deals with intense readings of 'moments' in time that this leads him to construct a complex but apparently static picture of societies – or whether this is an inherent outcome of his theory of practice – he does seem to acknowledge that his interpretations, and *habitus*, are historically contingent.

> If one ignores the dialectical relationship between the objective structures and the cognitive and motivating structures which they produce and which tend to reproduce them, if one forgets that these objective structures are themselves products of historical practices whose productive principle is itself the product of the structures which it consequently tends to reproduce, then one is condemned to reduce the relationship between the different social agencies (*instances*). (83)

What would seem difficult to incorporate into Bourdieu's theory of practice, however, is the inability of disabled people to fully access the embodied life or cultural capital of any or at any level of society, and how this is one means by which prejudice succeeds.[9] Nor, as we shall see in relation to Mary Douglas in the following chapter, does he attend to the subjective experience of the ethical or moral consequences of breaking the rules of a game.

The idea of *habitus* and bodily hexis do, however, signify a major turn away from much of the philosophical work from the time of Descartes. Bourdieu is quite right that scientific objectivism, and its (bastard) off-spring psychology, privilege the intellect and the intellectually perceived, constituting it as a field of play viewed from an enlightened perspective. Descartes's observing or thinking thing deliberately forgot its body, or at least consciously distanced itself from it. As a result, as this became the dominant and legitimised form for perceiving knowledge, the body and embodied relations became reformulated and recognised only from a cognitive point of view. This has been seen as a weak point in Foucault's work. An action becomes a given, and is thereby reduced to a symbolic representation, a playing out of a series of actions and reactions. In 'reviv-ifying' the body, Bourdieu opens the way for a much more textured and deeply layered understanding of social knowledge(s).

Another valid criticism of Bourdieu that has been addressed by some of his 'inheritors', is that at first glance it has little to offer feminism, a field of theorisations inextricably linked to embodiment. While Richard Jenkins's related criticism that Bourdieu is looking down on working-class women in *Distinction* is unwarranted (Robbins 2000: 114–15) – I don't discern any value judgement – it is true that gender does not figure in his discussion of embodiment until very late in his career. As we have seen though, while he does not deal with it in detail and his central preoccupation is definitely class, gender is not altogether absent from his work. In the culture under discussion in *Outline of a Theory of Practice*, he observes differentiations in disposition while looking mainly at the Kabyle as representing *a habitus*. And yet inherent, implicit and glossed over is that there is more than one *habitus*, at least along gender lines. He shows that there are radically dif-ferent worlds for men and women, particularly his allusion to the different meanings of gift and lending practices. He also treats the Kabyle as discrete – like a nation unto themselves. I am ignorant of the numbers and patterns of tribes of Bedouin, but I would have thought there is potential to find *habitus(es)* distinct and yet connected amongst the other Bedouin with whom they interact: that like the Native American 'nations', there were separate groups who cohered at another level.

Inheritors

There are countless sociologists and anthropologists who have been influ-enced by Bourdieu and use his theoretical approaches to the body in their work. This has extended into disability studies, most notably in Australia by Jan Branson and Don Miller in their work on deafness and deaf society. The number of critical readers or edited collections devoted to his work, and the number of memorialising seminars since his death – no doubt soon to be Festschrift – stand witness to how important his work became in English-speaking sociology and anthropology from the late 1970s onwards. However, given the prolific and often prolix nature of the work of his 'inheritors', I am going to limit myself to a discussion of two writers who have worked towards finding the potential to extend his work into the *habitus* of gender.

In her essay 'Appropriating Bourdieu: Feminist Theory and Pierre Bourdieu's Sociology of Culture', Toril Moi does so through a re-viewing of Simone de Beauvoir's achievements, particularly her educational and career achievements, in relation to her *habitus*. The attraction of Bourdieu's theories for Moi, particularly in their potential for feminist appropriation, is that in his 'microtheoretical approach ... Bourdieu makes sociological theory out of everything' (Moi 1990: 268). It makes everything in day-to-day life 'socially significant' and a worthwhile object or subject of study. As a literary theorist, Moi finds Bourdieu's 'thick' anthropology or sociology appealing because it opens out the range of texts and inter-texts available for analysis. It makes possible a thick description of the social and cultural components of gender. Moi builds upon Bourdieu's attention to gender late in his writing and argues that feminism can usefully appropriate his ideas to demystify or deconstruct gendered inequities within societies. She argues that if gender is a *habitus*, it is most usefully seen as functioning along with class within the 'whole social field' (289) rather than a specific field (such as education, art, etc.). She then uses this turn to assess Simone de Beauvoir's success within academe, casting her as one of those 'exceptions' who prove the rule of a *habitus*. Moi points out that de Beauvoir's middle-class access to the cultural capital of education, in which she excelled but to which she had no greater access than her male social contemporaries, only took her so far. Without being unkind, Moi argues that by de Beauvoir's embodied relation to Sartre, her 'social capital' was raised in a way that otherwise would not have been the case. De Beauvoir's expertise or power within the *field* of play – the *habitus* – was made possible by her deployment of the high social capital she had in her gender. Despite Moi's protestations against sexist denouncements of de Beauvoir on the very same grounds, and her belief that she is reclaiming agency through showing how de Beauvoir used her 'interest' and feel for the game, paradoxically Moi ends up confirming them. While her reading of de Beauvoir's intellectual success within Bourdieu's framework is elegant, in a cultivated and roundabout way she simply agrees that de Beauvoir slept her way to the top.

Terry Lovell, feminist cultural materialist, compares Bourdieu's approach to the body with Judith Butler's (see Chapter 5) on the basis of a shared interest in and use of performativity in language. Lovell supplements Bourdieu's 'inflexibility' on the subject within society by attempting to combine it with Butler's gender 'voluntarism', that is, her arguments around subjects being able to construct and perform their gender at will. At the same time she tones down Butler's disaggregation of the socialised body by introducing into it Bourdieu's attention to the class details of *habitus* and hexis. Using examples of females who have successfully passed as males throughout history, particularly in military and naval service, Lovell unsettles the static nature of Bourdieu's late-career gender categories. While standing back from Butler's radical gender 'voluntarism', Lovell shows that if one takes the documented existence of people who have successfully 'passed' as they appear in Butler's work, and approaches them with Bourdieu's textured readings of class, one can see that while gender passing has succeeded, it is not universally available to women of all classes. The ability to pass as an infantryman is made possible by a working-class woman's *habitus* and hexis, by the musculature and bearing imbued by her social origins. Lovell also makes the important point that while in Bourdieu women are generally seen as cultural 'objects', repositories of cultural capital to be traded between men, his theories can be used to show that women of all classes do also use and construct their femininity as cultural capital over which they retain control.

It is fitting that these particular re-readings of one the progenitors of the sociology of the body should close the first part of this book. In their attempts to combine social theory and psychoanalysis, they begin to draw us into the concerns of the following section. Elias, Foucault and Bourdieu provide the grounded social, sociological and anthropological object that is the body in their work – from which we can now differentiate the abject and the subject. In looking to the body as abject, we find at once a closer attention to the messy physicality of the body but a deep ambivalence towards its products. The abject – as the construction of the word implies – is the not-subject, not-object, and most importantly the not-'me' of the body. We will see how Mary Douglas, in a comparison of social formations not unlike Bourdieu's, finds concordances between what is abjected in different social formations. And in the work of Judith Butler, we shall begin to wonder if it is not the body as a whole that is being ab- or re-jected in favour of the power and reason of the mind.

Notes

1 Goudsblom and Mennell have recently returned to Elias's allied use of the term 'habitus' in their re-edited and revised translation of *The Civilizing Process*, p. xvii.

2 One of the most serious criticisms of Bourdieu's work is that it does not actually manage to do this, a point to which I shall return at the end of the chapter.

3 Implicit in Bourdieu's discussion of male and female spheres of power and influence is a possible second *habitus*, gender: see Moi as discussed later in this chapter.

4 I am referring specifically to *The Civilizing Process* here. As my anonymous reviewer quite rightly pointed out, in Norbert Elias and John Scotson (1965) Elias deals directly with race and ethnicity.

5 For a recent re-reading of this area, see Christopher Ziguras (2004).

6 As footnoted in Chapter 1, these arguments go back at least to the Renaissance art theory, and the proper gestures assigned for representation of the refined and the rustic. It is the differential of civility through *habitus*.

7 See Derek Robbins (2000) for a detailed summary of the major criticisms of Bourdieu's work as a whole.

8 See Bourdieu (1990b) and (1998).

9 See outspoken critic of Bourdieu, Richard Jenkins (1998) and for other attempts to fully encompass the embodied experience of disability see Chapter 7 below.

Part II

Abject – the Bounded Body

FOUR Blood, Bile and Phlegm

Ritual Bodies and Boundaries that Blur

Mary Douglas (1921–) is an anthropologist who has spent her working life writing on and around the anthropology and sociology of religion. The daughter of a career colonial officer in Italy, she was sent home at the age of five to be educated in Britain. She enjoyed a deeply formative secondary education, thanks to a bursary, as a boarder at the Sacred Heart Convent, Roehampton. Growing up a Catholic in the oldest Protestant state – where at that time Catholicism had been an impediment to social inclusion and much else since the Reformation – has had a clear influence on her work, as we shall see throughout this chapter. At Oxford University she completed both an undergraduate degree (1942) and, after four years war service with the Colonial Office, a doctorate in social anthropology (1951). From that time she worked at University College London until 1977, when she retired from her position as professor of anthropology. Her approach to anthropology was formed out of a particularly British stream of social anthropology, embedded in the works of Durkheim and Talcott Parsons.

Though she retired relatively young, like Elias, she did so only to continue to work for a further eleven years in a series of professorships in the United States. Since her second retirement in 1988, she has continued to research and to write. But it was during the 1960s that she published her best-known and most influential works of social anthropology: *Purity and Danger* (1966/2002) and *Natural Symbols* (1970/1996). Since their publication, these two books have been cited across the full spectrum of the humanities and social sciences and between them been translated into more than a dozen languages. When they appeared they caused a furore amongst Douglas's contemporaries and colleagues 'by her dragging social anthropology into engagement with contemporary issues' (Fardon 1999: xiv):

that is, by turning the anthropological gaze onto the institutions and rituals of the West. But as disputed and as influential as her writing has undoubtedly been within British social anthropology, and subsequently across the humanities and social sciences, she positions herself at the margins of that field.[1] Given her background, her gender, and the period in which she began her academic life - the kind of social context that is so central to her own anthropological methodology - this is hardly surprising.

Douglas

In looking at the work of Mary Douglas, this chapter focuses on her attempts to understand the messiness of corporeality, as it is interpreted through rites and rituals. Both particular parts and various products of the body have been treated as ritually significant symbols across time and across cultures, to varying degrees and in different ways. As we have seen, she is not the first to pick up on the importance of embodiment. Her work - like that of Elias, Bourdieu and Foucault - builds upon ideas of the body in society that were hinted at but not yet fully realised in the writings that had formative influences upon her. Durkheim was neither concerned with the individual in society, nor more particularly for our purposes that individual's body, and so is not included in this book. But, as adverted to in the Introduction, his pupil and direct inheritor Marcel Mauss did recognise that the body was a socially deployed tool, used variably across cultures.

> The body is man's first and most natural instrument. Or more accurately, not to speak of instruments, man's first and most natural technical object, and at the same time technical means, is his body. (Mauss 1979: 104)

In Chapters 1–3 of the present volume we clearly saw the human body as a 'natural technical *object*'. Even though Mauss never wrote the book that 'Body Techniques' could have become, he was working within the chain of intellectual associations from which Douglas's work emanates. The direction in which she took it, however, was entirely original.

Douglas laid the groundwork for the interpretation of the body as symbolic of power, both positive and negative, through the study of its *abject* parts and excretions (the concept of the 'abject' will be defined in a moment). She has done this through the study of a selection of tribal cultures and their responses to bodily attributes. Douglas has compared those cultures's 'cosmological' (ritualistic or religious) responses to such matter with that of the cultures and institutions of industrialised societies. Essentially her work encompasses an approach to the power and importance of belief over sacral bodies. Douglas's personal experience of Catholicism is a constant reference point within her work, particularly in the two books concentrated upon here. It is natural enough that someone whose life has been steeped in one of the most potent and successful disseminators of Christian ritual and symbolism should appeal to that system, given her chosen academic speciality. But as we shall see, it has also led to a certain limit of focus in what is on the whole a useful, important and highly influential body of work.

Kristeva and the Abject

Before moving into Douglas's theorisations around pollution and taboo, however, I want to expand on the use of the word *abject*. I have used this term to characterise the work encompassed by the chapters in this section of the book. This is not Douglas's term, rather it is a word that comes out of a discipline with which she displays some impatience – psychology – and from a period that postdates her work. The sense in which I am using it comes from the work of psychoanalytic theorist, Julia Kristeva, and is most fully elaborated in *Powers of Horror: An Essay on Abjection* (Kristeva 1980).

Kristeva writes on psychoanalytic theory and semiotics ('the science of signs'). Her aim is to try to find a way to make Freud and Lacan relevant for feminists. Her means to that end is in retheorising the connection between the earliest formation of language in infants and the formation of subjectivity. She describes two stages in the formation of the individual subject, the pre-linguistic and the linguistic, and places great emphasis on the shift from one to the other. The pre-linguistic mental and physical state of infancy, known as the *chora,* is chaotic. Kristeva argues that in it knowledge is based in and on the self and that there is no recognition of the self as an individual 'subject' separate from other beings or the world at large. Nor is one's body or one's bodily products understood as discrete. In this period the child identifies with the mother, from whom s/he is not differentiated. By contrast, once a young child acquires language, entering the stage known as the Symbolic, the world becomes ordered and coherent and the child recognises him or herself as a separate entity, and the emanations of the body as other than the self. The child has become a 'subject', entered the realm of the social and now identifies with the (differentiated) father. In short, language makes us social.

This is a crude and simplistic condensation but it allows us to come to the point central for our purposes. To move from the *chora* to the Symbolic, from self to social, chaos to coherence, one must learn distance and detachment. This is a simultaneously mental and physical detachment whereby the sense of self is formed through the acceptance of what is considered 'good' into, and the rejection of what is considered 'bad' from, the self. Most importantly this involves the body of the self.

That rejection is played out through *abjection*. Abjection is a semiotic (linguistic), but also an embodied, phenomenon. It is the rejection of and revulsion at what both is and is not the body. This largely centres on bodily wastes because this is a point at which the infant understands that those products are not 'me'. Blood, bile, phlegm, faeces, mucus, etc. are both of the body and not the body. They are *abject* and *abjected*. Dealing with this evidence of the body's boundaries is both necessary and dangerous to the self-constituting subject. One must abject (expel) the waste and enter the clean and ordered symbolic state to function effectively as a social being. But at the same time, the abject hovers at the margins of life, never fully abolished: one bleeds, one is sick, one shits. Abjected matter is a remnant of the uncontrollably chaotic *chora*, which threatens to 'irrupt' into (disrupt) the Symbolic order. In Kristeva's semiotic theorisations that 'irruption' by which coherence is threatened – and that she sees as potentially socially revolutionary – happens in avant-garde literature, most particularly poetry.

Here we part company with Kristeva until the final section of this chapter where we will look at the outcome of the cross-over between her work and Douglas's, and in Chapter 5 where we will look to a psychoanalytic turn in sociology and anthropology. For, while Kristeva gestures towards the infant's literal rejection of bodily excretions and ingestions and the adult return of such early feelings of disgust, she is really more concerned with a metaphoric of abjection. This is not the case in the work of Douglas. Certainly, all of Mary Douglas's writing around pollution and taboo is implicitly concerned with the effects of abjection. The difference is – and it is a significant difference – Douglas is interested in how abjection functions materially in social relations, amongst adults and differently in different social formations.

Purity and Danger

In her introduction to *Purity and Danger* ([1966] 2002), to set up the parameters within which pollution and taboos function, Douglas contrasts dirt and impurity. From a cross-cultural, pan-historical and universalising viewpoint, Douglas finds that across time, space and societies what constitutes dirtiness or defilement may differ but *how* they are defined is common. Dirt is an objective or 'real' fact, but the reactions of an individual or a culture to it are relative. One can easily take on board Douglas's point. Anyone who has lived in a shared household will be aware that one's sense of dirt is not necessarily the same as that of one's housemates. The fact that mice have gnawed the end off a food-caked wooden spoon left maturing on a sink will not bother one person and will lead to violent thoughts in another. The ageing, caked-on food is objectively dirty to both, but tolerance is relative. You can be dirty without being impure. On the other hand, Douglas argues that defilement or pollution is subjective, particular to a person or a culture, and is absolute. Something is either a source of pollution or defiled, or it is not. To return to my example of nose-blowing in the Introduction, carrying around snotty handkerchiefs is abominable in one culture, blowing one's nose directly into one's hand and discarding the product onto the street is entirely appropriate in another. There is nothing intrinsically dirty about mucus – but it is perceived as polluting, depending on where and how it is deployed. This is the crux of the argument in *Purity and Danger*: that problems of pollution and taboos appear when you cross boundaries, and in particular, bodily boundaries.

Richard Fardon succinctly defines the trajectory of *Purity and Danger* as one that moves

> from an erroneous account of difference, through an account of sameness, to a new and more detailed account of difference. The joker in the pack is the final chapter which is ambiguous but can plausibly be interpreted, in some respects, as a further corrective to the account of difference that tends to lead us back to a concluding account of human similarity. (Fardon 1999: 84)

What Fardon is referring to is Douglas's tendency to homogenise across social formations, to point up differences between social behaviours between tribal people and city-dwellers and then collapse those differences into similarities. We shall return to this tendency later in this chapter. Douglas uses the place of the body in religion to explore comparative religions and to explore how cosmologies are similar and different across cultures. What is of concern here is how that movement back and forth between sameness and difference shapes conceptions of the human body.

Acknowledging that we (in Western industrialised societies) are not immune to systems of pollution and taboo – 'we shall not expect to understand other people's ideas of contagion, sacred or secular, until we have confronted our own' – Douglas insists that it is important to look at Judaeo-Christian or biblical notions of purity and impurity in coming to 'try to compare peoples' views about man's destiny and place in the universe' (Douglas [1966] 2002: 29). Clearly and openly embedded in her own Catholicism, the aim of her method is to try to unpack the cultural relativism behind 'symbolic rites' and 'hygiene'.

Pollution can come from what is put into, or excreted from, the body. It can also come from contact with unclean bodies, and its manifestation is characteristic of the society in which it is formed. '[O]ur ideas of dirt also express symbolic systems'. However, for Douglas, 'the difference between pollution behaviour in one part of the world and another is only a matter of detail' (36). It is the symbolic systems as they relate to social forms, far more than the specific content of a taboo, that are under scrutiny. Douglas is concerned to clarify the ways in which patterns of inclusion and exclusion are formed. While throughout her work, religions or cosmologies are the means through which this patterning is identified, she does not believe that sacred systems are intrinsic to the definition of pollution. Nor does she believe that this involves any

> special distinction between primitives and moderns: we are all subject to the same rules. But in the primitive culture the rule of patterning works with greater force and more total comprehensiveness. With the moderns it applies to disjointed, separate areas of existence. (41)

She does, however, believe that all pollution notions are based on cultural world-views, which she specifically relates to spiritual ritualism and defines as 'rituals of separation' (42).

> A private person may revise his pattern of assumptions or not. It is a private matter. But cultural categories are public matters. They cannot be so easily subject to revision. Yet they cannot neglect the challenge of aberrant forms ... This is why, I suggest, we find in any culture worthy of the name various provisions for dealing with ambiguous or anomalous events. (40)

That is to say, by their very nature, events that cross boundaries are sources of pollution and taboo. Holiness is constituted in wholeness, in events and artefacts that do not cross boundaries, which are inseparable from the 'unity, integrity, perfection of the individual and of the kind' (55). Douglas expands upon this point through a detailed explanation of why some foods are considered unclean in the Bible. She builds up a complex picture of patterning that defines exclusion by a given food's lack of specificity to a recognised category. Cereals or animals are classified as impure because they are not discrete, neither one thing nor another.[2]

In this, ritual is a framing and focusing device – often centred on bodily matter or material control of bodily functions – that sharpens these distinctions. In the case of bodily effusions, as opposed to ingestions, Douglas notes that like many tribal cultures there were Christian teachings on ritual cleanliness, based particularly on blood pollution with respect to menstruating women, but they have gone by the wayside or been transmuted into something else (62). Rituals of bodily cleanliness and purification persist in tribal societies, however, surrounded by rites of power.

> More wonderful than the exotic caves and palaces of fairy tales, the magic of primitive ritual creates harmonious worlds with ranked and ordered populations playing their appointed parts. So far from being meaningless, it is primitive magic which gives meaning to existence. This applies as much to the negative as to the positive rights. The prohibitions trace the cosmic outlines and the ideal social order. (73)

According to Douglas, in Western industrialised societies, 'pollution' is subject to social sanctions; in 'primitive' societies, it is still primarily a matter of 'religious offence' (74).

Douglas argues that amongst 'primitive' peoples the universe is presumed to be 'responsive to signs', it is 'personal', though neither naïvely nor directly so. By contrast, in modern societies the universe is impersonal and unresponsive, though it is perceived as 'discerning'.

> It may discern between fine nuances in social relations, such as whether the partners in sexual intercourse are related within prohibited degrees, or between less fine ones such as whether a murder has been committed on a fellow-tribesman or on a stranger, or whether a woman is married or not. (88)

But whether personal or impersonal, responsive or discerning, pollution's effects are the same.

> A polluting person is always in the wrong. He has developed some wrong condition or simply crossed some line which should not have been crossed and this displacement unleashes danger for someone. Bringing pollution, unlike sorcery and witchcraft, is a capacity which men share with animals, for pollution is not always set off by humans. Pollution can be committed intentionally, but intention is irrelevant to its effect – it is more likely to happen inadvertently. This is as near as I can get to defining a particular class of dangers which are not powers vested in humans, but which can be released by human action. The power which presents a danger for careless humans is very evidently a power inhering in the structure of ideas, a power by which the structure is expected to protect itself. (114)

Douglas sees in the human body, and the symbolism attached to it in various cultures, a reflection or representation of society as a whole. What she is fighting against is any interpretation of bodily symbolism as exclusively aligned with the individual. In psychology or psychiatry, bodily meaning is restricted to the experience of the individual. The Oedipal moment is a symbolic crisis of the individual. Bodily matter such as faeces, spittle or breast milk is symbolically significant through the individual's experience of them. To give a flippant but commonly recognisable example which emphasises Douglas's point: blaming unacceptable adult behaviour on poor potty-training has a social resonance, but the criticised behaviour is dependent on the individual's experience. Douglas admits that the symbolic interpolations of neuroses, psychoses and disordered behaviours in psychology and psychiatry may have meaning in and through a social context but they are situated in and symbolically expressive of the individual. This will not do for Douglas's anthropology.

> The body is a model which can stand for any bounded system. Its boundaries can represent any boundaries which are threatened or precarious. The body is a complex structure. The functions of its different parts and their relation afford a source of symbols for other complex structures. We cannot possibly interpret rituals concerning excreta, breast milk, saliva and the rest unless we are prepared to see in the body a symbol of society, and to see the powers and dangers credited to social structure reproduced in small on the human body. It is easy to see the body of a sacrificial ox is being used as a diagram of a social situation. But when we try to interpret rituals of the human body in the same way the psychological tradition turns its face away from society, back towards the individual ... There is no possible justification for this shift of interpretation just because the rituals work upon human flesh ... when [Bettleheim] argues that rituals which are explicitly designed to produce genital bleeding in males are intended to express male envy of female reproductive processes, the anthropologist should protest that this is an inadequate interpretation of a public rite. It is inadequate because it is merely descriptive. What is being carved in human flesh is an image of society. (116–17)

Douglas is rejecting a psychological approach because it individualises symbolism as it pertains to the rites and rituals of the human body. She sees in the codification of the purity of breast milk or the impurity of menstrual blood an expression of society – in a manner not unrelated to Bourdieu's notions of the *habitus* and hexis. A society is embodied through its rituals of purity and defilement. Her rejection is aimed most squarely at anachronistic and culturally inappropriate psychological readings of 'primitive' rites and rituals. Although Douglas does not go into historical interpretations of the human body, this argument from anachronism is also applicable to earlier forms of bodily symbolism in Western cultures. When it comes to contemporary Western cultures, which are implicitly post-psychoanalytic societies, her point becomes more complicated. Psychology has become a part of the social system that is represented on and through the body, and society is individualised. This has particular relevance in relation to bodily modification, as we shall see in the analysis section below.

However, if as Douglas says, the body is symbolic of social systems through rites and rituals, and it is the crossing of boundaries that bestows or determines impurity, the next step in the argument is clear. Whatever crosses the boundaries of the body is in danger of materialising or transmitting impurity within society. Douglas is prepared to admit that infantile psychological drives (death, sex) are common to humanity and she uses that to refute psychological interpretations of rites and ritual.

These erotic desires which it is said to be the infant's dream to satisfy within the body's bounds are presumably common to the human race. Consequently body symbolism is part of the common stock of symbols, deeply emotive because of the individual's experience. But rituals draw on this common stock of symbolism selectively. Some develop here, others there. Psychological explanations cannot of their nature account for what is culturally distinctive. (122)

And bodily symbolism and its material expressions, as she shows quite clearly, vary from culture to culture.

Second, all margins are dangerous. If they are pulled this way or that the shape of fundamental experience is altered. Any structure of ideas is vulnerable at its margins. We should expect the orifices of the body to symbolise its specially vulnerable points. Matter issuing from them is marginal stuff of the most obvious kind. (122)

Hence the bodily matter most likely to be identified as symbolically powerful (polluting and impure or purifying and sacred) is that which crosses bodily boundaries, depending on where it issues from and whether it is contained or free-flowing.

The mistake is to treat bodily margins in isolation from all other margins. There is no reason to assume any primacy for the individual's attitude to his own bodily and emotional experience, any more than for his cultural and social experience. This is the clue which explains the unevenness with which different aspects of the body are treated in the rituals of the world. (122)

Variation in cultural or societal identification of pollution and purity is beyond the individual psychological experience. If psychological universals held, all cultures would find the same bodily products abominable or divine in the same way. To return to Fardon's point, Douglas sees all peoples as similar insofar as notions of pollution and attendant rituals appear in all cultures, but we are all different in those similarities, with wide divergences in what we find sacred or fetid.

Social and symbolic rituals guide and regulate bodily acts. Both are, in turn, constitutive and expressive of particular cultural forms and discrete cultures. They are the means by which meaning is constructed and the world is known and understood.

Any culture is a series of related structures which comprise social forms, values, cosmology, the whole of knowledge and through which all experience is mediated. Certain cultural themes are expressed by rites of bodily manipulation ... The rituals enact the form of social relations and in giving these relations visible expression they enable people to know their own society. The rituals work upon the body politic through the symbolic medium of the physical body. (129)

In a dual action, the human body is the symbolic expression of a society and the means by which a society maintains itself. It is the religious or ritualistic *habitus*. Bourdieu would see this as only one field of play within a larger complex of rituals that make up either a tribal or modern *habitus*, but there is a definite correlation between his idea of embodiment and Douglas's recognition of the centrality of bodily rituals across societies. Bourdieu understands the 'rules of the game' and has explanations of how one wins or loses on the fields of cultural capital, but he pays scant attention to the subjective, sacred or emotional reactions brought on by breaking the rules. In fact, he is much more likely to account for that aspect of social behaviour – to extend the metaphor of the game – by categorising it as a relegation or exclusion. There are value judgements and qualitative distinctions in Bourdieu's work – high and low, desirable and worthless – but no ethical or moral register in the rationalism of the *habitus*. This is precisely what Douglas offers us, a way of accounting for 'good' and 'bad' – terms that are central to pollution and taboo and common to all societies.

What Douglas makes clear is that not only is it the crossing of bodily boundaries that brings bodily matter under suspicion, but that by the same token whole bodies are endangered when either their boundaries are breached, they breach the boundaries of others, or they are implicated in the crossing of social boundaries. The moral and ethical aspects of embodiment are inseparable from issues of transgression:

> [W]herever the lines [of social sanctions] are precarious we find pollution ideas come to their support. Physical crossing of the social barrier is treated as a dangerous pollution, with any of the consequences we have just examined. The polluter becomes a doubly wicked object of reprobation, first because he crossed the line and second because he endangered others. (140)

So, the body is symbolic of society not only in its parts and excretions but also as a whole, and in all aspects is both emblematic of and influential upon the body politic. Douglas uses this to explain why in insular social forms, always under threat as a whole, bodily inviolability becomes so important. On this explanation, virginity becomes important and valuable in early Christian society, based

> in a small persecuted minority group. For we have seen that these social conditions lend themselves to beliefs which symbolise the body as an imperfect container which will only be perfect if it can be made impermeable. (159)

Implicitly virginity – and by extension a secure and identifiable bloodline – is less important in societies that are not under threat and where resources are ample.[3] But, Douglas argues, a society with overly strict rules of pollution and taboo cannot resist internal contradiction, constant taboo breaches and eventually hypocrisy. To counter this there has to be a means of reabsorbing or accounting for the impure. For as the body will not survive if a crucial part is excised, a society cannot survive if the incidence of pollution, and therefore the incidence of casting out, is too high.

> The body as we have tried to show, provides a basic scheme for all symbolism. There is hardly any pollution which does not have some primary physiological reference. As life is in the body it cannot be rejected outright. And as life must be affirmed, the most complete philosophies, as William James puts it, must find some ultimate way of affirming that which has been rejected. (165)

Thus, the abominable can become the revered and a bodily excretion or boundary-crossing may become the exception that proves the rule. Douglas, referring to the Lele tribe's cult around the pangolin, extends upon this theme in the closing chapter with a meditation on the ultimate bodily act or attribute that is inseparable from physical corruption and therefore implicit pollution: death.

> Just as the focus of all pollution symbolism is the body, the final problem to which the perspective of pollution leads is bodily disintegration. Death presents a challenge to any metaphysical system, but the challenge need not be squarely met. I am suggesting that in treating each death as the outcome of an individual act of treachery and human malice the Lele are evading its metaphysical implications. Their pangolin cult suggests a meditation on the inadequacy of the categories of human thought, but only a few are invited to make it and it is not related explicitly to their experience of death. (174)

Death is abject and horrifying, awe-inspiring and revered. In many cultures it is welcomed. Whether accounted for positively or negatively, it is universally respected and attended by ritual practices: 'we find corruption enshrined in sacred places and times' (180). In the same contradictory counterpoint that Douglas used to balance extreme pollution and its re-absorption, the ultimate form of corruption affirms life and in this we are again 'all the same'.

It is important to understand, however, that Douglas's arguments evolved after *Purity and Danger*. She took seriously several criticisms of this early book and adapted her work accordingly. Most importantly, while maintaining the position that boundary-crossing was central to the identification of pollution and taboo, she moved away from the position that the sacred was only identified with wholeness and impermeability. She states this most clearly in *Implicit Meanings: Essays in Anthropology* (1975) in admitting that her inability to account for the reverence for the (boundary-crossing) pangolin by the Lele which contrasts so strongly with the Biblical abomination of the pig.

Foul monster or good saviour, the judgment has little to do with the physical attributes of the being in question and much to do with the prevailing social pattern of rules and meanings which creates anomaly ... Such a response to a mixed category is essentially a gut reaction. (Douglas 1975: 285)

Boundary-crossing becomes a sign of liminality, and the liminal has the potential to confer either sacredness or defilement. And Douglas situates that judgement firmly in the embodied response: these are indeed 'gut' reactions.

Natural Symbols

Natural Symbols Explorations in Cosmology ([1970]1996) extends upon the themes and arguments of *Purity and Danger*, taking a closer look at the forms in which codifications of bodily symbolism appear. In it Douglas reiterates her argument from similarity, that all cultures – tribal, traditional, modern, industrial – have systems of cosmological symbols. These systems have embodied forms and effects. And they are different in their similarity, similar in their differences. For Douglas, given types of culture exhibit a characteristic symbolic expression. This is the essence of her arguments on 'grid and group' and the reason for constructing the metaphoric table that she uses to try and separate out four categories of social formation. It is an attempt to make concrete the differences, relations and progressions between one type of group and another. She argues that particular social formations will give rise to particular types of symbolic systems and characteristic forms of communication. Each of the quadrants of her table, discussed in more detail below, describes a social form.

While Douglas acknowledges cultural influence on appropriate behaviour (and difference), at the same time she insists that it is possible to make cross-cultural comparisons. Those characteristic symbolic systems can be compared across cultures, and symbolic systems from different social formations can also be compared. She believes that the point of doing ethnographic work with tribes – 'them' – is to be able to gain further insight to bear on 'us'. Again she is arguing that, somehow, we are all the same in our tendency to group things symbolically just as societies are grouped. While the approach of *Natural Symbols* is to look at societies as a whole and to try to account for the importance of the symbolic within societies, at several points this leads to a more particular focus on language and discourse. While this is important, it is the place of the body in these symbolic systems that concerns us here.

In the original introduction,[4] Douglas frames her approach by first appealing to the embodied symbols of *Purity and Danger* and then (if I can translate her words into the conceptual language of the constitutive abstraction approach) by arguing that the further away from face-to-face embodied culture the dominant integrative relations of a society become, the more abstract the systems of embodied control tend to be.

> According to the rule of distance from physiological origin (or the purity rule) the more the social situation exerts pressure on persons involved in it, the more the social demand for conformity tends to be expressed by a demand for physical control. Bodily processes are more ignored and more firmly set outside the social discourse, the more the latter is important. A natural way of investing a social occasion with dignity is to hide organic processes. Thus social distance tends to be expressed in distance from physiological origins and vice versa. (Douglas [1970] 1996: xxxii)

In other words, the more 'civilised' the social form, the more the body will be subjected to rules of suppression and control, the less important bodily symbolism will be in its cosmology, and the further that symbolism becomes incorporated into discourse. This fits well with Elias's explanation of the rise of manners and with Foucault's description of institutional repression. She takes it a step further however, and also links it to an increase in secularism. The more secular the society – or the more secularised a religion becomes – the less symbolism inheres in the body.

Working with a stated method aimed at making comparisons in and across given social environments, Douglas works on the basis that there are four separate types by which systems of 'natural symbols' can be identified. This is a long excerpt, but it bears quoting in full:

> These will be social systems in which the image of the body is used in different ways to reflect and enhance each person's experience of society. According to one, the body will tend to be conceived as an organ of communication. The major preoccupations will be with its functioning effectively; the relation of head to subordinate members will be a model of the central control system, the favourite metaphors of statecraft will harp upon the flow of blood in the arteries, sustenance and restoration of strength. According to another, though the body will also be seen as a vehicle of life, it will be vulnerable in different ways. The dangers to it will come not so much from lack of co-ordination or of food and rest, but from failure to control the quality of what it absorbs through the orifices; fear of poisoning, protection of boundaries, aversion to bodily waste products and medical theory that enjoins frequent purging. Another again will be very practical about the possible uses of bodily rejects, very cool about recycling waste matter and about the pay-off from such practices. The distinction between the life within the body and the body that carries it will hold no interest. In the control areas of this society controversies about spirit and matter will scarcely arise. But at the other end of the spectrum, where the vast majority are controlled by these pragmatists, a different attitude will be seen. Here the body is not primarily a vehicle of life, for life will be seen as purely spiritual, and the body as irrelevant matter. Here we can locate millennial tendencies from our early history to the

present day. For these people, society appears as a system which does not work. The human body is the most readily available image of a system. In these types of social experience, a person feels that his personal relations, so inexplicably unprofitable, are in the sinister grip of a social system. It follows that the body tends to serve as a symbol of evil, as a structured system contrasted with pure spirit which by its nature is free and undifferentiated. (xxxvi)

In this litany of social and symbolic forms we can see some concordances with Paul James's (1996) work on constitutive abstraction. In James there are characteristic forms of embodiment allied with the dominance of tribal, traditional, modern and postmodern social formations – here in Douglas there are characteristic forms of embodiment allied with each of her proposed social symbolic systems. In James none of these terms is epochal, nor are they linear: tribal social forms can, for example, live within and across postmodern social forms, though not without tension. In this instance, neither are the descriptions that Douglas gives necessarily linear or epochal. They could apply to historical traditional societies as easily as to tribal or modern industrial ones. What is clear in this passage is Douglas's motivation to define forms and categories so that they have correlations across social forms, which is precisely the opposite of the thrust of James's arguments on constitutive abstraction. James constructs a matrix of imbrications or palimpsests of difference, where Douglas would have us accept correlated ranks of sameness. And in James there is a direct correlation between a social formation and those characteristic forms of embodiment, something which is not true of Douglas's schema. For her, the form of embodiment understood by pygmies could as easily represent the social symbolic system of the Bog Irish. Further, what is not clear in this passage of Douglas's – at least at this point – is which society might be an example of any given system of symbolic representation.

Douglas acknowledges the complexity of symbols as they are used within systems of communication – that in day-to-day language words can function both specifically and in multiple ways – but she wants us to concentrate on the function of symbols that work beyond that to connect to, and act as, representations of cosmological meanings: what she calls *condensed symbols*. She appeals to Victor Turner's work on the Ndembu.

This people in Zambia experiences human society as a complex structure of descent groups and local groups stratified by age and cult associations. To symbolize this they fasten on the colours of the juices in the human body and in the earth and trees. The active principles in humans are black bile, red blood and white milk; in the world of living nature there are trees with milky saps and red, sticky resins and charred black wood; likewise, minerals include black earth, white and red clay. From these colours they work out a complex representation of male and female spheres, and destructive and nourishing powers interlocking at more and more abstract and inclusive levels of interpretation. So economical and highly articulated in this system of signs that it is enough to strike one chord to recognize that the orchestration is on a cosmic scale (Turner 1968). For Christian examples of condensed symbols, consider the sacraments, particularly the Eucharist and the Chrisms. (10)

For the Ndembu, wearing one colour brings into being a wealth of associations that resonate for the society that is represented in them. Douglas, appealing to her own Catholicism, finds a parallel in the rites of Christianity. Yet again, for Douglas, we are different but we are the same.

By contrast Douglas notes, in the ethnographic study by Barth of the Basseri who are a nomadic society of secularised 'Persian' Muslims, there is a seeming dearth of symbolic ritual.

> For one of the most obvious forms of religious behaviour, which Barth was looking for and failed to find, is the use of bodily symbols to express the notion of an organic social system. But it would seem that unless the form of personal relations corresponds in some obvious way to the form or functions of the body, a range of metaphysical questions of passionate interest to some people becomes entirely irrelevant. (19)

It is in the chapter 'To Inner Experience' that Douglas, following Basil Bernstein, teases out these problems and presents us with a diagram that is a concrete visualisation of the four categories that she brings up in the introduction. She argues that two facets form the framework for defining different kinds of societies: family/societal control and speech codes. In the first, she argues that the family is the basic form of social control in 'primitive' societies and the more developed a society becomes, the further the mechanisms of control move into the hands of community and eventually states. She represents this with an arrowed 'x axis' pointing from left to right, suggesting progression from the positional (family) to the personal (internalised social). On a perpendicular trajectory (the 'y axis') aimed from top to bottom, speech moves from being in the power of 'the immediate social context and elaborated for its use in the widest social structures of all' (28). Put these two axes together and you get a quartered representation of speech codes and social formations as they relate to cosmologies (religious world-views). Intuitively appealing, it accounts for shifts in language and upwardly mobile social groups from the tribal to the petite bourgeoisie.

> For the cosmology, based on its particular hierarchy of values and upholding a particular pattern of behaviour, is derived from society. As the grip of his immediate society on the individual tightens or slackens something happens to his religious attitudes. There is an awkward paradox in this presentation. For as a Londoner gets drawn more and more into the vortex of industrial society his religious ideas seem to approximate more and more to those of the pygmy ... This paradox is due to a distortion of the comparison caused by the effects of the division of labour. Pygmies cannot be equated with preachers, journalists and dons. The argument will have to go a long way before we can pick up this paradox and resolve it. In the meanwhile, note that what the Bernstein effect amounts to. As a

result of definable pressures on home and school there is an increasing tendency to rear children by personal, elaborated speech code methods. This produces a child acutely sensitive to the feelings of others, and interested in his own internal states. It follows that such an education will predispose a person to ethical preoccupations, for while it opens up his vocabulary of feeling it also denies him any sense of pattern in his social life. He must therefore look for some justification of his existence outside the performance of set rules. He can only find it in good works on behalf of humanity in general or in personal success, or both. Hence the drive towards a purely ethical religion. (36)

In this progressive narrative, the body becomes decreasingly significant. Moreover, as speech codes become more elaborated, and controls move into the hands of community and state, cosmologies become more personalised and more individualised. The gaze turns in upon the individual. An example comes to mind that may help to open this idea out, and one that Douglas would have had fresh in her experience while writing. With Vatican II the Catholic Church moved from a system of the individual confessing to a priest before God – verbalising one's sins, atoning and being publicly penitent – to one of massed, internal (unspoken) reconciliation with the Lord. One can see why Douglas in fact opines the move away from mysteries towards secularised ethical religion: it has direct connections to the secularisation of her own Church.

In her anthropological colleagues Douglas saw a contradiction in their modern desire for personal relationships devoid of status, in their averring of ritual, and their frustration at their professional inability to capture unspoken communication.

These very people, who prefer unstructured intimacy in their social relations, defeat their wish for communication without words. For only a ritual structure makes possible a wordless channel of communication that is not entirely coherent. (51)

Douglas is at base arguing for the maintenance of ritual, that only in mystery and rite are community and society maintained. She is an unabashed social conservative.[5] In Protestantism, and even in the arguments of the New Left, she finds an affirmation of the importance of the

follower's inside and of the insides of all his fellow members, together with the badness of everything external to the movement. Always we find bodily symbolism applied, from the values placed on internal and external parts of the body, on reality and appearance, content and form, spontaneity and established institutions. (51–2)

But, she argues, because the 'social body constrains the way the body is perceived' (68), follow this logic to its conclusion and you end up with social formations that deny the possibility of the kind of community that people crave.

Natural symbols will not be found in individual lexical items. The physical body can have universal meaning only as a system which responds to the social system, expressing it as a system. What it symbolizes naturally is the relation of parts of an organism to the whole. Natural symbols can express the relation of an individual to his society at that general systemic level. The two bodies are the self and society: sometimes they are so near as to be almost merged; sometimes they are far apart. The tension between them allows the elaboration of meanings. (87)

In secularised social formations you lose natural symbols and therefore you lose meaning. In this, Douglas makes perfectly clear that she is in favour of restricted speech codes, rites, ritual and natural symbolism – all of which are familiar and personally dear to her.

Analysis

There is much in Douglas's writing that is of great worth, but it has to be said, her faith is her Achilles' heel. Because she concentrates so firmly on cosmologies, she leaves out the vast majority of the secular systems of meaning. She is quite right that increasing individualisation leads to an intensification of the abstraction of personal relations – but that need not be directly attributable to the decline in religion. As I have already intimated, if instead one looks at the shift in social formations involved from the perspective of constitutive abstraction in the work of Paul James (1996), one finds that increasing abstraction of interpersonal relations and increasing individualisation go hand in hand, but religion is only one level at which this occurs. The ways of ordering things 'in-the-world' (knowledge systems of which religion might be one), of framing 'thing-in-the-world' (the modes of practice of classical sociology), the ways in which people order and frame themselves and others (including by embodied difference), along with the ways in which these levels come together and fan out in different social formations, all exist in increasingly intense levels of abstraction that have correlative links to the increasing individualisation within social formations. Douglas shows us one way into this process, but the process is much wider and far more complex than her arguments from cosmology allow.

Her arguments on the emptying out of meaning in embodied symbolism, or in our terms on the intensification of bodily abstraction, also carry weight. Within Western postmodern societies bodily modification is increasingly an expression of individualism, far more than social grouping. By and large, if it is related to social grouping, it is in a very abstract and disjointed way. The act of modification may in some ways be a means of identifying with a group (young, rebellious, autonomous) but the choice of symbols is rarely ritualistic – as it is in tribal societies – instead it is aesthetic and personalised. Postmodern embodied symbolism is much more about autonomy and personal narrative than community, more about inward self-creation than outward melding. To carry through the point above, this need not be attributed to lack of spirituality – far from it – but when symbols become commodities (or more simply fashion), their content is emptied of that resonance. But, to reiterate, just because this may be the case amongst individuals who happily and self-consciously use body modification to recreate themselves in a postmodern social formation, it does not follow that this also the case for tribal or traditional peoples who live at an intersection with such a society.

Much of Douglas's anthropology is usefully compatible with arguments from abstraction, particularly in relation to embodiment as I have gestured to above. Douglas's descriptions of particular symbols as characteristic of particular social formations is also useful, up to a point. Where these two theories part company is when it comes to her equation of different social formations in the abstract. She implicitly and explicitly draws parallels between different societies and finds the sameness in them. If one argues from abstraction, one argues that different social formations may have points of similarity, particularly in terms of content, but not only does that content have differently contextualised meaning, it is also practised in fundamentally different ways.

What Douglas cannot account for is simultaneous difference within social groupings or societies. Like Bourdieu's work, there is a static tendency in her theorisations. If there is a shift in social formation, it is characterised as a Fall: Paradise is lost. She could describe but not account for the co-existence of tribal social formations in a secularised society, such as one might hope to account for in the co-existence of indigenous communities who maintain traditions and rites while at the same time taking advantage of satellite technology to facilitate those traditions. The danger in such implicit pessimism in fact ignores the viability of traditional ways of being and that they do survive in her own terms: as boundary-crossers.

On the other hand, Douglas's account of abjection – the construction of self and other, the rejection of the body (or parts and products thereof), persons (or parts of society) and the delineation of outsides and insides – is acute. She finds a place for abjection that goes beyond the psychological, individualised explanations of Freud, Jung and their many inheritors. She finds the social and communal sense of abjection that psychoanalysis avers, and as we have seen she quite clearly rejects any individualised interpretation in tribal cultures. Douglas doesn't describe abjection to that end, she is interested in the social dynamic: what brings people together or what they believe in common that is made concrete by their exclusionary or systematising beliefs.

There is a great irony that her work is then regularly appealed to by psychoanalytic feminists in support of their arguments. For example, Julia Kristeva with whom we began and who has written a core text on abjection (Kristeva 1980). She cites Douglas and then uses her examples of pollution and taboo to move back to a universalised abject, utterly missing (and implicitly dismissing) Douglas's rejection of such moves. Kristeva pounces on the sacred symbolism as some kind of psychological universal; Douglas is quite adamant that it's not. The whole thrust of her social anthropology is that people react differently in different societies and under different circumstances. Otherwise Douglas's observations on the *differences* between societies, what is taboo or abject in one and not in another, would not make sense.

There are, as I have already noted, limitations in and a tension between Douglas's stated recognition of cultural difference and a simul- taneous assertion of homogeny, which leaves her open to such misappro- priation. In the chapters thus far I have offered brief comments on subsequent writers ('Inheritors') who have followed in the footsteps of the main theorists discussed. Rather than doing so here, Chapter 5 as a whole performs that function for Douglas's work on abject embodiment. Judith Butler, the subject of that chapter, is open to just such a charge of misappropriating Douglas's work. Butler is certainly one of a 'new wave' of feminists who turned to psychoanalysis in theorisations of embodi- ment and who, in their popularity across a wide range of interdiscipli- nary studies, have become influential in anthropology and sociology. It is at this point that we leave authors whose feet are in modernity as they scan tribal, traditional and modern societies and move on to writers whose heads are instead filled with postmodern turns on the body.

Notes

1 Richard Fardon (1990).

2 We can see here correspondences with other explanations of embodied boundary-crossing that imply purity and pollution. In (1984) *Rabelais and His World*, Mikhail Bakhtin's theorisations of the carnivalesque, open-orificed, impure female bodies are contrasted with impermeable, classical male bodies. The female body is impure precisely because it is always open to boundary-crossing, a leaky vessel, whereas – in his explana- tion at least – the (proper) male body does not admit penetration.

3 One can see in this an implicit explanation of the decreasing importance placed upon virginity at the time Douglas was writing. In relation to the earlier note on Bakhtin, the Western cultures in which his notions of open-orificed female bodies and closed male bodies thrived were not persecuted minority cultures – far from

it — they were characteristic of Christian European cultures in the sixteenth and seventeenth centuries. But they were the historical inheritors of those persecuted minorities, in whom the symbolism had become entrenched, experiencing a disruptive shift from a traditional to an early modern social formation.

4 In the second edition published in 1996, from which all quotations here are taken, there is a revised introduction in addition to the original.

5 Coincidentally, her husband was a long-serving economic researcher with the British Conservative Party, who fell out of favour with the fall of Ted Heath and the rise of Margaret Thatcher.

FIVE Mind over Matter

Psychoanalysis and 'Putting On' the Body

At the very beginning of this book, in contrasting Elias with his predecessors, I said that the focus of sociology and anthropology had been systems of thought (beliefs) and the intellectual connections between peoples. This had been at the neglect of the materiality of the human body. If the body was dealt with at all, it was as the container in which the important part – the thinking thing – was housed. The writers as discussed in Part I rediscovered the body as a social object. The concept of the 'abject' was introduced in the last chapter in relation to the work of Mary Douglas and Julia Kristeva, and we have seen how Douglas finds social meaning and social functions in the boundary-crossing of bodies and bodily matter. Following this direction, the writers who are addressed in the present chapter and the following Part III explicitly write about the body, about the boundary-crossing or liminal potential of the body, and/or its products. Paradoxically, many of them do so by expressly reinvesting controlling power in the mind even as they cry out for the importance of bodily materiality. While they would not necessarily express it in these terms, in the work of writers like Judith Butler and Donna Haraway the body – as a whole – becomes the abject of the mind. Discussing this line of theoretical development will be a necessary prior step for the concerns of the final section of this book to emerge: there we will see the body as subject, the individual as self-creation in a proliferation of permutations. In looking at the work of Judith Butler, the focus of this chapter, we will encounter some of the strains of thought that have come out of psychoanalytic feminisms, particularly those that have attempted to reconceive the body as malleable matter. Butler has been influential in theorising embodiment as 'performed' in an individual act of creative volition.

Up to the point where I introduced the work of Julia Kristeva and Mary Douglas in the preceding chapter, the theorisations around the body I have written about have come from writers directly concerned with social history, social theory or anthropology. Foucault, even as a poststructuralist, was still a social historian. They are also writers whose major works were written prior to 1980. It was around this time that cultural studies started to emerge as an interdisciplinary field in its own right in the English-speaking academic world. While this is a book on the body in sociology and anthropology, these disciplines can no longer be separated off with any ease from the effects of cultural theory and cultural studies as it has waxed and waned since that time. English-speaking literary and cultural theorists – particularly in America and Australia – began to read French poststructuralist, psychoanalytic and postmodern theory and take it to their collective bosoms. This in turn had a flow-on effect across the disciplines, with cultural theorists being influential upon comparative sociology and anthropology. And vice versa, as we have seen has been the case with the work of Mary Douglas.

Butler

Judith Butler is a case in point. An 'out' and politically active lesbian, she entered her academic studies at the height of the influx of French theory into American academe in the late 1970s and was a graduate student during the rise of gay and lesbian activism that mobilised in the early days of the AIDS epidemic. She is a feminist concerned with challenging and reformulating feminist theory and her work could be included in any of the disciplines of philosophy, women's studies, comparative literature and queer theory. In her introduction to the second edition to *Gender Trouble*, she explicitly recognises the kind of double translation that I gestured towards above, one that occurs between the work of anthropologist Douglas and psychoanalytic feminist Kristeva. Butler consciously blends a particular strain of French theory with 'the Anglo-American sociological and anthropological tradition of "gender" studies, which is distinct from the discourse of "sexual difference" derived from structuralist inquiry' (x).

It is important to note here that in her adherence to French psychoanalytic theory, Butler also imports a particular 'style' of writing. As I explained in relation to Kristeva in the last chapter, psychoanalysis depends heavily on particular notions around language and language acquisition which are, in turn, gendered. The pre-linguistic *Imaginary* phase is feminine; the post-linguistic *Symbolic* order is masculine. Like Kristeva, French feminist theorists Irigaray and Cixous both promote the use of a more 'poetic' or 'chaotic' language and reject 'clarity' as phallogocentric (male-word/logic-centred). In such feminists' writing, metaphor and 'slippage' between the meanings of words is consciously employed as a part of that rejection.[1] Sympathy with these theorists' linguistic agenda provides one basis for Butler's prose style. The other is a postmodern theoretical turn to 'language games' as method. Lyotard, the touchstone for many postmodernists on this point, defines language games thus:

> [E]ach of the various categories of utterance [denotative, performative, prescriptive, etc.] can be defined in terms of rules specifying their properties and the uses to which they can be put – in exactly the same way a the game of chess is defined by a set of rules determining the properties of each of the pieces, in other words, the proper way to move them. (Lyotard 1984: 10)

Lyotard goes on to say that 'to speak is to fight, in the sense of playing ... [and further] the observable social bond is composed of language "moves"' (10–11). So, when we utter words – give orders, make claims to truth, describe and thereby define an occurrence – we not only communicate, we also enter into a battle over meaning and the shaping of social action. As we shall see below, Butler relies heavily on this metaphoric style in her work on gender as performance.

What we also see here, as far as the overall theme of this book is concerned, is the shift from modern to postmodern embodiment in the terms of bodily abstraction. Up to this point the theorisations of the body we have looked at have been modern, if very late-modern (and post-structuralist) in the case of Foucault. Even in Douglas's readings of tribal peoples, which describe tribal and traditional social practices, her theorisations are inevitably through a 'modern' lens. From this point on, we are dealing with postmodern theorisations of embodiment. The postmodern body is even more intensely abstracted from itself than the modern body. Ironically but perfectly logically, the more central the body has become, the more abstract it has become: it is a disembodied body. Butler's contribution to this level of bodily abstraction has been in terms of contributing to the deconstruction of sex and gender distinctions.

Gender Trouble

Judith Butler's aim in *Gender Trouble* (1990) is to disrupt boundaries. Taking earlier feminist arguments that gender is a 'cultural interpretation' of sex, she extends the same logic to sex. If gender is a construct, so too is sex a gendered construct. Gendered individuals frame sex, which frames gender. She believes that patriarchal orthodoxies and feminisms like de Beauvoir's are inherently universalising. They can lead to a homogeneous idea of 'women', that elides further differences such as race, class, and sexual orientation: 'the insistence upon the coherence and unity of the category of women has effectively refused the multiplicity of cultural, social and political intersections in which the concrete array of "women" are constructed' (Butler 1990: 19–20).

Butler argues that if one takes it 'to its logical limit, the sex/gender distinction suggests a radical discontinuity between sexed bodies and culturally constructed genders.' If sex and gender are not necessarily linked, then there is no reason why gender categories should be confined to given bodies: 'man and masculine might just as easily signify a female body as a male one, and woman and feminine a male body as easily as a female one' (10). Butler believes that in the 'substantialising view of gender', sex and sexuality of de Beauvoir and others there is a heterosexist political bias that confirms and consolidates a naturalised heterosexual norm. 'The act of differentiating the two oppositional moments of the binary results in a consolidation of each term, the respective internal coherence of sex, gender and desire' (30–1). Through definition – a move in a language game – other ways of viewing gender and sex are rendered illegitimate. She aims to shift the rules of the game.

Butler wants to do so by going beyond arguments that are based in notions of 'construction'. To stake out the boundaries of her field, she goes through a detailed survey of different constructivist accounts of the sex/gender distinction, looking at the writing of de Beauvoir, Irigaray, Wittig and Foucault. She investigates

some aspects of the psychoanalytic structuralist account of sexual difference and the construction of sexuality with respect to its power to contest the regulatory regimes outlined here as well as its role in uncritically reproducing those regimes. The univocity of sex, the internal coherence of gender, and the binary framework for both sex and gender are considered throughout as regulatory fictions that consolidate and naturalize the convergent power regimes of masculine and hererosexist oppression. (44)

Butler assiduously wades through high-psychoanalytic approaches to gender roles, gender formation and gender transgression. This involves re-reading Lacan and Freud and their interpreters. She supplements this with an essay on the work of psychoanalytic feminists Kristeva and Wittig – who have attempted to recuperate Lacanian and Freudian analysis for feminism. Into this she weaves a further account of Foucault's constructivism. In this counterpoint of theories, working one off the other, she concentrates on and develops an account of the language (game) of sex and gender. She wants to be able to maintain the notion of construction while, at the same time, holding to psychoanalytic principles. In this she sets herself a hard task for the former and insists on the importance of social and historical context while the latter are by their nature universalising.

Psychoanalytic theories are also fundamentally tied to particular ideas of language and that understanding of language is filtered through (unacknowledged) ideas of sex and gender, particularly in the writing of Lacan. Indeed, Butler criticises Kristeva for being complicit in Lacan's deep heterosexism and for attempting to recuperate Lacan to feminist ends, precisely because it carries forward those unacknowledged heterosexist ideas of the sex/gender distinction.

> Kristeva constructs lesbian sexuality as intrinsically unintelligible. This tactical dismissal and reduction of lesbian experience performed in the name of the law positions Kristeva within the orbit of paternal-heterosexual privilege. (111)

Instead, Butler aims to meld Foucault's way of expressing the social construction of embodied being with psychoanalytic feminism as a means of supporting her disruption of normative heterosexuality.

> [I]f we apply the Foucaultian critique of the repressive hypothesis to the incest taboo, that paradigmatic law of repression, then it would appear the law produces *both* sanctioned heterosexuality and transgressive homosexuality. Both are indeed *effects*, temporally and ontologically later than the law itself, and the illusion of a sexuality before the law is itself a creation of that law. Rubin's essay remains committed to a distinction between sex and gender which assumes the discrete and prior ontological reality of a 'sex' which is done over in the name of the law, that is, transformed subsequently into 'gender'. (94)

As we saw in Chapter 2, Foucault's 'repressive hypothesis' is a broad claim that the more sex became a subject to be repressed from public discourse, the more it became the subject of endless chattering in the confessional and the clinic. The incest 'law' is what is at stake in the Oedipal moment referred to in the previous chapter, the moment when a child rejects the early maternal sphere and moves into the paternal order. As we saw then in relation to Kristeva (and therefore Lacan), this is intimately linked to shifts in language. So Butler's point is that the incest taboo, which is supposed to mark the moment of sex/gender differentiation, is already informed by the sex/gender distinction. She sees Gayle Rubin's essay 'The Traffic in Women: The "Political Economy" of Sex' as an exemplary feminist appropriation of Foucauldian method and therefore a good starting point, even though it still upholds an unproblematic 'sex'.

> If we accept Foucault's framework, we are compelled to redescribe the maternal libidinal economy as a product of an historically specific organization of sexuality ... The culturally constructed body will then be liberated, neither to its 'natural' past, nor to its original pleasures, but to an open future of cultural possibilities. (Butler 1990: 118–19)

> Foucault invokes a trope of prediscursive libidinal multiplicity that effectively presupposes a sexuality 'before the law', indeed, a sexuality waiting for emancipation from the shackles of 'sex'.
> (Butler 1990: 123)

While I will leave a further discussion of this point until the end of the chapter, it is worth noting here that Butler is using Foucault – a man who dealt in contingents – to support universalising claims. Butler does go some way to acknowledging this tension herself, noting that Foucault would argue that 'recourse to a sexuality before the law is an illusory and complicitous conceit of emancipatory politics' (124).

Butler sets up this long re-reading of a heterosexist hegemony because she wants to find a way of expressing embodiment that can account for what has become known as the 'queer' body: an account of embodiment that is neither homo- nor hetero-sexual. As an entry point she gives a detailed reading of Monique Wittig's turning upside-down of the Law of the Father in the name of radical lesbian feminism. In the end, however, she disagrees with Wittig:

> [T]he radical disjunction posited by Wittig between heterosexuality and homosexuality is simply not true ... there are structures of psychic homosexuality within heterosexual relations, and structures of psychic heterosexuality within gay and lesbian sexuality and relationships.' (155)

More than two-thirds of *Gender Trouble* is spent on this 'survey of the literature'. But in dismissing Wittig, she introduces her own intervention into the debate. She proposes her own take on 'language games', which relies specifically on the 'performative' utterance as a means to invoking the idea of the performativity of gender. If performatives in language games bring meaning into being, and that language is 'written' on the social body, then one can bring one's body into being through language.

> Is 'the body' or 'the sexed body' the firm foundation on which gender and systems of compulsory sexuality operate? Or is 'the body' itself shaped by political forces with strategic interest in keeping that body bounded and constituted by the marker of sex? The sex/gender distinction and the category of sex itself appear to presuppose a generalization of 'the body' that preexists the acquisition of its sexed significance. This 'body' often appears to be a passive medium that is signified by an inscription from a cultural source figured as 'external' to that body. (164)

To expand her point, Butler returns to Foucault's constructivism and also picks up on the idea of 'boundary-crossing' to formulate a notion of self-defining gender subversion.

Butler rightly points out that by 'maintaining a body prior to its cultural inscription, Foucault appears to assume a materiality prior to signification and form' (166). Because she is committed to maintaining a level of psychoanalysis in her system, Butler believes signification (understood in that specific theoretical sense) comes before embodied materiality. In psychoanalysis, embodiment is constructed at the levels of both sex and gender, and that construction is brought about through language. And the psychoanalytic linguistic dynamic is played out through descriptions of bodily boundary-crossing and the differentiation of self and other at the bodily boundaries: Oedipal crises, phallic signifiers, etc.

Butler uses Mary Douglas's early work from *Purity and Danger* on bodily limits and the dangerousness of boundary-crossing to support her assertions. As we have seen, at that point in Douglas's theoretical evolution she argues that the body is *the* symbol of society and that society is 'inscribed' upon and through the body in ritual. Crossing the boundaries of the body transgresses social boundaries and is inherently dangerous. Appealing to this isolated point of Douglas's, Butler brings up the (putative) notion that homosexuality is a danger to society, and redefines that danger in terms of both social and bodily boundary-crossing. Homosexuality crosses the sex/gender boundary.[2] Butler further appeals to Kristeva's directly related theorisation of the abject to support her point.

Building on this, Butler argues that bodily signification, or signification through or on the body, brings coherence to being:

In other words, acts, gestures, and desire produce the effect of an internal core or substance, but produce this *on the surface* of the body, through the play of signifying absences that suggest, but never reveal, the organizing principle of identity as a cause. Such acts, gesture, enactments generally construed, are *performative* in the sense that the essence or identity that they otherwise purport to express are *fabrications* manufactured and sustained through corporeal signs and other discursive means. That the gendered body is performative suggests that it has no ontological status apart from the various acts which constitute its reality. This also suggests that if that reality is fabricated as an interior essence, that very interiority is an effect and function of a decidedly public and social discourse, the public regulation of fantasy through the surface politics of the body, the gender border control that differentiates inner from outer, and so institutes the 'integrity' of the subject. (173)

If the body is not a 'being,' but a variable boundary, a surface whose permeability is politically regulated, a signifying practice within a cultural field of gender hierarchy and compulsory heterosexuality, then what language is left for understanding this corporeal enactment, gender, that constitutes its 'interior' signification on its surface? (177)

Gender is also a norm that can never be fully internalized; 'the internal' is a surface signification, and gender norms are finally phantasmatic, impossible to embody. (179)

So, embodiment is then, open to reconstruction. And in the terms of the 'language games' of our beginning, the appropriate type of utterance to make a successful move in the game is the 'performative'.

Bodies that Matter

Bodies that Matter: On the Discursive Limits of 'Sex' is an extension upon and a filling out of the project undertaken in *Gender Trouble* that starts with a rehearsal of her premise that gender is always already prior to sex definitions and that both are cultural constructions (Butler 1993: 28). She wants to explore the idea that the very ways in which the supposedly irreducible material grounds for bodily existence are themselves the product of a 'problematic gendered matrix' (29); that the body, which is often purported to be a blank slate upon which gender is inscribed, is always and already instituted in terms polluted by the assumptions implicit in a gendered system. Therefore, as she warns in *Gender Trouble*, the basic appeal to bodily materiality upon which much feminism is grounded also encapsulates a notion of matter which is inherently problematic for that feminism. To illustrate her point, Butler introduces a historicisation of theories of bodily materiality. She looks back to classical ideas of bodily formation to see how they inform more contemporary concepts, by looking for traces of Aristotelian thought in Foucault's work and analysing Irigaray's re-reading of Plato.

Butler sees within Foucault's understanding of the body an 'implicit reworking of the Aristotelian formulation' (33) of women as the contributors of matter to the human body (the wax) during gestation, and men as the contributors of form (*schema*, the shape given by a stamp to the wax). In this 'the principle of [matter's] recognisability, its characteristic gesture or usual address, is indissoluble from what constitutes its matter' (33). For Foucault the soul, as an instrument of power, re-enacts the force of the *schema* upon the body by shaping and forming it so that it conforms to the tenets and ideals of the soul (34). We saw this effect in *Discipline and Punish*, in Chapter 2. This is not to say that power is a purely external controlling force, it is itself implicated in the formulation and regulation of the subject at the material level. What Butler objects to in Foucault's work is that his formulation of the subject and its subjection may 'fail to account for not only what is *excluded* from the economies of discursive intelligibility that he describes, but what *has to be excluded* for those economies to function as self-sustaining systems' (35), that being the 'feminine' and the female body.

Butler then outlines Luce Irigaray's attempt to render visible what has been excluded from Plato's formulation of the distinction between form and matter. Using metaphors of gestation, Plato theorises about a receptacle (the *chora*) into which matter is inserted and takes on form. However, matter is already matter before entering: this feminised vessel does not transmit anything of itself (44). The world of form is intelligible therefore the *chora*, being pre-intelligible, is excluded from articulation within that sphere. Irigaray happily claims this 'unintelligible' space for the feminine. She rejects the attempts to articulate the feminine within patrilineally determined system of representations, for these only present poor copies. She uses her writing strategically to 'mimic', and thereby comment upon, the traditional discourse of metaphysics 'showing that what cannot enter it is already inside it (as its necessary outside) ... until this emergence of the outside within the system calls into question its systematic closure and its pretension to be self-grounding' (45). Butler points to a danger in this strategy, that to figure the feminine as the 'chora ... in such a way that the feminine is "always" the outside, and the outside is "always" the feminine' (48) is, firstly, to risk re-enforcing exactly what you intend to subvert. Secondly, to posit the 'other' to the xenophobically constructed male body as always and only the female body displaces all the 'othered' bodies of the Platonic republic – slaves, foreigners, children, animals.

As has been noted above, Butler is warning against the problematic of feminisms which make the naïve move of grounding their theory in an inherently gendered materiality that is left unchallenged. Butler insists that matter be read as a '*sign* which in its redoublings and contradictions enacts an inchoate drama of sexual difference' (49). She returns to Plato's injunction against the *chora* that it never 'assumes' its form from that which penetrates it. Irigaray reads this assumption of form as a conception, re-enforcing the notion of masculine autogenesis, but Butler looks at another possible interpretation of it as 'to have or take a wife', that is assume the role of the penetrator. Butler reads this as invoking a notion of a deliberately heterosexual *matrix* (Latin for uterus), casting the she/*chora* as the penetrated and the he/Form as the penetrator. Butler asks:

> Can we read this taboo that mobilises the speculative and phantasmatic beginnings of Western metaphysics in terms of the spectre of sexual exchange that it produces through its own prohibition, as a panic over the lesbian or, perhaps more specifically, over the phallicization of the lesbian? (51)

So, not only is Western metaphysics misogynistic, it is homophobic at the moment of the inscription of matter.

> There is no singular outside, for the Forms require a number of exclusions, they are and replicate themselves through what they exclude, through not being the animal, not being the woman, not being the slave, whose propriety is purchased through property, national and racial boundary, masculinism, and compulsory heterosexuality. (52)

Butler, like Irigaray, wants to use this marginal position to criticise the normative centre, while still preserving that marginality. She argues that

Plato's prohibitions (not to assume/conceive/penetrate) are prefigurings of the kinds of prohibitions that appear in Freud and Lacan 'which presume the phallus as the synecdochal token of sexed positionality' (55). Given how steeped in classical and literary allusion psychoanalysis is, this is hardly surprising.

Butler extends this analysis into a critique of the phallus as theorised by Freud and re-theorised by Lacan. She investigates the ways in which Freud's discussion of narcissim and ego formation formulates the (mental) interpretation of bodily pain as the grounding for bodily experience, and particularly libidinal experience. This is especially important for her project because Freud explained homosexuality in terms of narcissism. In narcissism pain in a given body part becomes the object of self-preoccupation. The psyche works on this pain, libidinising it to the point where the over-imagined sensation becomes a site of pleasure. This is the basis of hypochondria (58). A similar notion is incorporated into the idea of ego formation: 'Freud argues that libidinal self-attention is precisely what delineates a body part as a part' (59). This therefore precedes and is the condition of possibility for self-knowledge. This also situates the experience of excitation in the male sexual organ as the prototype for the initial recognition by which all bodily parts come into being. Freud claims that the libidinal experience of the male genitalia is spread across the body to various erotogenic zones which act as substitutes for those genitals. Butler also gives Lacan's notion of 'the symbolically encoded phallus' (60) that explains the genitals 'as the (symbolic) ideal that offers an impossible and originary measure for the genitals to approximate, and as the (imaginary) anatomy which is marked by the failure to accomplish that return to the symbolic ideal' (61). Put more clearly, the phallus becomes the symbol of erotogenic investment in all organs of the body.

So the body is 'materialised' or made conscious through the experience of pain/pleasure, in which the psyche acts like the *schema*, shaping the matter into a form. But as Butler points out, this is effected by pathologising both desire and bodily self-awareness; that in Freud's theory sexuality is prone to pathologisation at a general level, and homosexuality is particularly so. It is seen as the archetypal narcissistic identification. It is through guilt-induced, psychosomatic and organic illness that embodiment becomes known. The narcissist is guilty over the prohibition against self-love and becomes suffused by the pain brought on by that guilt. However, for Butler this leaves open a space for postulating 'variable body surfaces or bodily egos [which] may thus become sites of transfer for properties that no longer belong properly to any anatomy' (64). She proposes alternative Imaginaries and, importantly, an alternative Imaginary phallus, which will bypass defining homosexuality as narcissistic, one that resists the traditional phallic *schema* which informs scientific and social discourse on the body (67).

In search of this ideal, she turns her attention to Lacan's work in which bodies are the product of signification within language. Lacan rewrites the moment of narcissism, ego formation and bodily self-knowledge. Freud's body comes into being through the ego's recognition and projection of pleasure/pain via a pre-existing libidinal economy. The body is there and consciousness comes to recognise it. Lacan's body and ego come into existence simultaneously at the Mirror stage, the moment of self- and other-recognition. This provides the frame within which the ego forms. The child enters the Symbolic order, making coherent the chaotic experience of the Imaginary order through a (reflected) self-recognition and other/self-rationalisation:[3] 'mirroring transforms a lived sense of disunity and loss of control into an ideal of integrity and control (*"la puissance"*) through that event of specularization' (75). The external and internal worlds are unified as the self is unified, and this movement is ruled over by the privileged signifier, the phallus. But as Butler says, 'this account of the genesis of epistemological relations implies that all knowable objects will have an anthropomorphic and androcentric character. Secondly, this androcentric character will be phallic' (78). So in Lacan's work meaning is human-centred and masculine.

Butler believes that Lacan wants to have the phallus stand for something which is neither the organ it symbolises (the penis), nor an imaginary effect of that organ, but something that is capable of having significatory content in the (coherent) Symbolic. Butler asks why other parts of the body may not be substituted as the privileged site of symbolisation. She wants to make the phallus just another indeterminate body part of the (incoherent) Imaginary that is made recognisable and reified in the Symbolic, rather than something beyond these two terms. Because, if this is so, 'its structural place is no longer determined by the logical relations of mutual exclusion entailed by a heterosexist version of sexual difference in which men are said to "have" and women to "be" the phallus' (88). To this end, and most famously, she posits a lesbian phallus: 'The offering of the lesbian phallus suggests that the signifier can come to signify *in excess* of its structurally-mandated position; indeed the signifier can be repeated in contexts and relations that come to *displace* the privileged status of that signifier' (90). She thinks that by this move she opens the way to subvert a hegemonic heterosexist Imaginary by positing another, or multiple other, imaginaries of sexual difference.

I don't want to dwell too much on the detail of her exposition on these two psychoanalytic father-figures, which as in the first two-thirds of

Gender Trouble serves mostly as a survey of the field. However, it is important to understand where the lesbian phallus has its genesis to understand the way in which Butler applies it when she eventually returns to her own theorising. In this she pushes her point on the gendered constructedness of the sex/gender distinction one step further to challenge the basic gendering inherent in language *per se*, as it is understood in classic psychoanalytic theory.

Reiterating the abject position of male and female homosexuality within classical psychoanalysis and the pitfalls of constructivist accounts of gender, sex, sexuality and sexual difference (100), she returns again to the possibility of a means of self-identification that is malleable and of one's own making: gender performativity.

> [T]he heterosexual presumption of the symbolic domain is that apparently inverted identifications will effectively and exclusively signal abjection *rather than* pleasure, or signal abjection without at once signalling the possibility of a pleasurable insurrection against the law or an erotic turning of the law against itself. The presumption is that the law will constitute sexed subjects along the heterosexual divide to the extent that its threat of a punishment effectively instils fear, where the object of fear is figured by homosexualized abjection. (110)

In effect, normative heterosexual hegemony 'talks' itself into the position of power. Through the power of language, it relegates homosexuality to the incoherent and illegitimate Imaginary. The aim of her project is for homosexuality to lay claim to a position in the Symbolic without becoming normalised and contained within it.

This is to be realised, in part, through the recognition that the rejection or abjection (othering) of something is always implicit in the act of constitution (112). But how is one to articulate a subject position without abjecting and erasing someone else, or a group of someone elses in a 'logic of mutual exclusion' (113) that seems always to constitute the other as a threat? In an attempt to get around this problem, Butler puts in question the need to adhere to a coherent identity of any kind. This is not to say that she wants to adhere to a radically inclusive identity with all the imperialistic and colonistic overtones inherent in such an idea. Rather, she wants to open the possibility of a free flow of multiple identifications – race, class, gender, etc. – from amongst those that constitute any given subject. In essence she argues for a kind of radical individuality.

Interestingly, for someone concerned to deconstruct dominant containers of the self, this idea of radical individuality was, during the time that Butler was writing, becoming a dominant ideology of self-formation whether expressed in Coca-Cola advertisements, romantic political notions of personal liberation, or neo-liberal ideas of the self-constituting person.

Butler presses for a subject's self-recognition and self-realisation through those multiple identifications, for tracing 'the ways in which identification is implicated in what it excludes, and to follow the lines of that implication for the map of future community that it might yield' (119).

Ultimately, her answer is to return again to the subversive possibilities of performative language against the linguistic 'Law' of heterosexist psychoanalytic theory. In this she gives particular attention to the power of parody (122). Parody calls into question the legitimacy of authoritative language. In parody, she argues, social norms are mobilised by those abjected by those very norms as a means to critique.

Butler uses the documentary film *Paris Is Burning* (1991) to illustrate her point. This film follows individuals competing in and the events surrounding an annual drag ball in Harlem, New York. In it socially marginal men in drag – Latin-American and African-American, transvestite, transsexual, transgender – 'subvert' heterosexual norms by playing out parodies of stereotypical female personae. Individuals are fostered towards their performances in the competitive ball through the familial kinship system of the drag 'houses'. Butler analyses the film in an attempt to 'move to a consideration ... [of] what it suggests about the simultaneous production and subjugation of subjects in a culture which appears to arrange always and in every way for the annihilation of queers' (124).

For Butler the thrust of the film is that heterosexuality is a form of drag itself, that gender is the product of a hegemonic reiteration of the norms which heterosexuality needs to affirm to itself to maintain its boundaries. Drag in the hands of the people in *Paris Is Burning* is 'subversive to the extent that it reflects on the imitative structure by which hegemonic gender is itself produced and disputes heterosexuality's claim on naturalness and originality' (125). Butler writes that bell hooks's criticism of the film – that the drag within it is misogynistic – carries too narrow a view of the dynamics of drag. She argues that hooks seems to see male homosexuality as being about women, which is in turn a colonialist move on hooks's part.

Butler sees drag as far more powerful, that it bears out her idea of the performativity of gender, and that the drag in this film is an appropriation and subversion of 'racist, misogynistic, and homophobic norms of oppression' (128). These African-Amercian and Latin-American 'men' take stereotypical social norms and vamp them, norms which play on straightness, class distinction, gender roles and racial distinctions, with each of these categories crossing the others in various permutations. For her the contest performs and exposes the 'phantasmatic' nature – the unrealisable idealisation of the signified – of those norms. Butler says that the Lacanian symbolic 'assumes the primacy of sexual difference in the constitution of the subject' but that in this film it is made clear that 'the symbolic is also and at once a racializing set of norms, and that norms of realness by which the subject is produced are racially informed conceptions of "sex" (this underscores the importance of subjecting the entire psychoanalytic paradigm to this insight)' (130).

This is not a uniformly happy tale, however; there are qualifications and constraints to be made on the subversive power and message of the film. Venus Xtravaganza, a young Latino/a pre-operative transsexual, invests such hope in the phantasmatic norm that she falls victim to it. Presumably found out to be 'passing' by a straight male lover, she is murdered. 'As much as she crosses gender, sexuality, and race performatively, the hegemony that reinscribes the privileges of normative femininity and whiteness wields the final power to *re*naturalize Venus's body and cross out that prior crossing, an erasure that is her death' (133). Further, bell hooks questions the political position of the film's maker, Jennie Livingstone, as a white middle-class Jewish lesbian specularising 'black' gay males as if on an ethnographic expedition – though as Butler points out, neither the film-maker nor hooks differentiates between the ethnic alignments in these houses. Nor do they recognise that Venus is not 'black', s/he is a light skinned Latino/a who is capable of 'passing' as white as well as female.

This connects directly to what I find the most interesting focus of appropriation and subversion, that is the norms of kinship in the idea of the 'houses'. These houses are run by men who 'mother' each other, and produce and 'rear' 'children' who perform in the contests. According to Butler, this is a resignification of the normative family relationships in a way that she sees as holding out great hope: '[W]e see an appropriation of the terms of domination that turns them towards a more enabling future' (137). They colonise and reinscribe heterosexist kinship relations. I have a slightly different reading of the kinship dynamic to which I shall return below.

I have paid significant attention to the details of Butler's philosophical and theoretical scene-setting and (in my opinion) her strongest example. Much of the remainder of the book is exegesis, giving literary and theoretical 'evidence' of the ways in which gender can be performed or subverted. She does this through reading the fiction of Willa Cather and Nella Larsen and the psychoanalytic theory of Žižek. Butler makes much of the gender ambivalence of Cather, in both her own name and her naming of her characters. Similarly, she foregrounds the Larsen's place as an author of the Harlem Renaissance and the importance of both racial and sexual boundary-crossing in her writing, coyly gesturing towards and yet avoiding discussion of Larsen's sexuality. Like Kristeva, Butler implicitly appeals to the revolutionary potential of creative language but sadly ends up being far less convincing.

In Cather's work Butler looks towards the 'misrecognition' or manipulation of names in her fiction, where 'the name not only designates a gender uncertainty, but produces a crisis in figuration of sexed morphology as well' (139–40). She argues that Cather subverts patrilineal authority by her play on masculinised and feminised names, and by her refusal to be confined to either. The proper name is instituted as a tool of the phallic order, again underscoring the gendered biases of the construction of Lacan's phallus. Butler argues that gender-ambivalent Cather's use of a text within a text, with a male narrative voice in the internal story and an anonymous narrative voice in the framing story, makes this a subversive text because it upsets gender boundaries.

In these two rather weak examples from literary fiction there is a surprising degree of conflation between the biographies of the two female authors with the contents of their novels and the narrative voices they create. One does not have to be convinced of the death of the author to recognise that there is no necessary connection between a writer's life and their fictional creations. Some of the observations are simply silly, as for example, that the 'W'-shaped snake in Cather's *My Antonia* is an expression of Cather's own gender ambivalence. The killing of this snake by the male narrator is supposedly a suppression of lesbian desire on Cather's part.

The love that dare not speak its name becomes for Cather a love that proliferates names at the site of that non-speaking, establishing a possibility for fiction as this displacement, reiterating that prohibition and at the same time *working, indeed, exploiting that prohibition for the possibilities of its repetition and subversion.* (152)

With respect to Larsen, Butler reads in Nella Larsen's work a means of laying bare the way sexuality and race are intertwined in their construction. The subject of Larsen's book *Passing* is the tale of a light-skinned black character named Clare who 'passes' for white, and her consequent death. For Butler, by her racial boundary-crossing Clare subverts the 'law' of the (white heterosexual) Father – that is she does not conform to the constraints of the phallic order of the Symbolic. Clare is also openly sensual and sexual. This supposedly makes her an object of suppressed lesbian desire for another female character, Irene, who is similarly light-skinned but who lives as black. Clare cannot survive under the 'law' of the Father. Irene is compliantly labouring under a set of racialised gender conventions and can. In trying to live otherwise than as the exotic/erotic black woman, in trying to be a chaste good girl, Irene is obeying the 'law' of a white heterosexual Father. In rejecting the pit, she aims for the pedestal, but she still interpolates a racialised sexuality. 'Trapped by a promise of safety through class mobility, Irene accepted the terms of power which threatened her, becoming its instrument in the end' (185).

Extrapolating on these two threads of naming and boundary-crossing, Butler uses Žižek to try and add depth to her earlier assertions about performatives. And again we find an unhelpful slippage between psychoanalytic metaphors, discourse metaphors and the philosophy of language – at least on Butler's part. Žižek rejects 'discourse' in favour of psychoanalytic language metaphors and theories. Butler both agrees and disagrees with him, by maintaining an idea of historicism and contextualisation (187) but at the same time wanting to use his idea of phantasmatic language that fits with her idea of perpetually liminal identity and radical performativity (188).

Žižek subscribes to a Lacanian description of the workings of language, and its formation of the subject via threat, abjection and regulatory law. Butler agrees with Žižek insofar as he postulates that rallying points for political struggle (based in unifying names or terms like 'women') are necessarily 'phantasmatic' ideals:

Political signifiers, especially those that designate subject positions, are not descriptive; that is, they do not represent pre-given constituencies, but are empty signs which come to bear phantasmatic investments of various kinds. (191)

In other words, Žižek wants to argue that while implicated in them, such terms cannot be bounded by historical or social context. Rather, the overall signifier of 'woman' (or any other such rallying point of difference) is symbolic/Symbolic and can never be pinned down: 'every discursive formation must be understood in relation to that which it cannot accommodate within its own discursive or symbolic terms' (192), that is the 'real'. Žižek sees in this a possibility for a radical democratic project which ensures a notion of futurity, something he sees as missing from poststructuralism, feminism and Foucauldian projects. He sees these as disempowering and paralysing. Žižek's is an anti-essentialistic, anti-descriptivist project which is reliant on a contingency and lack of fixity in its political signifiers.

While Butler argues back and forth on Žižek's attacks on historical contextualisation and discursive construction (which, we have seen, she has a significant investment in) and the inherent sexism in his theorising, she does find worth in his work on language as an 'identity-constituting performance' (208). A name like 'woman' is phantasmatic, and as such

> orders and institutes a variety of free-floating signifiers to an 'identity'; the name effectively 'sutures' the object ... the name designates a contingent and open organizing principle for the formation of political groups. It is in this sense that anti-descriptivism provides a linguistic theory for an anti-essentialist identity politics. (208)

Names of political groups function as unifying principles in as much as they operate as proper names. For Žižek, they are not strictly referential, 'but act as rigid designators that institute and maintain the social phenomena to which they appear to refer' (209–10). They are performative, they don't just cohere pre-existing groups, they invoke the coherent existence of a group. Butler queries the implications of a theory based on proper names, and the implicit assumptions involved in the use of a performative notion of symbolisation: 'In the end, it is profoundly unclear whether Žižek's effort to understand political signifiers on the model of a performative theory of names can provide for the kind of variation and rearticulation required for an anti-essentialistic radical democratic project' (211). But while she sees problems in the formulation, she is convinced by the overall project. If the Law and the phallus can be re-imagined as Butler believes, then agency can be re-imagined, rather than cancelled out by its dependence on prior phantasmatic signification (220). Butler does not want a closure to the play available within a phantasmatic signifier, she sees it as liberating and inclusive, and for that sees hope in Žižek's project.

Butler uses this to extend her own ideas into the liberatory possibilities of the term 'queer'. As was the case in *Gender Trouble,* Butler makes us wait until the final chapter before she offers her own piece of 'futurity'. And, similarly, though it is relatively brief, it has had a deep effect on body and gender theory. She tries to envisage a way in which queer politics can use some of the theoretical moves which she has seen as possible through Žižek's work. She looks at the possibility of seeing the proper name/noun 'queer' as an identity-politics rallying point, a phantasmatic signifier, built on a history of social and performative interdictions.

> Neither power nor discourse are rendered anew every moment, they are not as weightless as the utopics of radical signification might imply. And yet how are we to understand their convergent force as an accumulated effect of usage that both constrains and enables their reworking? ... If the power of discourse to produce that which it names is linked with the question of performativity, then the performative is one domain in which power acts *as* discourse. (224–5)

Here Butler adds a further level of sophistication to her comments on performatives, adding now that performatives themselves have historical contexts within which they are formed. The 'I' of any linguistic performative presumes, she believes, a heterosexual 'I' as invoked in 'I pronounce you ...' and as such is based in an abjection of the 'queer'. The appellation 'queer' is necessary to the constitution of that 'I' in its prohibition, its rejection, its othering: 'a performative "works" to the extent that *it draws on and covers over* the constitutive conventions by which it is mobilized.' (227).

One cannot master a term like 'queer', however, because it is in Žižek's terms 'phantasmatic'. It is constitutive and exclusionary, can never be wholly identified with as a totem of identity politics, which allows it the potential of a radically democratic futurity. It has within it the potential to shift and change, accommodate diverse interests without descending to a destructive factionalism. Or, it can be discarded as it loses its usefulness as a unifying signifier.

> The expectation of a self-determination that self-naming arouses is paradoxically contested by the historicity of the name itself: by the history of the usages that one never controlled, but that constrain the very usage that now emblematizes autonomy; by the future efforts to deploy the term against the grain of the current ones, and that will exceed the control of those who seek to set the course of the terms in the present. (228)

The limits imposed on 'queer' agency are also their most enabling conditions, the slur becomes an effective political standpoint, and it is in its non-totalising effect that it is most effective. 'The political deconstruction of "queer" ought not to paralyse the use of such terms, but, ideally, to extend its range, to make us consider at what expense and for what purposes the terms are used, and through what relations of power such categories have been wrought' (229).

Butler likens linguistic performativity to drag, illustrating the links between 'discursive resignification' and 'gender parody or impersonation' (230). She says that gender formation is itself a phantasmatic ideal, albeit a dictated one, but 'it is an assignment which is never quite carried out according to expectation, whose addressee never quite inhabits the ideal s/he is compelled to approximate' (231). So we are all marked by a set of stereotypical expectations of how we ought to form our gender identifications. Drag allows the performativity of heterosexuality to be exposed, taking up and performing a role against the grain shows up the contingency of that role. Performing queerness does the same thing, it exposes the constructedness of both the 'pure' and the 'abject', the centre and the margin. 'This kind of citation will emerge as *theatrical* to the extent that it *mimes and renders hyperbolic* the discursive convention that it also *reverses*' (232).

Butler goes back to psychoanalytic metaphors here. The external performance of gender is not to be read as the external workings of the fixed truth of the psychic identification with gender. Performativity should not be reduced to performance. What is performed conceals the 'what cannot be expressed' of the psyche.

> [D]rag exposes or allegorizes the mundane psychic and performative practices by which heterosexu-alized genders form themselves through the renunciation of the *possibility* of homosexuality, a fore-closure that produces a field of heterosexual objects at the same time as it produces a domain of those whom it would be impossible to love. (235)

To constitute homosexual relations as melancholic – as Freud does – proscribes them from the start as legitimate positive affiliations. If all gender is performed, then straight relations are melancholic of a lost or foreclosed homosexuality. Gay melancholia is constituted against the foreclosed possibility of straight melancholia (237). Heterosexuality, by trying to claim to stabilise gender relationships cannot do so for in its constitution it always already includes the site of its contestation. That site should remain multi-focal and multi-vocal, proliferative and radically democratic: 'The heterosexual logic that requires that identification and desire be mutually exclusive is one of the most reductive of hetero-sexism's psychological instruments: if one identifies *as* a given gender, one must desire a different gender' (239). But there is no one femininity, no one masculinity with which to constrain this dynamic. Heterosexism is an '*imaginary* logic' (239) that proves its own unintelligibility:

> Performativity describes this relation of being implicated in that which one opposes this turning of power against itself to produce alternative modalities of power, to establish a kind of political con-testation that is not a 'pure' opposition, a 'transcendence' of contemporary relations of power, but a difficult labor of forging a future from resources inevitably impure. (241)

So self-identification or self-naming as queer and accepting gender performativity are politically liberatory. There are no boundaries, and we are all boundary-crossers. The sex/gender distinction is a construction informed by a prior gendering, as is the psychoanalytic phallus that gov-erns meaning and self-identification, and so too are performatives in uttered language based on a pre-existing gendered assumptions around speech and speakers.

Analysis

So where in *Gender Trouble* Butler had begun to question the power of the phallus, by the time of writing *Bodies That Matter* she had found the means to do so, taking that one step further to question the constructedness of psychoanalytic terms. Has she taken that questioning far enough though?

There are several thematics that run through these two books which will reappear in many of those we shall be touching upon in the remaining chapters. The first has already been mentioned in preceeding chapters. We will remember one telling criticism that neither Elias, Foucault nor Bourdieu paid sufficient attention to the different bodily experience of women. The body in their work is implicitly the male/masculine body – as it has been at least in the Western world 'since Adam was a pup'. In Douglas's work we began to see some accommodation of difference across cultures and at least different practices and meanings in relation to men and women. Feminist politics takes the sex/gender distinction to be central in any understanding of embodiment. Butler takes this a step further, as we have seen, questioning the implicit heterosexism in many feminist writers and leading the way in queer theory body politics.

The second thematic, which borrows explicitly from the anthropological work of Mary Douglas, is the notion of boundary-crossing. We have already seen how problematic the appropriation of theorisations that come directly out of deep ethnographic studies – into generalised studies that do not – can be from the discussion of Kristeva's borrowings from Douglas. And we already know from Chapter 4 that by the time she came to write *Natural Symbols*, Douglas had adapted her work and come to the conclusion that boundary-crossing can confer both danger and sanctity. We also saw in Chapter 4 that Kristeva misread and misrepresented Douglas in using her to support the notion of abjection.

The third thematic is language – the psychoanalytic Symbolic, philosophical performative, Foucauldian discursive – and its potential for shaping the world. In analysing Butler's arguments, I shall work my way through the implications of these thematics in this order, but I shall reserve most of my criticisms for this final theme.

To take the first, what are some of the implications of focusing so firmly on the sex/gender distinction and its clear problematics? What does this mean for the body in society, the body in sociology and the body in anthropology? When so much emphasis is placed on psychoanalytic theory, which Butler rightly points out is fixated on drives and impulses focused on pleasure and pain, the body risks becoming *just* the sexualised body, even as theorists like Butler claim to be making a space for radical inclusion. How successful radical inclusion of difference is will be looked at in Part III, but it is worth noting here that crucially necessary as it is to understand and accommodate the differential bodily experiences of men and women, there is always a danger of suppressing and diminishing other experiences of embodiment that are, if not common, at least comparable across that division. And there are some experiences of embodiment for which performativity even in Western cultures is largely irrelevant – advanced dementia, being one example. Here, in *Gender Trouble*, we come up against a basic split between theorisations of the body – those reliant on psychoanalytic theory and those that are not. By appealing to psychoanalysis and its basic preoccupation with the erogenous or erotic potential of the body, writers end up becoming obsessed with that potential to the detriment of any other bodily potential. The body becomes a matter primarily of pleasure and pain, deeply individualised, and (to borrow a term from psychoanalysis) unconsciously deeply Western and postmodern.

Butler argues that the lesbian phallus is radically transferable and has the potential to take into account all socially constructivist referents. But lesbian or otherwise, the phallus inevitably implies a basic universalising principle that there is an Imaginary and a Symbolic brought into being by the capability for creating coherence invested in the psyche. Though by the time of writing *Bodies that Matter*, Butler had taken that further step and started to deconstruct the heterosexism of the first principles of psychoanalysis and offer an alternative view, I don't actually see that she has avoided the first unstated universalising principle in the notion of the phallus, that there is something irreducibly common in the human 'psyche' in the first place.

Moira Gatens argued that in trying to 'neutralize difference' between men and women, as is implied by the sex/gender distinction, 'the implied neutrality is not a neutrality at all but a "masculinization" or "normalization" (where men are seen as the norm or standard) of women' (Gatens 1983: 156). So too there is a real potential to inflict a similar neutering or normalisation of other cultures' social and historical understandings of embodiment by theorisations of performativity. The lesbian phallus is not neutral. It is Western, postmodern and potentially as colonialising as any nineteenth-century explorer confronting a Hottentot Venus.

This is also the main problem with Butler's second thematic, the appropriation of the notion of boundary-crossing from Mary Douglas's anthropological theory. As I noted earlier, Douglas's ideas on boundary-crossing evolved and she came to believe that such behaviour was not simply reviled, it could confer either or both sanctity and danger. Butler, like Kristeva, picks up only on the earlier formulation, seeing boundary-crossing as dangerous and/or subversive. Douglas's theories are based on long ethnographic interaction and first-hand observation of *practices* with a range of peoples whom she met and knew. They are steeped in cultural contextualisation even if Douglas herself slips into cross-cultural equivalences at times. Butler tries to universalise culturally specific observations using appropriations of ethnographic theory to formulate second-hand interpretations of very particular *narratives* (*Paris Is Burning*, Cather and Larsen's fiction).

This leads me to the criticism of the third thematic in her work. Her reading of *Paris Is Burning* and the subject matter of the film are both her strongest case for her proposals on the power of language to remake the world through taking charge of meaning, but also most clearly show up the incommensurability of universalising principles and historical contextualisation.

In Butler's reading of *Paris Is Burning* and in the criticisms of it she looks at, nothing is made of the possible connection between these 'houses' and the samba schools in the *favelas* (poor neighbourhood enclaves) in Rio de Janeiro which promote contesting teams in the annual carnival (festival of the flesh). These operate very much along kinship lines with patrons/ mothers of each team, and are a speculative explosion of irruptive glamour and pure joy in music by extremely poor people. It would seem to enact a similar politically relevant dynamic to the drag balls and, given the cultural background of the participants in *Paris Is Burning*, also provides a direct social context of a 'world turned upside-down' that has thrived for at least six centuries (in Europe and Latin America). Indeed, though the Rio carnival's formation as a competition between *favela*-based samba schools originated in the 1930s, there is now a parallel gay carnival. Butler's recasting of the drag balls as a rewriting of the phallic order actually suppresses and neutralises the social and historical context of a display of power in community (not individuality) on the part of the poor.

Overall, Butler attempts to formulate an all-encompassing explanation for difference, but in doing so her theories simply do not work across cultures nor across the social formations of the tribal to the postmodern. It is inappropriate and colonialising to try and use these ideas of volitional embodiment outside a postmodern society. It has the power to fracture social identity by pushing individual, in preference to social, identity. In terms of a postmodern society, however, this is quite an effective and revolutionary way of looking at the ways in which we live in and through a hegemonic discourse which has been influenced by Freudian and post-Freudian psychoanalysis for the majority of this century. Psychoanalysis is pervasive in popular culture. However, it still works as a universalising discourse, culturally specific in its insistence on the means of mediating bodily experience, and is historically and culturally contingent in itself.

If 'we' look back at Plato and his world, or the seventeenth century, it is impossible to reconstruct those worlds as they were perceived at the time (indeed there are always a panoply of views within a given time). But to import psychoanalytic notions back to them is to do them a violence, just as it is to do so to cultures that do not subscribe to that particular epistemology. To give her credit, Butler does at some level recognise cultural sensitivities, consciously moderating her reading of Nella Larsen's stories because she seems not to want to speak for a black woman writer of the Harlem Renaissance, even if (strangely) she does not see the need to do so for either Cather or the subjects of *Paris Is Burning*.

So Butler's assertions that language can empower one has little cross-cultural relevance, but the problems with trying to use language as a means of reworking embodiment go deeper. They go to the way in which she constructs her case in the first place. Butler uses three distinct metaphorics of language: psychoanalytic theories of identity formation, philosophical theories of meaning formation (epistemology), and Foucault's poststructuralist theory of the historical contingency of epistemes. By slipping between psychoanalytic theorisations that hinge on a very particular idea of language and philosophical games that make claims about the social effects of utterances, with an appeal to a third linguistic metaphor – Foucauldian 'discourse' – to support her claims of constructed embodiment through utterance, Butler theorises that embodied being is 'performative'. Gender is an outcome of that performance. In essence Butler, trained in philosophy, is using a classical form of argument: syllogism. The problem, however, is that the terms of her syllogism are not comparable. Psychoanalysis uses linguistic terms metaphorically on the one hand and treats language as an all-powerful determinant of meaning on the other. Language-games deal specifically with the social and the interpersonal in subjective communication, the ways in which people interpret and make the world through agreed meaning. Foucault's discourse is the outcome of epistemes, systems of meaning and knowledge accorded authority by social beings but which are prone to shifting across time and cultures. These are three quite different ideas of language, the first ahistorical and universalising, the second social and contextual but dependent on direct communication (utterance). The third, different again, describes a series of socially and historically contextualised knowledge systems: epistemologies. They are comparable to a dictionary, a grammar and a set of encyclopaedia – not quite 'apples and oranges' but the strongest connection being that they deal in metaphorics of language. The universalising principles of the first, however, are simply incommensurate with the contextualising intentions of the latter two.

And this over-dependence on metaphoric connections instead of argument extends into other facets of Butler's propositions, particularly in her allusions to the work of Foucault. In *Gender Trouble* (134–5) Butler slips between the juridical law that is imposed on Herculine Barbin and The Law of the Father. In discussing *Discipline and Punish*, she jumps from the 'inscription' of penal law on the body to the masquerade of gender, as if both were equivalent 'writing' on the surface of the body. To do so is squarely at odds with Foucault's contextualised and historicised constructions. Butler also depends rather heavily on a metaphoric 'slip-page' between Foucault's use of the word 'discourse', his notion of diffuse power, and his 'repressive hypothesis' with semiotics, phallic power (the Law) and psychoanalytic notions of 'repression'. The basic problem is that she conflates two metaphors of writing – acts and gestures are not merely surface phenomena, they are fully embodied across space and time. They are more than just text. Certainly, they can be superficial, but they are three-dimensionally embodied. And in another example, of which there are many, she slips between metaphors of fabrications and fabric, as if one 'puts on the body' like a piece of clothing. Metaphors are incredibly suggestive and useful linguistic means of amplifying meaning, but it weakens her argument considerably to rely so heavily on what are often tenuous metaphoric connections. She says she is trying to import ideas of construction or historical contextualisation into psychoanalysis with the aim of breaking down its universalism, but what she ends up doing is universalising 'postmodern playfulness' across history or, more disastrously, across cultures. Even if she succeeds in creating a multiplicity of genders, by basing it in psychoanalytic terms she implicitly and necessarily does so across cultures. And that, as Mary Douglas would agree, is simply not tenable. Unfortunately holding to pyschoanalytic signification that is prior to materiality, as we saw was the case with the implications of Kristeva's work, ignores difference across and between cultures.

This is a problem that we will see besets most of the writers discussed in the two chapters in Part III. They come to grips with the vagaries and pitfalls of trying to account for different experiences of embodiment with varying degrees of success. It seems, however, that with the turn to post-modern theorisations and the proliferation of writing on the body that has followed on from the work of the writers dealt with thus far, the more elusive embodied being becomes.

Notes

1 This can lead to some unhelpfully dense prose but this is not a necessary outcome of their politics. Liz Grosz's writing, for example, has a beautiful clarity.

2 I shall return to this below, but we already know from Chapter 4 that by the time she came to write *Natural Symbols*, Douglas had adapted her work and come to the conclusion that boundary-crossing can confer both danger and sanctity. We also saw in Chapter 4 that Kristeva misread and misrepresented Douglas in using her to support the notion of abjection.

3 See Chapter 4, on Kristeva.

Part III

Subject – the Body of Difference

SIX Technoscience

Remodelling and Redefining Boundaries

The theorisations analysed in these final two chapters that make up Part III take the body as subject – the embodied subject in society, the body as a subject of analysis and the body as subjectively experienced. The defining characteristic of this body is the plethora of ways in which it displays 'difference'. Subject, subjected and subjective bodies, even when spoken of in terms of groups, are not bodies of social concordance, they are the bodies of groups of individuals whose focus is on their own experience of embodiment. It has undoubtedly been crucially important for the subjective experience of embodiment to be recognised and given weight – so much oppression has been based in the unthinking acceptance of an ideal of bodily sameness, from which large proportions of the world's population are excluded on one basis or another.

Both the 'lead' writers used in these final two chapters, Donna Haraway and Susan Bordo, are feminist theorists. Given that the proliferation of theories of difference is certainly, even if not solely, indebted to feminist critiques of sex and gender differences, this is hardly surprising. We have seen in the work of Elias (Chapter 1), Bourdieu (Chapter 3) and Douglas (Chapter 4) that class difference has long been taken into account in relation to the sociology and anthropology of embodiment. Theorisations of gender difference, however, have helped pave the way for a far greater range of different experiences of embodiment to be legitimated as academic concerns: race, gender, sexuality and disability all affect how the body is lived. Many of the cognate writers briefly mentioned at the end of each of these two chapters are the intellectual inheritors of this shift.

In this and the subsequent chapter I have chosen to concentrate on two writers whose work is emblematic of what I see as the two strands to which the work on the body has turned. As a consequence I have also chosen to mention only briefly a selection of cognate work as it can been seen to fall into those strands, rather than trying to cover the plethora of work on bodily difference in sociology and comparative anthropology and thereby deal only glancingly with any of them. Others have given more specific and far more expert commentary on the work to be found in those fields of difference and I would direct the reader to those texts to fill in the gaps that I quite consciously leave (Shilling 1993; Turner [1984] 1996).

My point in taking this approach is not to claim that Haraway and Bordo are the most important theorists amongst those who explore issues of difference – influential as their work undoubtedly has been. Rather, my intention is to show how their approaches are emblematic of the bifurcation that has occurred in theorisations of embodiment. On the one hand, we now have a group of theorisations in which the (organic) body retreats from the picture: it is implicitly abjected or rejected. On the other hand, we have theories that, while recognising the importance of boundaries and border-crossing, look to physical subjectivity and social context to ground their understanding of embodiment in society. Haraway, Kristeva, Scarry and many others whose work is founded upon arguments from semiotics and psychoanalysis still privilege the mind as the dominant partner in our dualistic being, even as they argue for new visions of materiality. This is evident even at the level of their exemplary evidence: they conflate the importance of narratives, representations and fiction with lived realities. Bordo, Douglas, Martin, Seymour and innumerable social and anthropological writers who speak to and work from the lives of people recognise the life of the mind and its power, but they also remember the physical expressions and exertions that accompany them. At the simplest level this comes out in Bordo's recounting of her students' daily experiences or in Martins' or Seymours' relating what comes out in interviews with people who have lived experiences of physical difference. To my mind this split comes not so much out of being a divide between the empirical and the theoretical – no one could say Mary Douglas or Susan Bordo did not write theoretically – but between those who have a more embodied approach to their subject matter and those who have a more abstracted approach. Our first writer, Donna Haraway, belongs to the latter group.

Haraway

Donna Haraway began her academic career as a biologist, became a historian and philosopher of science, and through various byways in anthropology has come to be one of the most influential postmodern feminists writing on the body to date. Drawing on science fiction, Haraway's best-known assertion (dealt with in detail below) is that because we have already accepted the technologisation of our bodies through the interventions of medical science – immunisation, pacemakers, transplants, ultrasound, the human genome, etc. – we are all already biotechnological beings. We are cyborgs, cybernetic organisms. In her early writing it is clear that she had a lot of sympathy with historical materialism and constructivist arguments. However, Haraway reached a point where her thought shifted. As we saw (in Chapter 5) was the case with Butler, though in a different way, Haraway too began trying to meld social context and/or construction with self-construction. Indeed, though Haraway is of a slightly older generation, Butler seems to have been a formative influence on her move into cyborg theorisations. And in this, Haraway also uses the idea of bodily boundary-crossing – and the idea of the Trickster – thereby directly appealing to the work of Mary Douglas.

Where she differs from Butler, however, is in her early grounding in empirical research and in the manner in which she re-embraces the embodied subject, if in a highly abstracted way. The fact that she was trained in the sciences and in science studies means that much as she works towards a transcendental embodiment in her later work, she knows the worth of detailed case studies and the close reading of data. Her background, undoubtedly, also has had some influence on her hope for the possibilities of technoscience, even when she is perfectly aware and highly critical of its effects in practice. She seems to fall within that camp of philosophers of science who believe that the basis of 'good' science is a properly defined methodology and best practice, and that, conversely, 'bad' science results from poor methodologies and poor practice. Science itself cannot be bad, but there are certainly inadequately rigorous scientists. In relation to embodiment, her answer to poor scientists and poor scientific practice – science used to support gender, race and class oppression – is to propose a feminist technoscientific practice that reinvents the body in a technoscientific form. That reinvention is the cyborg. The cyborg body transcends simple materiality and is, in keeping with the overall concern of this section, a body that is centred in and on the subject.

While Haraway's first book, *Primate Visions*, was extremely influential, I turn rather to her second book, the collection of ground-breaking essays *Simians, Cyborgs, and Women: The Reinvention of Nature* (1991), through which one can trace the progression in her thought. Whether one accepts and agrees with her arguments or not, it is not overstating the case to say they have shifted the course of studies of human materiality, particularly the pivotal essay 'The Cyborg Manifesto'. To be fair to my reader and to try and ameliorate any bias that may creep in on my part, I shall state at the outset that while there is much to agree with in Haraway's analysis of technoscience – and her early work on primatology is keenly observed and convincing – I am far from persuaded by Haraway's overall arguments for embracing her cyborg vision. Nor am I comfortable with some of the implications of accepting her world-view, as I make clear in the concluding chapter. That said, I shall do my best to bring out what is useful in it and to give it its due place in the sociology and anthropology of the body.

Simians, Cyborgs, and Women

Because this book tracks a theoretical progression, it is worth commenting in some detail upon the way in which this collection has been structured. The essays within this work range from the late 1970s to the early 1990s and they are arranged almost chronologically. The essays in the first two sections cover the periods 1978–79 and 1981–88, with only the last essay of the second section reaching into the middle of the period covered by the third section (1985–91). Haraway leads off the third section with an essay on the history of the terms 'sex' and 'gender'. This bridges the timeframe of sections two and three, having been written over six years (1981–87), pre-dating and overlapping the original publication of 'The Cyborg Manifesto' (1985) which is the second essay of the third section. This 'fold' in the middle of an otherwise strictly chronological order is important. It allows us to see how the technoscientifically informed Cyborg Manifesto influenced her work in women's studies, and also how her thinking on sex and gender is an inseparable basis for that Manifesto.

In her early work, as it is represented in the first section, Haraway's writing is pellucid and her analysis is acute. She is utterly convincing in tracing the connections between the reliance of comparative psychobiology from the 1920s onwards on two factors. The first is the importation of assumptions about human behaviour into psychobiology's supposedly objective empirical studies of primate societies, and the second, its subsequent re-importation of those prejudiced assumptions back to human models. Researchers 'found' that dominance and aggression were fundamental to the social structuring of primate groups, which in turn gave them the bases for arguing that, as highly evolved primates, human societies 'naturally' work on a similar hierarchical basis. The studies Haraway looks at argue that dominance is cultural, not gendered, but

144

the association of 'leadership' and biological dominance was considered natural ... With respect to the division of labour in the family, which was the model for the division of labour in all of society, the logic of naturalization provided a cornerstone of historical explanation based on reproduction' (53)

Haraway, positioning herself firmly as a Marxist, concludes that:

In rationalizing the market exchange of marriage and the productive machinery of industry, comparative psychobiology took its place among the life of human sciences theorizing nature and humanity according to the logic of capitalist patriarchy. (57)

In comparative psychology studies, primate and other animal behaviour was extrapolated to humans, but she shows that it was clearly already informed by sexist (masculinist) ideas of what social behaviour should be based on. Historically, this has been used to support ideas of the body politic in human societies. Haraway gives a wonderful contextualisation of the continuation of anthropomorphism that runs through behaviourism and some strains of psychology – particularly in relation to extrapolating from studies of primate social interaction to humans. Her aim is to try to answer the question in the closing heading of the first part of this collection – 'Is Feminist-Socialist Science Possible?' (67).

The second section marks the first shift in Haraway's interests. Clearly influenced by the same influx of theory that marks Judith Butler's writing, Haraway continues to question the assumptions of science from a feminist perspective. However, though she maintains her pursuit of the biases of primatology and comparative psychobiology, her focus has moved. She turns to the power of language in science and the political implications of who holds that power.

In the history of science, the fathers of things have been first of all fathers of words – or so the story is told to student of the discipline. Aristotle named being and thereby constructed the rules of logic; Bacon denounced Aristotle in a project for the reform of language so as to permit, at last, true knowledge. (81)

So while there is undoubtedly some influence here from the concerns of French theory, as we have already encountered it, this is not simply a matter of the problems brought on by a (straightforwardly) gendered language: it is a problem of (patriarchal) science across time and across languages. And there is no doubt that science has been obsessed with taxonomy.

[S]cientific debate is a contest for the language to announce what will count as public knowledge. Scientific debate about monkeys, apes, and human beings, that is, about primates, is a social process of producing stories, important stories that constitute public meanings. Science is our myth. (81)

And that myth has changed over time, reflecting societal shifts and contextual prejudices.

[In the 1920s], primates seemed models of natural co-operation un-obscured by language and culture. During the 1930s, in early field work on wild primates, the sexual physiology of natural co-operation (in the forms of dominance of males over females and of troop demographic structure) emerged in arguments about human social therapeutics for social disorder – like labour strikes and divorce. (84)

From the 1950s primate models have been used in the naturalisation of nuclear families and as clinical evidence for human depression studies. Indeed, though Haraway does not cite these examples, there has been an increasing interest in the social importance of sexual activity amongst Bonobo monkeys since the 1960s. More recently, a recognition of the carnivorousness of chimpanzees – largely made visible because their habitats are contracting – has become a matter of portentous fascination in a violent, conflict-ridden, globalised world. Indeed, it is not hard to see how the history of comparison she does elucidate could lead to simplistic (racist) equivalences being made between chimpanzee behaviour and atrocities committed during political upheavals.

Female primatologists experiencing first-wave feminism started to change this: 'some of these changes have been a function of, and have in turn contributed to, major political struggles over the social relations of human reproduction and over the political place of all primate females in nature' (94). They have taken the 'social authority to author scientific stories' (106). Haraway applauds the rewriting of primatology and the recognition of the importance of social relations involving females and infants – not just aggressive males. She rightly observes that scientific studies are 'shaped materially by contemporary political struggles, in particular conflict over the reproductive social behaviour of women ... People in particular historical settings make the meanings: it is in the nature of primates' (108). This last statement is, one hopes, ironic.

It is around this point in the book, and her career, that her essays start to draw more heavily on literature, art and popular culture. Haraway by no means abandons the history and philosophy of science nor, she protests, does she move away from her socialism. 'The politics of difference that feminists need to articulate must be rooted in a politics of experience that searches for specificity, heterogeneity, and connection *through struggle*, not through psychologistic, liberal appeals to each her own endless difference. Feminism is collective; and difference is political, that is, about power, accountability, and hope. Experience, like difference, is about contradictory and necessary connection.' (109) Haraway does, however, spend less time analysing scientific processes and more time concentrating on other kinds of narratives that tell similar if competing stories. For example, through reading the fiction of Buchi Emecheta, she self-consciously (and painfully) positions and repositions herself.

> From our very specific, non-innocent positions in the local/global and personal/political terrain of contemporary mappings of women's consciousness, each of these readings is a pedagogic practice, working through the naming of the power-charged differences, specificities, and affinities that structure the potent, world-changing artefacts called 'women's experience'. In difference is the irretrievable loss of the illusion of the one. (124)

While undoubtedly it was a fresh feminist argument at the time of writing, this now seems a fairly standard postcolonial, postmodern polemic – except that she builds it on an analysis of the scientific invention of 'race', which is directly connected to her work on primatology. It is ironic, though, in the light of her later work, that here she claims not to be interested in 'liberal appeals' to 'endless difference'.

This is also the point at which we begin to experience the 'fold' in her work, and her subsequent embracing of the explosion in multi-disciplinary feminism starts to take the sting out of her Marxism and draw her firmly into playful fields of 'endless difference'. During this period when popular culture became more central to her work, Haraway wrote an entry for a Marxist dictionary of keywords on the evolution of the sex/gender distinction. Through this survey of the field, and the writing and rewriting of it over some years, she appears to have gradually aligned herself with a position of gender performativity. Here Haraway acknowledges the influence of the writing of Judith Butler, who 'argued that agency is an instituted practice in a field of enabling constraints. A concept of a coherent inner self, achieved (cultural) or innate (biological), is a regulatory fiction that is unnecessary – indeed, inhibitory – for feminist projects of producing and affirming complex agency and responsibility' (135). In the process Haraway moves from clear critical analyses of high modern science to postmodern irony and irruption of the popular cultural reception of science, including through science fiction. The effects of this 'sea-change' flow through her arguments and extend to a noticeable shift in her prose style.

And it is here that she formulates her arguments on the connection between the invention of race and the invention of sex/gender.

> The refusal to become or to remain a 'gendered' man or a woman, then, is an eminently political insistence on emerging from the nightmare of the all-too-real, imaginary narrative of sex and race. Finally and ironically, the political and explanatory power of the 'social' category of gender depends upon historicizing the categories of sex, flesh, body, biology, race, and nature in such a way that the binary, universalizing opposition that spawned the concept of the sex/gender system at a particular time and

> place in feminist theory implodes into articulated, differentiated, accountable, located and conse-
> quential theories of embodiment, where nature is no longer imagined and enacted as a resource to
> culture or sex to gender ... Phallogocentrism was the egg ovulated by the master subject, the brood-
> ing hen to the permanent chickens of history. But into the nest with that literal-minded egg has been
> placed the germ of a phoenix that will speak in all the tongues of a world turned upside down. (148)

Postmodern feminism will have the means of demystifying all forms of oppression: a large claim. This polemic for a political lexicon becomes, in turn, a staging post for the arguments that inform the essay which as I flagged at the beginning of this chapter, confirmed her position as one of the most influential theorists on the body today.

'The Cyborg Manifesto', like Butler's notion of performative gender, is unabashedly utopian. It is in some ways surprising, but in other ways perfectly understandable, that Haraway should move from being a trained scientist, to a historian and philosopher of science, through women's studies to becoming a card-carrying believer in the possibilities of liberation through technoscience and its metaphorics. In doing so she doesn't quite turn away from her Marxism so much as turn it inside out: eviscerate it, if you will. She is certainly right that Marxism, Marxist-feminisms and some radical feminisms tend to flatten out, or, 'have simultaneously naturalized and denatured the category "woman" and consciousness of the social lives of "women"' (158). She is also right to connect this to the centrality of economic forces (modes of production) in Marxist theory and the implicit reduction in most endeavours to account for women's lives or women's labour to reproduction.

> In my taxonomy, which like any other taxonomy is a re-inscription of history, radical feminism can
> accommodate all the activities of women named by socialist feminists as forms of labour only if the
> activity can somehow be sexualized. Reproduction had different tones of meaning for the two ten-
> dencies, one rooted in labour, one in sex, both calling the consequences of domination and ignorance
> of social and personal reality 'false consciousness'. (159–60)

Haraway offers a different place for women in the modes of production, one in which the body and labour take an altogether different turn. She argues that technologies, and in particular communications technologies, are a means of remaking 'our bodies, our selves' (180). 'The cyborg is a kind of disassembled and reassembled, postmodern collective and personal self. This is the self feminists must code' (163).

She does this by first setting up lists of terms that are differentiated along the lines of societal, political and technological shifts that characterise modern and postmodern life – in her chronology, respectively, pre- and post-World War II. She looks to communications technologies and coding (yet another linguistic metaphor) as the means of taking control of meaning and redefining the world anew. Re-crafting the body, women's bodies, is a matter of accepting and arresting technoscience to one's own (feminist) ends. Like Butler, she argues that the self can be made or remade through the power of language.

> Communications technologies and biotechnologies are the crucial tools re-crafting our bodies. These tools embody and enforce new social relations for women world-wide ... communications sciences and modern biologies are constructed by a common move – *the translation of the world into a problem of coding*, a search for a common language in which all resistance to instrumental control disappears and all heterogeneity can be submitted to disassembly, reassembly, investment, and exchange. (164)

Language is the code of the 'software' and the 'operating system' of embodiment. Code is the underpinning logic of communications technologies and biotechnologies. Women can take control of the logic of communications technologies and biotechnologies to their own ends and 'rewrite' embodiment. In this narrative, computers, the internet and the integration of medical technologies with the human form open the way for women to use them to their own ends. Biotechnical, cyborg bodies are bodies beyond patriarchal constraints of sex and gender. They are bodies beyond 'nature': 'A cyborg body is not innocent; it was not born in a garden; it does not seek unitary identity and so generate antagonistic dualisms without end (or until the world ends); it takes irony for granted' (180). Cyborgs are cybernetic organisms, hybrid boundary-crossers that are visible in the techno-soldier and the biotechnological body – each in their different ways now inextricable from highly sophisticated means of distancing and abstracting the self from intimate relations of life and death. Haraway is linking a linguistic metaphor for empowerment over embodiment in yet another way, but still using the ideas of sex/gender and boundary-crossing as the fulcrum of her argument.

> Exploring conceptions of bodily boundaries and social order, the anthropologist Mary Douglas (1966, 1970) should be credited with helping us to consciousness about how fundamental body imagery is to world view, and so to political language. French feminists like Luce Irigaray and Monique Wittig, for all their differences, know how to write the body; how to weave eroticism, cosmology, and politics from imagery of embodiment, and especially for Wittig, from imagery of fragmentation and reconstitution of bodies. (173–4)

Here, again like Butler, we see the blurring of the line between psychoanalytic theories of irruptive language and the observations of ethnography. Haraway does not take Douglas's work quite so out of context as Butler and Kristeva, but like them she does not recognise that the boundary-crossing body of Douglas's work is both potentially dangerous (which she wants the cyborg to be) and sacred: that is, a force for the status quo. Rather for her, cyborg bodies

> are maps of power and identity ... Up till now (once upon a time), female embodiment seemed to be given, organic, necessary; and female embodiment seemed to mean skill in mothering and its metaphoric extensions ... Cyborgs might consider more seriously the partial, fluid, sometimes aspect of sex and sexual embodiment. Gender might not be global identity after all, even if it has profound historical breadth and depth. (180)

Further, the cyborg body and cyborg gender are a means to demystify all forms of prejudice. Haraway is very clear that this does not mean it is therefore universalising or a 'totalising theory' but that it is 'taking responsibility for the social relations of science and technology'. It flies in the face of what she sees as the simplistic demonisation of technology.

> Cyborg imagery can suggest a way out of the maze of dualisms in which we have explained our bodies and our tools to ourselves. This is a dream not of a common language, but of a powerful infidel heteroglossia. (181)

Cyborg bodies do not reproduce, they regenerate, so there is no need for women to have their labour reduced to the ability to procreate or fulfil a maternal role. Nor need sex or gender be constrained in the ways that Butler has made so clear marginalise any body other than the straight male body. Here endeth the Manifesto.

The essays that follow on from the Manifesto serve to expand upon its basic claims and refine the lists of terms that are divided along the lines of what in Foucault would be called an epistemic shift. For, though she adamantly resiles from Foucault (n.4, 245), Haraway is telling a story of social construction and historical contextualisation. She recognises this, and it makes her 'nervous'.

> Like all neuroses, mine is rooted in the problem of metaphor, that is, the problem of the relation of bodies and language. For example, the force field imagery of moves in the fully textualized and coded world is the matrix for many arguments about socially negotiated reality for the postmodern subject. This world-as-code is, just for starters, a high-tech military field, a kind of automated academic battlefield, where blips of light called players disintegrate (what a metaphor!) each other in order to stay in the knowledge and power game. Technoscience and science fiction collapse into the sun of their radiant (ir)reality – war. (185)

So Haraway has a consciousness, unlike Butler, that relying on metaphors can obscure the material relations and material effects of embodied being. Her answer, however, is to try and take control of those metaphors, specifically the metaphorics of vision which so dominates 'objective' scientific endeavours and has done since the seventeenth century. When Haraway writes

'I am arguing for politics and epistemologies of location, positioning, and situating, where partiality and not universality is the condition of being heard to make rational knowledge claims' (195), she is, I think, arguing that vision is presented as clear and reliable but it too is never objective. Instead, we can be empowered by locating and identifying ourselves with a particular 'point of view' (pov). And in taking control of that metaphorics and becoming 'visionaries', we can use bodily boundaries to our advantage in a techno-poetics of self-construction.

> [B]odies as objects of knowledge are material-semiotic generative nodes. Their *boundaries* material-ize in social interaction. Boundaries are drawn by mapping practices, 'objects' do not pre-exist as such. Objects are boundary projects. But boundaries shift from within; boundaries are very tricky. What boundaries provisionally contain remains generative, productive of meanings and bodies. Siting (sighting) boundaries is a risky practice. (200–1)

At this point Haraway identifies herself with postmodernism, perhaps more than with Marxism or socialism. She seems to have had a crisis of faith, like many other Left-leaning academics at the time of the fall of the Berlin Wall, in reaction to which she apparently 'reinvented' her social-ism through postmodernism. This is a difficult move to make convincing when postmodernism is so very centred in and on the individual and individual experience, rather than society and the social.

Haraway correctly notes that the 'extraordinarily close tie of language and technology could hardly be overstressed in postmodernism':

> The 'construct' is at the centre of attention; making, reading, writing, and meaning seem to be very close to the same thing. This near-identity between technology, body, and semiosis suggests a particular edge to the mutually constitutive relations of political economy, symbol, and science that 'inform' contemporary research trends in medical anthropology ... Bodies, then, are not born; they are made. Bodies have been as thoroughly denaturalized as sign, context, and time. Late twentieth-cen-tury bodies do not grow from internal harmonic principles theorized within Romanticism. Neither are they discovered in the domains of realism and modernism ... one is not born an organism. Organisms are made; they are constructs of a world-changing kind. The constructions of an organism's bound-aries, the job of the discourses of immunology, are particularly potent mediators of the experiences of sickness and death for industrial and post-industrial people. (208)

Haraway gives 'discourse' around the immune system as an extended example of the shifts in understanding and the consequent retelling and remaking of the 'story' of how the immune system works. She asks us to accept her postmodern breaking down of the boundaries not only between bodies but also between bodies, machines, texts and 'nature' in a further move that opens the way to introduce fantasy, metaphor and poetics into 'scientific' domains.

> [N]either is there any ground for opposing the *mythical* to the organic, textual, and technical ...
> Bodies have become cyborgs - cybernetic organisms - compounds of hybrid techno-organic embod-
> iment and textuality (Haraway 1985). The cyborg is text, machine, body, and metaphor - all theorized
> and engaged in practice in terms of communications. (212)

We are rewritable because we are text. And other texts - such as science
fiction and science fantasy - become tools at the service of this rewriting.
Haraway happily offers the narratives of science fiction as utopian alter-
natives to current lived conceptions of sex, gender, embodiment, society
and politics.

> From this field of differences, replete with the promises and terrors of cyborg embodiments and sit-
> uated knowledges, there is no exit. Anthropologists of possible selves, we are technicians of realizable
> futures. Science *is* culture. (230)

Rewriting the female body as a replicator - linked in to the creative potential of the internet and reproductive technologies - not a reproducer, is part
of this freeing us all from the bonds of a science pretending to 'naturalism'.

Modest_Witness@Second_Millennium.FemaleMan©_
Meets_OncoMouse™: Feminism and Technoscience

Just as Judith Butler's *Bodies that Matter* was an attempt to refine the
thoughts expressed in *Gender Trouble*, Haraway's subsequent book is an
extended treatment of and elaboration upon 'The Cyborg Manifesto'. And
like Butler's later work, it too is suffused with appeals to popular cultural
references: science fiction, art, science-trade advertising. It is concerned
with communications technologies, feminism, racism and future possibilities for embodiment. It recognises the real exploitation in the world
that is hidden by the hype of technoscience but at the same time clings
to the liberatory possibilities of technoscience and science fiction. Where
the place of sex and gender had been articulated in the entry in the dictionary of Marxist keywords and present but relatively understated in the
Manifesto, here it is elaborated at length and the interconnection with
racism is fully, if obfuscatingly, articulated.

Here again, structure is very important to understanding the content of
Haraway's work. She consciously sets out to highlight the importance of
communications to her understanding of the coding of the world and the
body through science. To this end she uses a conceit based on grammar
(yet another metaphor of language) to weave her way through a complex
narrative. The book is divided into three unequal parts and the conceit of

the structure plays out sequentially as 'the formal structure of signification', 'the contents or figures of communication' and 'the physiology of meaning-making' (Haraway 1997: 14). The field of the 'formal structure of signification' is technoscience. The 'figures of communication' (agents) are the observers and the observed in technoscience: that is scientists and cyborg organisms (both material and fictional). The 'contents' of their communications include the context of their world-views. The 'physiology of meaning making', a mysterious phrase, is what is observable in case studies: how technoscience creates meaning in practice. Haraway's intent is to be deliberately postmodern, to be ironic, to diffract meaning. While I do not want to become bogged down in a direct recounting of the text, it is important to recognise the effect her structuring – or refusal to structure – has on her assertions.

Haraway asks us to revision our bodies and ourselves to inhabit technoscience as cyborgs. She wants us to bear witness to its problematics, and also to take control and to disrupt it: to create our own multiply identified, embodied point of view (pov). The title of the book is a materialisation of this appeal. Using the metaphor of cyberspace, she casts herself as an inhabitant of an internet domain – Second_Millennium.FemaleMan©_Meets_OncoMouse™ – who bears the username Modest_Witness. We shall have reason to return to this metaphor in the analysis, for in the years since this book was published its aptness has become revealing.

Syntactics

Because cyborgs are not just human-technical or human-mechanical hybrids but also animals that have had human matter introduced into them, Haraway includes non-humans in her studies of how 'social relationships get congealed into and taken for decontextualized things' (8). Technoscience relies on crossing boundaries of all descriptions. To Haraway's mind it is also integral to globalisation:

> [it] is a semiotic-material production of some forms of life rather than others. Technoscience is the story of such globalisation; it is the travelogue of distributed, heterogenous, linked, sociotechnical circulations that craft the world as a net called the global. (12)

In this world, as she stated in 'The Cyborg Manifesto', there are replications or regenerations, not births. The meaning of corporeal matter is potentially pluripotent – infinitely malleable – and cyborgs are the expression of that pluripotency.

> The offspring of these technoscientific wombs are cyborgs – imploded germinal entities, densely packed condensations of worlds, shocked into being from the force of the implosion of the natural and the

artificial, nature and culture, subject and object, machine and organic body, money and lives, narrative and reality. Cyborgs are the stem cells in the marrow of the technoscientific body; they differentiate into the subjects and objects at stake in the contested zones of technoscientific culture. (14)

While Haraway's prose can be annoyingly 'suggestive' and 'poetic', within this hyperbole is a simple statement that the intervention of technoscience into our bodies, our material lives, puts us in the position of being able to create and contest the meanings created within it. For Haraway, the historical and contextual construction of the cyborg is not necessarily something out of our powers of definition, and the rejection of the possibilities of technoscience is a romanticisation of prior understandings of embodiment. Like Caliban in Shakespeare's *The Tempest* – we can talk back.

Semantics

Haraway's answer to how we go about doing so in a world coded technoscientifically from the cellular level upwards, is through the codes and patterns of that discourse. Haraway allies herself with two other boundary-crossing 'fellow travellers': OncoMouse™ and FemaleMan©. By including these trade and copyright marks, Haraway is making the point that both these names also include their status as owned 'creations': the former is a strain of genetically modified laboratory mice, the latter is a fictional character. OncoMouse is Haraway's 'synecdoche for all of technoscience' (22). Haraway explains at length why she uses the ironic email address but the crux is succinct: 'My tendentious point is that apparatuses of cultural production going by the names of science studies, antiracist feminism, and technoscience have a common circulatory system' (22). So her domain name is a transcendental *habitus*, an alternate world. We have seen in her earlier work that she unpicks the supposed objectivity of scientific empiricism. Here she connects flawed drives to 'pure' observation back to Robert Boyle – one of the founders of the Royal Society in London in the late-seventeenth century. Boyle characterised the proper scientific observer as a 'modest witness', one who disappears before the truth that experimentation reveals. She styles herself as an ironic Modest_Witness, arguing that this attempt at invisible observation only serves to blind the (gender-laden and racially loaded) political content of scientific observations: 'Gender and race never existed separately and never were about preformed subjects endowed with funny genitals and curious colors. Race and gender are about entwined, barely analytically separable, highly protean, *relational* categories' (30).

Those categories have been used implicitly and explicitly to support white Western masculinity. Historically, there have been gender, racial and class barriers to being a proper modest witness to science (32). The bases for defining certain people as being unable to be objective observers has been the imputation that such people are insurmountably partial on the basis of their embodiment. Whole social groups have been constructed as inalienable from their own visible difference: and if you are visible, you cannot be modestly 'transparent'. But, she still sees a space for 'good science'.

> I am using the story of Boyle and the experimental way of life as a figure for technoscience; the story stands for more than itself. My claim is double: (i) There have been practical inheritances, which have undergone many reconfigurations but which remain potent; and (ii) the stories of the scientific Revolution set up a narrative about 'objectivity' that continues to get in the way of a more adequate, self-critical technoscience committed to situated knowledges. The important practice of credible witnessing is still at stake. (33)

So, for Haraway, the problem is not technoscience itself. The point of being a Modest_Witness is to be able to find a way of reaching a technoscience that will be at the behest of all. She wants to queer techno-science, not reject or dispose of it. And she uses the appeal to Christian tradition that was undoubtedly inherent in Boyle's original term, that of bearing witness to the 'Truth', to that end and by queering that tradition as well (43). She is bearing witness in the domain of FemaleMan and OncoMouse. Haraway is correct that there is no getting away from the physical fact that most of the developed world's inhabitants and many of the undeveloped world's inhabitants are already cyborgs by her defini-tion, insofar as we do not live unmolested in a state of nature. Many of us have been immunised in childhood. Most of us have taken antibiotics at some stage in our lives. There are few in the developed world who can afford the luxury and fewer still in the undeveloped world who can avoid ingesting commercial hybrid or non-organically treated crops. To use the word Haraway makes much of, she 'and hundreds of millions of people on this planet have been interpellated [within technoscience], whether we like it or not' (49).

And, as I have already said, Haraway does not see this as an intrinsi-cally bad thing. She situates anxieties over hybridity as historically and contextually intertwined with racism: 'Transgenic border-crossing signifies serious challenges to the "sanctity of life" for many members of Western cultures, which historically have been obsessed with racial purity, cate-gories authorized by nature, and the well-defined self' (60). Insofar as evolution is a process of intermixing, she is correct to argue that miscegenation (interbreeding) is simply a fact of biology, in flora and fauna. She is also right that historically this has been used to support theories of race, all of which are racist. But is that sufficient reason to accept technoscientific hybridisation, both within and across species? Surely, there is more at stake than racism in concerns about the intermixing of the base matter of life – exploitation, unimaginable consequences, devaluing the living and the dying, the commercialisation of life – issues to which we shall return in the analysis below. Haraway, who opposes genetic patenting, is in fact sensitive to some of these problems but she argues that

> the tendency by the political 'left' ... to collapse molecular genetics, biotechnology, profit, and exploitation into one undifferentiated mass is at least as much of a mistake as the mirror-image reduction of the 'right'of biological – or informational – complexity to the gene and its avatars, including the dollar. (62)

She wants to be related to OncoMouse and FemaleMan, seeing in them a preferable form of kinship to that embodied in the stereotypical nuclear family.

FemaleMan is a character from a mid-1970s science fiction novel. S/he is genetically altered. So too is OncoMouse, the generic name of a strain of laboratory mice that can be guaranteed to develop cancers – in particular, breast cancer. They are highly valued as research tools. Haraway feels particularly sympathetic towards and implicated in the fate of OncoMouse because as a woman she may well depend on the results of research into breast cancer on these mammals. To express her 'pov', she refers to the paintings of Lyn Randolph, one of which depicts a female OncoMouse as a caged, scientifically observed Christ. Haraway's goal is 'to help put the boundary between the technical and the political back into permanent question as part of the obligation of building situated knowledges inside the materialized narrative fields of technoscience' (89).

OncoMouse is a patented organism, the genetic make-up of which is the direct result of technoscientific intervention. They are commercial products. And they are 'interpellated' in what she has already identified as a coded world because they are valued for their genetic construction: for their altered bodies. They are defined by their place in the communications structure – by their genetic coding. Similarly, though fictionally, FemaleMan genetically (through code) crosses gender boundaries and epitomises a space outside normative physical and social categories.

We have seen in earlier chapters in relation to other writers (Butler, Kristeva) that this kind of reliance on metaphor can be problematic. Haraway recognises this but insists that there is a materiality to her use of metaphor.

Not only does metaphor become a research program, but also, more fundamentally, the organism for us is an information system and an economic system of a particular kind. For us, that is, those interpellated into this materialized story, the biological world *is* an accumulation strategy in the fruitful collapse of metaphor and materiality that animates technoscience ... The collapse of metaphor and materiality is a question not of ideology but of modes of practice among humans and non-humans that configure the world – materially and semiotically in terms of some objects and boundaries and not others. (97)

She believes technoscience deconstructs the binary opposition of nature and culture (102). Not only does Haraway want to be kin to these two fantastic 'creations,' she also sees them as equal Modest Witnesses to the acts of technoscience. They are at once produced objects and complicit, believing witnesses. They are 'products of genetic technologies', 'products of writing technologies', 'queer', 'gestated in the wombs of modernity and enlightenment, but their existence warps the matrix of their origin', and 'they come together in the energetically imploded conversation about constructivism and naturalism in transnational science studies and in multiracial, multicultural feminism' (120–1).

Pragmatics

The final and longest section of the book is devoted to giving detailed case studies of different facets of the effects of technoscience in gene mapping, human reproduction and arguments around 'race'. I will be inversely brief in dealing with it. Many of the political and social assumptions behind each of these areas of science are taken for granted. The metaphors that scientists, and those mass-marketing scientific products, use in relation to them both hide and uncover deep assumptions about embodiment. Discourses of colonisation pervade gene mapping, as does the breaking down of ourselves into constitutive, mappable fragments. Human reproduction has become infused with ideas of replication and representation, and is increasingly distanced from the self who is gestating, at least in the developed world. In the undeveloped world technoscience sells its (post)modernity at the cost of infants' lives. Deep unsupportable racism suffuses scientific practice from its origins. But her answer to the very real problems that she outlines in and through these case studies is to treat them promiscuously, as evidence of moments of connection in hypertext, or interconnected 'nodes' of stem cells.

By this metaphor she means that as stem cells can form clusters (nodes), so too in technoscience there are clusters of meaning production. In this she is not necessarily speaking of the embryonic stem cells that cause such heated ethical debate – the basic building-blocks of the human body – but the stem cells that replace and repair our bodies on a constant basis: adult stem cells. This is a confusingly apt metaphor because either kind of stem cell can metastasise (to form regrowth or tumours) and they can migrate. However, they do not necessarily remain connected when they do so, except at the most abstract level of being situated in the one organism. Though she designates the 'technoscientific body' as the 'organism' in which this abstracted interconnection is taking place, what she really seems to mean is the whole discursive practice of technoscience, or indeed, every level of the known universe.

> Objects like the fetus, chip/computer, gene, race, ecosystem, brain, database, and bomb are stem cells of the technoscientific body. Each of these curious objects is a recent construct or material-semiotic 'object of knowledge', forged by heterogeneous practices in the furnaces of technoscience. To be a construct does NOT mean to be unreal or made up; quite the opposite. Out of each of these nodes or stem cells, sticky threads lead to every nook and cranny of the world. Which threads to follow is an analytical, imaginative, physical, and political choice. (129)

Her cases studies are in effect a description of what she styles as nodes and the interconnections that are formed between them. She asserts that by tracing patterns of practices and connections, she is identifying 'situated knowledges in the worlds of technoscience' that include links between human and non-human participants (130).

In relation to mapping the human genome, she skips from the creation of alternate possible worlds in the 'Sim' series of games, which were originally dominated by ecology, geography and cartography;[1] to the difference between Indigenous and Western knowledge systems in relation to spatialisation in the determination of Wik Native Title in Australia; and finally to metaphors within and around the mapping of the human genome, via various byways in science journal advertisements and cartoons.

> The cultural productions of the genome produce a category crisis, a generic conundrum in which proliferating ambiguities and chimeras animate the action in science, entertainment, domestic life, fashion, religion, and business ... Borderlands are often especially heavily polluted and policed; they are also especially full of interesting traffic and powerful hopes. The gene and the genome constitute such borderlands on the maps of technoscience. The gene, a kind of stem cell in the technoscientific body, is enmeshed in a hypertext that ramifies and intersects richly with all the other nodes in the web. (148-9)

Her basis for connecting these disparate examples – nodes, in her terms – is that she sees these as moments of border-crossing. In this she is stretching Douglas's notion of boundary- or border-crossing. This pattern of interlinking is repeated in the discussion of the human foetus in technoscience. She first invokes popular images of foetal ultrasonography, from feminist cartoons to telecommunications advertisements. From this she moves to the place of creativity and productivity that

158

computers offer to women. Then we are drawn into a discussion of the place of the gynaecological speculum in feminism – taking back the techno-medical instrument as an object of self-definition in the 1960s and 1970s – and a descriptive discussion of the political implications of abortion for African American women. Finally she appeals to a description of the on-the-ground practices and (fatal) consequences of technoscientific intervention, in the adoption of infant formula by impoverished women in Brazil in preference to breast milk.

From her examples she wants us to see that reproduction is thoroughly technologised and that factors that were once taken as authoritative points of meaning in pregnancy – the first feeling of a baby moving, a purely maternal knowing – have lost ground to the ability to technologically 'visualise' a foetus *in utero*, and even an embryo at conception (177). But, again, the fact that the pregnant (female) body is largely mediated by technoscientific interventions as disembodied extensions is no reason for her to reject technoscience.

These ontologically confusing *bodies*, and the practices that produce specific embodiment, are what we have to address, not the false problem of *dis*embodiment. Whose and which bodies – human and non-human, silicon based and carbon based – are at stake, and how, in our technoscientific dramas of origin? (186)

To find and define the subject (human and nonhuman) in that act of creation, she proposes feminist technoscience:

Feminist technoscience inquiry is a speculum, a surgical instrument, a tool for widening all kinds of orifices to improve observation and intervention in the interest of projects that are simultaneously about freedom, justice and knowledge. In these terms, feminist inquiry is not more innocent, no more free of the inevitable wounding that all questioning brings, than any other knowledge project. (191)

That virtual speculum, it is proposed, allows us to fully explore the material facts of what lies behind the appalling number of babies that die under a year old in undeveloped countries as a direct result of the introduction of bottle-feeding. She shows how ideas of K- and r-species selection – that non-nurturing animals can afford to have high birth-rates and correspondingly high infant mortality, while nurturing animals have low birth-rates and low mortality rates – are implicit in the rhetoric of developed world discourses on the relative fates of human infants in developed and undeveloped countries (204).

One task of feminist technoscience studies is to construct the analytical languages – to design the speculums – for representing and intervening in our spliced, cyborg worlds ... The signifiers of choice for Bell Telephone and for Nestlé parody feminist reproductive freedom and knowledge projects and

> the dispersed, disseminated, differentiated, 'transnational' yearning that sustains them ... The right speculum for the job makes visible the data structures that are our bodies. (212)

This methodology is repeated in a discussion which builds on and extends her early work on primatology and theories of race from the late-nineteenth century to the present. In her discussion, ideas of blood and bloodlines and images of vampires and simians abound. She sets out several tables of ways in which representations that are infused with these images recur over time and wide range of publications and policies in the public domain.

> My chart does *not* argue that 'forces' such as political developments 'influenced' biology from the 'outside', or vice versa; nor does it imply that life science, or anything else, is the summation of its determinations. Biology is a complex cultural practice engaged in by real people, not bundles of determinations just waiting for the analyst's clever discovery. Biology might be politics by other means, but the means are specific to the located practice of the life sciences. These means are usually more about things like genes, graphs, and blood than about legislatures or supposed social interests of science. (230)

They are stem cell nodes, and she leaves it entirely up to the individual to make what he or she will of the multiple possible connections.

> That is simultaneously a political, cultural, and scientific question. From a biological point of view, symptoms point to functioning or malfunctioning, bodies and processes that might otherwise be invisible. The best metaphor, a technical device, for representing the kind of relationality implicit in this chart might be hypertext. (231)

There is no claim to be made, there is no position that is more or less valid than another. Her point and her project is postmodern, and the outcome is the granting of playful, free-floating, meaning-making to the individual. For several reasons, as I noted in my open remarks, I find this an unsatisfying approach.

Analysis

There is a paradox in Haraway's approach. In her early work she gives finely textured science studies criticisms of scientific practice and throughout her work remains committed to uncovering the prejudice and social injustice perpetrated in the name of science. Her insights are incisive, particularly in relation to the deep racism at work in social psychology and the mirror-image anthropomorphism in primatology. All her observations based on case studies are careful and at the very least useful. The point at which her arguments take a less convincing turn, even in her own terms, is directly attributable to her fascination with poststructuralist and postmodern theory. She loses touch with her materialism, and like many bioethicists who end up being apologists for the practices of medical scientists, she is too close to her subject-matter.

Without being overly simplistic, or falling into what she would see as a romanticisation of forms of embodiment prior to the postmodern, it has to be said that her own approach to technoscience is at the very least overly optimistic about its possibilities of overcoming what she herself admits are serious flaws in practice. For example, her claim that 'Bodies are not born they are made' – if you take this from de Beauvoir's perspective, that these things are contextualised constructs, then her claim is fair enough. The problem is that, though Haraway would deny that this is what she means, it then becomes very easy for such statements to be translated into claims that bodies can be infinitely made up. Beyond taking it as a metaphoric game which, frankly, is a nonsense that ignores agreed meanings about what it is to be embodied in a social complex. Embodied individuals do not live in a vacuum.

Further, while science fiction may offer possible alternate worlds, it also is deeply influenced by its context, displacing the fears and concerns of the relative, material 'here and now'. It is just as misguided to treat fictional texts – particularly science fiction and science fantasies – as having revolutionary potential in and of themselves as it is to treat people's narrativisation of lived experience as either 'truths' or 'only stories' – rather than as complex outcomes of their embodied, socially and materially embedded lives that may or *may not* have truth functions. This, like the effects of postmodern theory across many disciplines, goes further than giving weight to voices from below, which is a laudable aim. It flattens out experience and empties it of meaning – precisely because meaning that is entirely self-referential is meaningless. It is ironic that this seems to escape theorists who appeal so plaintively to linguistic metaphors.

Yes, we tell our stories and construct ourselves mentally throughout our lives: every day, and over time, retell them and mix them up. But, even though there are undoubtedly increasingly sophisticated ways of remoulding our physical appearance, no matter what the claims of gene therapies, it does not reshape the base matter of ourselves: those processes go on beyond our ultimate control. We age, we die. And on those grounds it is easy to see why poetry becomes an appealing chimera of revolutionary potential (Haraway 1991: 245). Poems can live indefinitely: 'So long as men can breathe and eyes can see,/So long lives this, and this gives life to thee' (Shakespeare, Sonnet 18). Our mortality is one of the fundamental ways in which our lives take on meaning.

In Haraway's work it is almost as if technoscience becomes a religion and science fiction its new cosmology. Of course, Haraway doesn't say this, and I am being provocative, but it is implicit in her metaphorics that science is her faith. Because she is so committed to the possibilities of both technoscience and postmodern self reinvention, by the time we come to *Modest Witness* her project ends up becoming a series of descriptions. There is hope, but it is hope of the kind that comes from cosmology – a belief in a future that will come about through transcendence – not one of or for agency. If you position yourself as bearing witness, no matter how ironically, you are bearing witness to a truth, not just exposing the grossness behind the New World Order Inc., and that truth resides in technoscience. Where then, in reality, is the difference between Haraway and Boyle? Why should her vision, her technoscientific witness, be any more or any less infused with prejudice than Boyle's?

Indeed, implicitly Haraway still assumes a Western-centric world-view precisely because it bases itself in technoscience which is intrinsically embedded in Western histories of thought. By merely citing snippets and narratives, by keeping criticism at a distance and resiling from taking an argued position – which from her early work she is clearly extremely adept at doing – she ends up shoring-up the power of technoscience's domination. If one steps back from it, however, one can see it as one in a range of epistemologies that are characteristic of different social formations. What she describes is characteristic of postmodern societies in the developed world. Who in the developing world has the time or the luxury of thinking of bettering their lives by becoming a node in a stem cell network or a hyperlink in the greater techno-body of the universe? At base, the cyborg body is, and only is, a postmodern body. It is a very sophisticated colonial body that is a part of the overwriting of other forms of embodiment that are integral to different social formations. So, much as it tries to avoid the pitfalls of 'objective' ways of viewing the world, it cannot get out of them and it cannot get around them. While she has a point that rejecting technoscience altogether risks romanticising prior ways of being, Haraway puts too much faith in science. Though admittedly problematic, other modes of practice like economics – which she explicitly rejects as part of her outmoded Marxist past – *are* cross-cultural, because every culture has some means of exchange relations. But perhaps that is the problem – she is not theorising a mode of practice.

To conclude I would like to pick up on my earlier gesturing towards the aptness of title of *Modest Witness* and Haraway's slippage into the notion of hypertext and hyperlinks. Haraway started out by claiming cyborg identity was liberatory because it is based in technology, and that this is especially important for women because they are more at home with computers and the personalised space of control they offer. In this she is following Kristeva, Irigaray and/or Wittig in the rejection of 'masculine' forms of writing. These arguments are suffused with the wonderment many felt with the technological advances that came with the dot.com boom, increasingly powerful computers, and the massive proliferation of information and connections via the internet. Even in the brief time between the publication of *Modest Witness* and the present, however, in the developed world computers and internet usage have become ubiquitous. To be perfectly personal, I work with websites all the time, constructing them and populating them with content.[2] The pace of advance in that short space of time allows one to see with blinding clarity that hyperspace in fact creates nothing new under the sun: it replicates all the thought systems, organisational structures and all the commercial imperatives of what Haraway 'fondly think[s] of as the real world'. The major difference is that it abstracts people from more physically immediate forms of communication. Finally, while it may be available in cyber-cafés for tourists, it means very little to people in developing countries except as an unattainable commodity. With the distance of only eight years, her appeals to the wonder of hyperlinks and hypertext ring as hollowly as the futurity of a Buck Rogers spaceship.[3]

Cognate writers

There are many writers who fall into what I am identifying as the disembodied branch of body studies. Not all of them can be classified as or would identify themselves as postmodernists, though those who are not would probably be fairly described as poststructuralists. Nor are they necessarily 'inheritors', as I used the term in relation to the writers in the first three chapters. Though some of them may have been influenced by or influenced Haraway themselves, they sit here more because they take part at that broader level in the intense abstraction of embodiment that, ironically, leads theorists of embodiment to give far more credence and power to the mind. I shall only briefly mention a very few examples to plot out the field.

Elaine Scarry's *The Body in Pain: The Making and Unmaking of the World* (1985) is, for example, poststructuralist rather than postmodern. In common with Haraway, however, she places a great deal of credence in both linguistic metaphors and bio-medical interpretations of the body. Scarry's focus on the subjective experience of embodiment is how individuals experience their bodies under torture – how their worlds are unmade through a process that literally renders them speechless. Extreme pain, Scarry argues, takes one beyond words, beyond thought and beyond coherence. Her understanding of pain is, categorically, taken from medical studies. Scarry's book stands as a testament to the stupidity and veniality of torture, and is in many ways laudable in attempting to unpick the politics of such acts even if in ways that do not necessarily lead to agency. What is notable in the present discussion, however, is the degree to which even as the most visceral of embodied acts and experiences are brought to attention, the power of being and knowing never really gets past the creation of the world through thought. In all that it is about a totally embodied experience, it is the mind that matters.

Margrit Shildrick, like Haraway, is clearly and openly postmodern. Her *Leaky Bodies and Boundaries: Feminism, Postmodernism and (Bio)Ethics* (1997) also covers some of the areas that Haraway deals with, specifically reproduction and technoscience from a feminist perspective. For her a feminist ethic entails no standpoint, apart from the valorisation of women, and a rejection of value judgement. She would rather take control of the metaphors of feminine lack of boundaries and lack of continence – negative constructions that go back to Eve and which have infused discourses on women in art and medicine to name but two – as empowering. She is also a proponent of the possibilities of assisted reproductive techniques to reshape embodiment, motherhood and subvert (or queer) the nuclear family. This is, in essence, an argument from radical individualism. She openly states, 'Although I have consistently had the ethical in mind, the approach that I have outlined makes no claims, and is not intended, to resolve the moral questions of how each of us should behave in concrete situations' (Shildrick 1997: 211). Indeed. Her argument, however, is more openly in sympathy with Derrida's postmodernism than Haraway's cyborg.

Sarah Franklin, an anthropologist who specialises in assisted conception and reproductive biology, is a far more considered and thoughtful researcher, but it is even harder to pin down any opinions in her work than in Shildrick's. Her approach to reproductive techniques in *Embodied Progress: A Cultural Account of Assisted Conception* (1997) is extraordinarily careful and detailed in its ethnography. She is one of the newer 'breed' of anthropologists whose focus is not the culture of an 'other' but facets of Western culture. The proposed outcome of her close reading of the experiences of women in the Midlands and North England is a revision of the understanding of kinship. She is quite right that assisted reproductive techniques do offer challenges to commonly held understanding of kinship, they rewrite what kinship lines mean and consist in. The coyness with which she implies her approval of this revision is not hers alone – it is something I have come to understand from my own brief ethnographic excursion into their world that is ubiquitous amongst latter-day anthropologists of science at least. Her work is unassailable in its disciplinary rigour. Its interest in our present context, though, is that it takes as read and promulgates quietly the instensification of the abstraction of embodiment. The kinship that Franklin argues for – by describing in gently positive phrases that stand back from outright comment – is a postmodern kinship. It is a kinship that does not require embodied relations.

There are many other writers who write in a similar vein. In many ways, despite the avowed intent of its main proponents that they want to reclaim embodiment for the new millennium, at heart they represent an idealising of radical disembodiment. This chapter has dealt with the future fantasies of un-bodies, the rejection of embodiment, and the embracing of cyborg or techno-bodies. The cyborg body represents the postmodern experience of embodied abstraction whereby the materially embodied subject is, on the one hand, romantically fused with technological apparatuses, and on the other hand, distanced and devalued by the reinterpretation of the body through bio-technological means.

The writing in the final chapter takes a rather different tack. While still dealing with the embodied subject of later modernity, the writers of the final chapter have more in common with the methodologies of Bourdieu and Douglas or the contextualisation of Foucault. In the final chapter we shall look at the ways in which difference is theorised as it is lived out in the body through direct examples of people's experiences. While one cannot say that this means that the body is spoken of in any less intellectual terms than we have seen across the last two chapters – or that it is in fact any less a product of a social formation that functions at a postmodern level of embodied abstraction – it does mean that embodied experience is more directly foregrounded. There is some sense in which the body is 'there'.

Notes

1 These are now better known for the pervasive and perverse 'Sims' – a create-your-own virtual life and death soap opera: multiple, interactive, sociopathic, humanoid Tamagotchi.

2 See www.rmit.edu.au/globalism, www.sourcesofinsecurity.org, www.communitysustainability.info, www.borderknowledges.info, www.globalism.nationalism.org and www.critical.ethical.org

3 Buck Rogers was an extremely popular US science fiction movie serial in the 1930s.

Life-Experiences, Lifestyles and Life-Stages

I have given over the previous two chapters to postmodern theories of embodiment because they have been accorded serious standing in disciplines, including and beyond anthropology and sociology. At this point I want to reintroduce four forms of social formation that I introduced at the beginning of this book – tribal, traditional, modern and postmodern. This list should not be taken as necessarily sequential. It would be easy to assume that because Western society can be characterised as postmodern, and that it is often seen to be at the vanguard of a positivist history of the present, that this is the next logical step in the globalising way of the future, in which prior cultural forms will follow 'our' example. Powerful and influential as the globalisation of postmodern embodiment is, it would be a mistake to take from the way those social formations are presented as a series that they are necessarily progressive. They can co-exist, even if in tension: and who is to say that what we now see as postmodern will not be seen, with the benefit of hindsight, as an intense and neurotic blip in modernity? For these reasons, instead of giving radical futurists the last word, I want instead to turn to writers who have learned from poststructuralist and postmodern theories of embodiment, but who maintain a grounded sense of embodied *lives*. I take Susan Bordo – who writes on gendered embodiment – as my detailed case study. She is one amongst many writers who continue to work on experiences of lived embodiment.

Bordo

Susan Bordo is of a similar generation to, though of a quite different social background from, Donna Haraway. Haraway, as we saw, insistently positions herself as a relatively privileged, white, middle-class woman with a Christian upbringing, a Marxist past and a postmodern future. I was almost going to say that Haraway 'laid herself bare,' but 'positioned' is more accurate and more apt, particularly in comparison with Bordo. Two years after Haraway's *Simians, Cyborgs and Women* appeared, Susan Bordo published *Unbearable Weight* (1993) which, similarly, consists of a series of formative essays written between the early 1980s through to the early 1990s. This provides a framing context that is illuminating for a number of reasons. In *Unbearable Weight*, and much more so in *The Male Body* (1999), Bordo does lay herself bare, making eloquent and detailed use of her own Jewish, lower-middle-class upbringing in 1950s and 1960s New York – her detailed cultural and historical context – from childhood to the present. Her approach could not be more different from Haraway's, nor could the quality of positioning evoked in her writing. Where Haraway aligns herself in an interior intellectual world with OncoMouse and the fictional FemaleMan, casting herself as a postmodern version of Robert Boyle's observing modest witness, Bordo positions herself firmly within the complex public, cultural and historical interconnections that structure the fabric of her arguments.

Bordo tells us through the course of *The Male Body* of her fascination with and submersion in film from an early age. She relates how she entered university in the early 1960s, dealt first-hand with the day-to-day sexism of the time, and only gradually came to (mostly) overcome the ingrained effects it had had on her. She has, since that time, taught across literary studies, cultural studies and women's studies and has undoubtedly been extremely influential in debates on contemporary culture and the body, particularly in relation to the effects of popular cultural images on lived experience. Her earlier writing concentrated on the female body – on eating disorders and cosmetic surgery – but her interests have extended to encompass masculinity and the male body, and the effects of various cultural forms on those constructions of identity.

In Chapter 6 we traced the direct line from Butler through psychoanalytic theory to Haraway's cyborg, noting along the way the misuse in both writers of the work of Mary Douglas. In this chapter we find a more likely inheritor of Douglas's deeply textured ethnographic work, and a reworking rather than a rejection of the work of Bourdieu and Foucault. This is not to say that Bordo's work is without its drawbacks, which include the kinds of blind-spots that Butler in particular wants to address. While homosexual- and lesbian-embodied experience are not invisible, they are certainly not foregrounded in Bordo's theoretical explanations of the human body. However, in truly situating herself, going back again and again to interrogate the way she has shaped her arguments, Bordo takes responsibility for the political implications of her situated standpoint rather than disingenuously distancing herself from that responsibility. We find in Bordo a path to encompassing more deeply textured, lived experiences of different lives under the pressure of dominant or hegemonic ideals than is available in the strands of postmodern theorisation of disembodied embodiment that we have looked at thus far. Butler uses Foucault but tries to equate his appeal to the power of language in historical contexts with universalising, transcendent language. Haraway scorns Foucault as 'old'. Bordo takes what is useful from the work of both Foucault and Bourdieu to address what they generally forget: lived female embodiment under pressure. Haraway implicitly accepts and thereby empowers techno-medical understandings of embodiment: indeed, the more biological Haraway gets, the more transcendent and the further away from social bodies she moves. Bordo looks at the power of the medicalisation of the human body but she does so as one amongst many modes or processes by which we experience ourselves as bodies in society.

Unbearable Weight

Unbearable Weight: Feminism, Western Culture and the Body is a study of the social bases and the lived experiences of eating disorders. It is worth noting that unlike the writers of the last two chapters, Bordo consciously resists linguistic playfulness. There is no shying away from clarity of argument here and her work is consequently a pleasure to read. She takes postmodern and poststructuralist arguments about language seriously but demurs from the assertion that women need to find another language in which to express themselves. Rather, she deliberately shows her reader that her ability to express herself clearly comes out of her cultural background and her lived experiences as a woman – from her father she learned what she had to say was worthwhile and in reaction to infantilising male lecturers she learned to defend her views. Indeed, it has always seemed foolish to me to argue that one should rescind the power one already has in language rather than wresting it: to burble rather than to speak back. But then Bordo, unlike Butler and Haraway who concentrate on language as an abstract system, gives full weight to the social, interpersonal and subjective power of language. This frames the way she explains her theorisations of embodiment in Western culture.

Bordo recognises that the human body, like other social objects, is constructed within and understood through various knowledges that have social bases: in this sense, she understands the body to be a construct.

In this we can see that she is clearly in sympathy with Foucault. She knows that the body has not always been seen in the way that it is seen now, but she argues that what is common across time is that the body has been constructed as something lesser than, at odds with and 'apart from the true self': 'That which is not-body is the highest, the best, the noblest, the closest to God; that which is body is the albatross, the heavy drag on self-realization' (5). This is the unbearable weight.

So the mind/body split is socially embedded in Western culture. This may have begun with philosophical argument and subsequently have been concretised within Cartesian dualism, but it is and has been for centuries part of normalised, dominant culture in the West. Under pressure from increasingly intense forms of globalisation, it is becoming a part of the normalised dominant culture for the majority of the world. This is ingrained throughout Western culture – 'in medicine, law, literary and artistic representations, the psychological constructions of self, interpersonal relationships, popular culture, and advertisements'. However, Bordo believes that if we understand the power and the effects of this dualism, we can bring about 'concrete transformation of the institutions and practices that sustain it' (Bordo 1993: 13–14). Though she uses one of Derrida's terms, 'deconstruction', she does so to insist that politics (institutions and practices) be brought back into the discussion. Bordo has little time for theories that attempt simply to reject this understanding of embodiment, that claim it is possible to transcend the limits of the body and make of it whatever one wants. As she states, 'it is not so easy to "go beyond dualism" in this culture' (15). The work of *Unbearable Weight* is to ground this claim in arguments that rely on thoroughly detailed historical, social and cultural contextualisations of female embodiment, using eating disorders as a focal point.

However, Bordo is careful to give full credit to the important insights that have come out of some poststructuralist feminisms, particularly that former views of the body (including feminist views) have been homogenising. As soon as a norm is proposed, it is inevitable that dissenting 'racial', class, gender, ethnic, chronological, etc. bodily experiences will differ from that norm and complicate any simplistic reading of 'the' body. And it is equally inevitable that 'unique configurations (of ethnicity, social class, sexual orientation, religion, genetics, education, family, age, and so forth)' (62) – mean people receive dominant images in different ways. What she does not agree with is that reading for difference be the primary aim or analysis: '[T]o focus *only* on multiple interpretations is to miss important effects of the everyday deployment of mass cultural representations of masculinity, femininity, beauty, and success' (24).

That is, Bordo acknowledges what is often left out in postmodern claims to absolute control over the self. Selves are still at the mercy of and live under the influence of mass cultural images that promote and support dominant views of embodiment. It is extraordinarily difficult to resist such images, and Bordo argues that it is extremely important to recognise their 'dominance, and not to efface such recognition through a facile and abstract celebration of "heterogeneity", "difference", "subversive reading", and so forth' (29–30). That is not to say that people (women) are gullible in falling prey to those views. People have agency – limited as Bourdieu has shown that might be against such images – but they can recognise the rules of the game and use them to their advantage.

Bordo is also quite right to question the tendency of postmodern theorists such as Butler and Susan McClary to recreate the body as yet another form of text, that is for privileging the notion of the free-play of meaning and forgetting to attend to the complex materiality of the body in time, space and culture: 'If the body is treated as pure text, subversive, destabilizing elements can be emphasised and freedom and self-determination celebrated: but one is left wondering is there a *body* in this text?' (38). Indeed, as we have seen, materiality ends up yet again taking a poor second place to the mind. However, Bordo is careful not to condemn people for using increasingly available postmodern medical interventions to reshape or manipulate their bodies. Her concern is rather 'to highlight a *discourse* that is gradually changing our conception and experience of our bodies, a discourse that encourages us to "imagine the possibilities" and close our eyes to limits and consequences' (39). In life there are *material* consequences.

Bordo tracks those consequences through a complex contextualisation of dominant ideas of the female body as they play out through regimes of beauty, fertility and weight control. She concentrates on four 'significations' that she believes appear and reappear to varying degrees in each of these regimes.

> (1) the promise of transcendence of domestic femininity and admission to the privileged public world ... (2) the symbolic and practical control of female hunger (read: desire), continually constructed as a problem in patriarchal cultures ... (3) the symbolic recircumscription of woman's limited 'place' in the world; and (4) the tantalizing (and mystifying) ideal of a perfectly managed and regulated self, within a consumer culture which has made the actual management of hunger and desire intensely problematic. (68)

This self-control is played out through dietary and exercise regimes. In terms of fertility, Bordo looks to the status of the female body within legal and medical discourse and the terms in which debates around abortion are fought. She argues that the polarisation (as often happens in moral debates) between individual rights and moral (read religious) sentiments leads to an imbalance that has had a material effect on the way the female body is treated in law and in fact. In current arguments that polarise between claims to personhood for the foetus and feminist counter-claims of individual choice for women, what gets elided is that the *personhood of women* is under assault. This has led to an increasing tendency to permit unwanted medical interventions into women's bodies (72). In American law, at least, other kinds of medical intervention cannot be forced on people – Bordo gives a telling example of a man who could not be forced to donate his bone marrow to a dying relative (77). The various means of 'assistance' in human reproduction have not had an uncomplicatedly positive effect on women's subjectivity.

> On the one hand, women now have a booming technology seemingly focused on fulfilling *their* desires: to conceive, to prevent miscarriage, to deliver a healthy baby at term. On the other hand, proponents and practitioners continually encourage women to treat their bodies as passive instruments of those goals, ready and willing, 'if they want a child badly enough', to endure however complicated and invasive a regime of diagnostic testing, daily monitoring, injections, and operative procedures may be required. (86)

Bordo argues that everything else in their lives (work etc.) is minimised and made a matter of guilt. And if a woman is not prepared to go through that regime, it is not uncommon for those around her, including medical professionals, to bring pressure to bear on her to conform. In the past few years there has been anecdotal evidence at least in my local newspapers of doctors reproving women for both declining to attempt and refusing to continue with IVF treatment. Bordo wants to see arguments that give more weight to women's 'distinctive embodiment' and 'social histories' in according us a certain moral authority 'to adjudicate the complex ethical dilemmas that arise out of our reproductivity' (94). This is without appealing to the bugbear of postmodernism – essence – but rather the validity of particular experience that comes with female embodiment.

In terms of the way *Unbearable Weight* is set out, what I have described so far forms the first (and most general) of three sections. The thrust of this argument on abortion debates sets the ground for further arguments on beauty by showing that women's embodiment does have particular resonances and is subject to more restrictive and more intrusive attempts at bodily control than has historically been the case for men. Bordo's arguments progress to focus around eating disorders as attempts at self-control that are supported and promoted by dominant cultural images of women's relation to food and to desire. This comes out of the rewriting of a series of essays that trace an evolution in Bordo's thoughts on the cultural factors and forces involved in women's development of gendered pathologies. This is worth noting because it allows one to see how her arguments have gradually become more firmly aligned with constructivist close reading approaches and the likes of Douglas, Bourdieu and Foucault.

Bordo sees in commercials that directly target women to advertise various foods an implicit projection of a view of female eating habits as behaviours that are (and putatively should be) constantly under self-management and self-control. Like Victorian guides to female conduct and manners, they promote an unhealthy attitude to food and appetite that is centred on self-restriction. This, she argues, is not just about 'food intake':

> Rather, the social control of female hunger operates as a practical 'discipline' (to use Foucault's term) that trains female bodies in the knowledge of their limits and possibilities. Denying oneself food becomes the central micro-practice in the education of feminine self-restraint and containment of impulse. (130)

Bordo argues that the bases of this endorsement of bodily control goes far deeper than any one ad campaign or even series of campaigns. It goes to the heart of Western culture in which the body has been normalised as an unworthy partner for the mind from classical philosophy (Plato, Augustine) through to Cartesian dualism that 'provide instructions, rules, or models of how to gain control over the body, with the ultimate aim – for this is what their regimen finally boils down to – of learning to live without it' (145). The body and its appetites are there to be overcome. When in that same normalised philosophical tradition the female body is cast as 'the' body, is it any wonder then that women have felt the power to conform at a different level of intensity? Bordo, picking up on Mary Douglas's arguments at the body being inscribed with culture, extends those terms.

> The body may also operate as a metaphor for culture. From quarters as diverse as Plato and Hobbes to French feminist Luce Irigaray, an imagination of body morphology has provided a blueprint for diagnosis and/or vision of social and political life. The body is not only a *text* of culture. It is also, as anthropologist Pierre Bourdieu and philosopher Michel Foucault (among others) have argued, a *practical*, direct locus of social control. (165)

Not a free-floating signifier, not an infinitely malleable lump of matter, the body is a concrete expression of the struggles for social power. And those struggles for power enact a 'double bind' on the body, most particularly the female body. That double bind presents images and ideals of empowerment for women by which the women who strive for those ideals 'may find themselves as distracted, depressed, and physically ill as female bodies in the nineteenth century', when the ideal of femininity being promoted was (basically) helplessness (184). If success resides in self-control, and self-control is signified by an ability to deny oneself food, success can lead to death. Using Douglas again, Bordo asks us what it says about the social body if success is signified by the slim, hard (masculine) body of exercise regimes? Without being the least psychoanalytic about it, her answer is that it speaks of a particular anxiety around the body politic.

> Bulimia embodies the unstable double bind of consumer capitalism, while anorexia and obesity embody an attempted resolution of that double bind. Anorexia could thus be seen as an extreme development of the capacity for self-denial and repression of desire (the work ethic in absolute control); obesity, as an extreme capacity to capitulate to desire (consumerism in control). Both are rooted in the same consumer-culture construction of desire as overwhelming and overtaking the self. Given that construction, we can only respond either with total submission or rigid defense. (201)

The double bind is that at the same time as consumer culture promotes an ideal of self-denial, it simultaneously asks that the subject does precisely that, consume. But again, Bordo shows that women are not 'stupid' to fall in with these pressures, they are recognising that in the cultural milieu – or the field of play in Bordieu's terms – these are the rules for 'winning'. In patriarchy, '"male" body symbolism' is the means to success. In this it is quite different from Victorian self-denial and 'female slenderness, which symbolically emphasised reproductive femininity corseted under tight "external" constraints', but in both cases 'no body can escape either the imprint of culture or its gendered meanings' (212). This is a significant blind-spot in Butler's and Haraway's feminisms.

Bordo directly addresses this myopia by looking at several developments within postmodern streams of feminist argumentation around the body – the most important two being a concentration on including difference, and a subsequent textualisation of difference. Bordo is careful to point out the real worth of feminists addressing matters of difference, given that so much repression and subjection has been based on gender biases. Indeed, it is quite right that feminists should acknowledge that one woman's experience is not every woman's experience – 'race', class, ethnicity, age, etc. have concrete effects. One cannot generalise across all women in all things; our historical and cultural contexts vary enormously. What Bordo does object to is the (false) rationalisation that women therefore have no common experiences. She attributes this problem to the melding of feminism with particular forms of postmodern and poststructuralist thought, and asserts that the outcome has been a political paralysis that infects much postmodernism because such 'methodologism ... often implicitly (and mistakenly) supposes that the adoption of a "correct" theoretical approach makes it possible to *avoid* ethnocentrism' (217). As we saw in relation to Butler and Haraway, this is patently untrue. The second development, in which everything becomes text, is equally paralysing for living embodied subjects. Gender becomes just another binary opposition to be displaced.

> But this ideal, I argue, although it arises out of a critique of modernist epistemological pretensions to represent reality adequately by achieving what Thomas Nagel has called the 'view from nowhere', remains animated by its own fantasies of attaining an epistemological perspective free of the located-ness and limitations of embodied existence – a fantasy that I call a 'dream of everywhere'. (217-18)

As we have already seen, Bordo is far from ready to give up the located-ness of embodied existence. She is motivated by social and cultural complexity. We saw in relation to Butler and Haraway that the wave of European theory that hit American universities in the 1970s had a context. Bordo adds a layer to this temporal narrative of the drive to theoretical transcendence of embodiment by showing how it had a direct effect on the structural, not just the teaching, practices in universities in the States. In the first instance, the academic recognition that there were multiple versions of women's experience, when confronted by a proliferation of narratives and arguments that challenged dominant cultural views, led to a positive and productive degree of reflexivity on the part of universities and academics. This required more 'humility' from academics and led to a broadening of the syllabus – both positive things (220). Bordo's concern is that this has resulted in

> the conversion of this insight into *the* authoritative insight, and thence into a privileged critical framework, a 'neutral matrix' (to borrow Rorty's term) that legislates the appropriate terms of all intellectual efforts and is conceived as capable of determining who is going astray and who is on the right track. (222)

Bordo is right to see in this a deep conservatism and a potentially self-destructive outcome. She argues, instead, for a conscientious locatedness that takes responsibility for its arguments and political stands. Generalised hypotheses still have a place, and are 'dialogically valuable', particularly when they admit that they are generalised hypotheses (223). Bordo's concern was that feminists would argue themselves out of relevance, that by trying so hard not to avoid the appearance of being implicated in oppression, there was a greater danger of a tendency to 'an increasingly paralyzing anxiety over falling (from what grace?) into ethnocentrism or "essentialism"' (225). Bordo believes, instead, that there is no more a dream of everywhere than there ever was a view from nowhere.

[T]he spirit of epistemological *jouissance* suggested by the images of cyborg, Trickster, the metaphors of dance, and so forth obscures the located, limited, inescapably partial, and *always* personally invested nature of human 'story making'. This is not merely a theoretical point ... [poststructuralists and postmodernists] refuse to assume a shape for which they must take responsibility. (228)

Bordo goes so far as to contextualise these rejections of feminisms that do not reject gender on the basis that they are in some way 'biologistic' as being the outcome of a historical moment – and a specifically academic paranoia (242).

Bordo is never dismissive of what is useful in postmodern feminisms, however. She thoroughly approves of Butler's explanation of performativity as a heuristic device that is extremely valuable in unlocking people's use of cultural gestures to construct gender. Bordo also admires Butler's uncovering of the blatant heterosexism of Kristeva and Foucault's unthinking biologism. But Bordo does find fault in Butler's extending this into privileging language and textuality above embodiment and implicitly according 'linguistic foundationalism' the authority of 'demystifying and liberating Truth' that is 'immune from cultural suspicion and critique': 'I would argue, against this, that both naturalist and textualizing notions of the body are culturally situated (the latter in postmodern culture), and that both are thus equally amenable to being historically utilized as coercive instruments of power' (291).

Importantly, Bordo quite rightly picks up that in *Gender Trouble* Butler does not ever look at the body in drag in social context, at who is performing and who is reading the body. She also notes (as I pointed out in Chapter 5) that when Butler does try to do this in *Bodies that Matter*, she doesn't do so by going to people but by relying on a film-maker's constructed representation or abstraction, reading a film and the bodies within it as text. Further, Bordo suggests that drag – with its reliance on stereotypes – may be less destabilising of gender norms than gender ambiguity that rejects stereotypes (293). But Bordo is still careful, as we have seen before, to leave open the door for the real agency that Butler does propose, which comes about in and through 'subversion'. For Bordo, though, that 'subversion is contextual, historical, and, above, all, social' (294). Texts and textualised bodies, whether irruptive or conservative, are always socially located.

Failure to recognize this can result in theorizing potentially subversive but still highly culturally contained forms of subjectivity as though they were on an equal footing with historically dominant forms, romanticizing the degree of cultural challenge that is occurring, and thus diverting focus from continued patterns of exclusion, subordination, normalization. (295)

Historical, cultural and social context have to be taken into account or political paralysis – even conservatism – ensues.

The Male Body

While *Unbearable Weight* concentrates firmly on the female body, Bordo is not so blind as to believe that those same dominant signifiers and images don't have or haven't had a material effect on men's embodiment and given embodied men. Again, to stage her arguments she uses a very personal relation of the male body, basing her arguments in her own experiences: of coming into contact with male bodies in different ways at various stages in her life; her submission to the power of the male body as relayed via imagery over time; and, finally in her very particular relation to it in the changing form of her ageing father. The most personal contextualisation is that her father died during the writing of that book.

The arguments within *The Male Body: A New Look at Men in Public and Private* (1999) build and extend upon her arguments against ignoring the culturally embedded and socially situated power of gender. Where in *Unbearable Weight* she made the connection between the hardening of the female body as a response to masculine ideals of restraint and self-control, in *The Male Body* Bordo historicises those ideals within late-twentieth-century American culture and looks at the concomitant pressures on male bodies to conform to a shifting ideal. The other side of the arguments from dualism – that women *are* the body – is that men are properly mind-oriented and therefore *are not* their bodies. Men are supposed to be above their embodiment: 'They are not supposed to be slaves to sexual moods and needs, to physical and emotional dependency. They are supposed to think objectively' (19). This is no less of a double bind for men than it is for women because, obviously, men do have bodies and they are subject to 'the thousand natural shocks/That flesh is heir to'. They are expected to be 'thinking things' and yet, as Shakespeare often punned, they have wilful bodies.

My references to the seventeenth century are not innocent. Part of Bordo's point is that bodies are 'flesh and blood' but that they also have an 'evolutionary history', a historical context. From my own research it is clear that the way we conceptualise embodiment is extraordinarily different from the ways people lived their bodies in earlier times, particularly before rationalist dualism took hold (Cregan 1999, 2002). However, even at that time, when male and female bodies were conceived of as reflexive complements, gender differences functioned with all the power that medical science accords sexual difference today. It is a gross misrepresentation (and an anachronism) to claim a concordance between contemporary appeals to gender malleability and the gender ambiguities of an earlier time that were only ever played out on the male body. Bodies and behaviours were conceived differently in a social and historical context. Bordo makes a similar point, that 'sexual dimorphism' is more than just 'a piece of ideology' (40), it does have a material component.

Bordo spends a lot of time pondering what the penis actually means within Western culture, particularly in American culture, and the ways in which it has been used to signify masculinity, power and lack of power. In contemporary culture, men are constructed as 'hard'. While she does not say so directly, Bordo points to one reason why the penis and/or the phallus has becomes so deeply symbolic and significant. In Douglas's terms, it is a boundary crosser.

All animals, of course, are made of mostly soft stuff, requiring various kinds of protection ... Human flesh is particularly vulnerable, but the soft penis seems especially so, not, I think, because (like the testicles) it *is* more easily hurt than other parts of the body, but by virtue of contrast with its erect state. No other body part offers that contrast. (44)

More significantly, in a deeply embedded philosophical tradition that expects thought and control to reside in the male and passion and uncontrolled desire in the female, it is the part of the male body that makes clear that a man's passions are aroused. As Sartre would have it, desire undoes thought and drags consciousness into undeniable awareness of its embodiment, 'endows it with the weight of the body' (67).

This bodily 'weakness' is itself a historical and cultural construct, though. In Western history and in non-Western cultures the erect penis is a sign of power – procreative, political and social. As philosophical traditions raised the mind out of the body and relegated the body to base animalism, this imagery became abstracted, divested of power and the penis itself as symbolic of 'irrational desires'.

Thus notions of male superiority ceased being grounded in sexual potency, and began to be grounded in the superiority of the male intellect, rationality, mind – qualities that advertised not the superior virility of an individual male or the sexual generativity of the race but the divinely bestowed fitness of men to rule the earth. (90-1)

Bordo recognises but retreats from the symbolic status of the phallus in psychoanalysis however, precisely because it has so insistently been removed from the historical, cultural and social context of its origins. This is precisely the opposite of Bordo's intent, which is to re-situate men and the male body *as* embodied. There is a historical basis to Lacan's symbol of the power of language. No matter how abstract now, the power of the phallus is 'grounded in the bodily image of the erect penis and ideas humans have attached to *it*' (94). Masculine strength, therefore, is simultaneously situated within and outside of physical hardness.

Through a very personal understanding of the ways in which images of masculinity functioned in film through the 1950s to the 1990s – Bordo was fortunate to have parents who took her to any movie they attended, regardless of rating – she shows us how in the second half of the twentieth century, ideals of masculinity shifted towards this ideal. Through a retelling of her youthful remembrances, and of subsequent viewings, she traces post-World War II images of masculinity. In Spencer Tracy's portrayal of middle-aged, middle-class fatherhood in the early 1950s she finds a model of the 'domesticated good provider' (119) who falls by the wayside in the face of rebellious 'angry young men' portrayed by a younger generation of actors including Marlon Brando, James Dean and Montgomery Clift. These actors played characters who displayed '*need*, helplessness, dependency' that was at odds with other male ideals that privileged heroic action.

> Even with Kowalski [in *Streetcar Named Desire*] – as brutally heterosexual as they come – Brando was 'queering' masculinity in ways that James Dean and others would develop still further, and that have remained a constant undercurrent of macho masculinity. (112)

Bordo sees these (then) new images of masculinity as part of a refusal to conform to middle-class values. Certainly Bordo is not alone in seeing in the characters portrayed in these films, and in films like *The Man in the Gray Flannel Suit*, a post-war reaction to the domestic life that boxed men into suits and offices, and women into girdles and the confinement of home. Men too felt the constraints of the gender roles they were expected to conform to. Unfortunately, however, male flight from constraint was not without its effect on women. What became liberation from conformity for men also led to a more explicit and intense sexual objectification of women.

> At the same time, Hollywood became less and less interested in how women saw and experienced things – as 'subjects', as it were ... the films with which we most strongly identify the 'sexual revolution' of the sixties ... are all told from the perspective of men's crises, desires, development. (147)

Certainly Hugh Hefner's idea of male liberation from the bonds of middle-class America was entirely focused on the busty bodies of middle-class women. Bordo cites a rather remarkable interview with Hefner, where he insists that his Playmates should come from 'nice' homes – and most certainly not from a 'poor' background. Bordo's larger point, however, is that in being accorded the status of matinee idols, Brando and Dean brought a particular objectification of the male body into popular culture and a vulnerability of the male psyche to the fore.

When Bordo turns her attention towards how men's bodies have been portrayed more recently, in advertising, she finds that men are increasingly portrayed in ads for underwear or beachwear in positions that have previously rarely appeared on other than the female body. Again, in my own research on medical anatomy, it is rare indeed to find a male body that is in any way sexually suggestive. The few that do exist show men in positions taken from female anatomical illustrations that are highly sexually coded (Cregan 1999). Poses that are *de trop* on a female model become all the more obviously sexualised on a male body – whether for the heterosexual female or the homosexual male gaze. Shifts in cultural representations of embodiment affect men's and women's sexualised responses (177). And yet, there is still resistance here. These male bodies may be hard and buff but there is also a 'double bind' in these representations' imperative, depending on the product. Bordo argues that the men portrayed also convey a disregard for their objectification, that we should not believe that they care too much about the way they look. Vanity still belongs to the feminine realm.

> The man who cares about his looks the way a woman does, self-esteem on the line, ready to be shattered at the slightest insult or weight gain, is unmanly, sexually suspect. So the next time you see a Dockers or Haggar ad, think of it not only as an advertisement for khakis but also as an advertisement for a certain notion of what it means to be a man. (200)

Even so, in these ads is a recognition that men are just as subject to the influence of images of embodiment. The kinds of bodily self-control, self-regulation and readjustment that *Unbearable Weight* argues Western women internalise are no longer (if they ever were) solely their 'problem'.

> To imagine that they are is to view black, Asian, Latin, lesbian, and working-class women as outside the loop of the dominant culture and untouched by its messages about what is beautiful – a mistake that has left many women feeling abandoned and alone with a disorder they weren't 'supposed' to have. (216)

And the same is increasingly the case for men. They are becoming subject to eating disorders in greater numbers. Men also are heading to the plastic surgeon for eye-lifts, nose-jobs and pectoral implants.

Even though the pressure to 'buff up' has been there for a long time for men, it has become more intense, along with the pressure towards an extremely low fat-to-muscle ratio. Celebrities and movie stars are prey to these pressures as much as they promulgate them – as Bordo succinctly puts it, they are 'fully dressed even when naked' (225). She gives the example of John Travolta hardening his body between *Saturday Night Fever* and *Staying Alive* under the instructions of his body-building director, Sylvester Stallone. Travolta spent seven months honing his body in imitation of a statue of a discus thrower. In one way this is an imitation of the Greek ideal, but what was an ideal in a traditional culture becomes intensely abstracted under the pressure of late modernity.

> Consumer culture, unfortunately, can even grind playfulness into a commodity, a required item for this year's wardrobe. For all its idealization of the beauty of the body, Greek culture also understood that beauty could be 'inner'. (223)

Bordo is quick to admit that there is a racial content here too. Particularly in American culture, with its history of slavery, black male bodies have long been subjected to a discourse of animality. She gives a detailed reading of the Clarence Thomas/Anita Hill trial and the far greater cultural sensitivity accorded to Thomas – avoiding any suggestion that he was a black man ruled by his desires – than to Hill, who was judged by all the stereotypes of black female sexuality. But with respect to the meaning of clothing, 'sartorial sensuality and decorativeness, as I've learned, do not necessarily mean "femininity" for African-American men' (208). Adhering to older traditions of masculine beauty was a means of resistance during slavery that has survived. Indeed, notions of white masculinity have drawn on black masculinity (and continue to), in an appropriative, patronising and stereotype-concretising way. Bordo cites the notion of the 'noble savage' as it functioned in nineteenth-century European culture. 'Savages' had qualities that 'the European gentleman lacked and needed. ... it was a time when the prestige of older notions of manliness was eroding, since those notions revolved around qualities no longer very useful to success in a market-driven economy' (249). Being less of a refined gentleman and more of a competitive animal was considered advantageous to succeeding in the 'jungle' of that economy. Women are in a double bind, asked to be like men (competitive, hard) and yet not lose their femininity. Young men are in a double bind too, on the one hand expected to be compassionate and caring and on the other hand not lose that hard-edged, competitive aggressiveness.

Bordo argues for difference but does not privilege it above other social and cultural influences. Nor, while she is in favour of social and cultural explanations for the construction of masculinity and femininity, does she believe that we can ignore the material physical differences of male and female bodies – even if the ways in which they are received are influenced by culture: 'In my opinion, this goes way too far in the direction of an arrogant homocentrism (an old impulse in a new "linguistic" form) that lifts human beings out of the evolutionary picture entirely' (263). In short, she does not believe we can transcend the materiality of our bodies, even if we can recognise and analyse the ways which the reception of our material being is formed, and act to redress social and political inequities that flow on as a result.

Analysis

As I have already mentioned, there is little in what Bordo writes that takes into account anything outside Western heterosexual embodiment. She gestures towards the importance of all forms of difference and notes important points of difference when they arise, but she does not attempt to theorise embodiment in a way that speaks directly to the panoply of differences that now populate discourses on embodiment. Instead she presents herself as having a very particular relation to embodiment, which she consciously and conscientiously presents to her reader. She does, however, leave a space for others to 'fill in the gaps'. She writes about the dominance of ideals and constructed understandings because, as she says, they have influence over more than the population at which they are explicitly aimed. Why else would perfectly beautiful women in non-Western cultures who do not conform to a Western ideal strive towards that chimera?

As such, Bordo's arguments still have political and social weight for cultures that are not Western because they analyse the mechanisms behind hegemonic representations that are being promulgated across cultures in an increasingly globalising world. This is in contrast to the theories of embodiment in our parallel stream (Chapter 6), where difference is implicitly absorbed and colonised. To claim that we are all cyborgs, or that performativity will allow all forms of embodiment to be liberated, is to wipe out social and cultural embodied differences. In consciously positioning herself, Bordo avoids what is a contradictory impulse in postmodern theories: they claim to avoid being universalising by naming differences and yet simultaneously they flatten out difference until it becomes meaningless and politically paralysed.

In relation to *The Male Body*, it would be easy and quite possibly founded to criticise Bordo on the grounds that her feminism has softened and that she has become an apologist for patriarchy, but it would also be simplistic. In elaborating on the ways in which the male body is just as much at the behest of those increasingly global images, she is taking from Bourdieu and Foucault their greatest strengths and extending it into the one area where they are weakest, the predicament of women. In Bourdieu's terms, no one has control over the power invested in the fields of play. We all contribute to that power and we are all influenced by it, though some have greater flexibility and more agency when it comes to manipulating the rules. From Foucault's perspective, power is diffuse. Though there are undoubtedly gender biases in who is and is not an 'authority of delimitation' or who has control over a discourse, those authorities are not immune from the discourse nor are they untouched by other competing discourses. Bordo offers us an understanding of gendered embodiment in a postmodern culture but one that reveals the potentially productive tensions between the social formations I reintroduced at the beginning of this chapter. If my criticisms of Bordo are less searching than they have been with regard to other writers, it is because her approach is commensurate with arguing from constitutive abstraction.

Cognate Writers

Without attempting to cover the wide range of perspectives on embodiment that take a similarly culturally and socially textured approach, I shall close this chapter with an extremely brief sample of other ways of analysing lived embodied being. There simply is not space to reflect on the preponderance of work that is related to the explosion of categories of bodily difference and the sociological studies devoted to them. Here again, I would direct the reader to the work of Shilling, Turner, Hepworth, Featherstone, Williams and Bendelow, Shakespeare, Synnott and the journal *Body & Society* for the range of sociological and anthropological approaches to embodiment that can be found. There are many areas of study I could sample – ageing, dying, sporty, musical, consuming bodies – but I will take only a few examples to make my point. I include Sander Gilman for his work on aesthetics and surgery, Wendy Seymour for her work on disability, and Emily Martin for her work on women and reproduction.

In *Making the Body Beautiful: A Cultural History of Aesthetic Surgery* (1999), Sander Gilman traces the origins of surgical body modification performed for cultural not medical reasons. Surgery for appearances's sake has been attempted since at least the late-sixteenth century, when the first instructions appeared for the reconstructive repair of war-wounds.

Another early form of aesthetic surgery included the reconstruction of decayed, syphilitic noses. The desire to try and conform to socially approved ideals of attractiveness and acceptability hardly needs stating, but Gilman extends his study into the power of dominant cultural norms on bodily attractiveness as they have affected individuals and groups. In this, he shows in careful detail how nose shape has been central to the racial and racist definition of peoples. As a consequence, rhinoplasty (a 'nose-job') has been inseparable from the social and cultural power dynamics that have supported the oppression of those whose noses do not conform to that ideal – in short the Irish and Jews. Jewish men and women have undergone rhinoplasty to 'pass' in a world where norms of beauty and acceptability specifically exclude them. While this provides Gilman with a clear example of the power of culturally and socially embedded norms to be internalised and acted upon, he also extends this to the pressure women have felt to reshape their breasts to meet ideals of beauty (whether by augmentation or reduction) and even into early attempts at what is now known as gender reassignment. In each of these examples, and in his discussion of the desire to avoid signs of ageing, his point is to uncover the strength of the imperative to reshape the body to conform to dominant ideas of embodiment: those who are excluded are driven to reshape themselves in order to attempt to 'pass'.

In looking at Wendy Seymour's *Remaking the Body: Rehabilitation and Change* (1998), I take it as an example of the explosion in disability studies that began in the early 1990s. Physical disability can come about for a great number of reasons, congenital or acquired, and Seymour looks to the latter through an ethnographic study of people with varying degrees of spinal cord injury. Studies of disability such as Seymour's or Tom Shakespeare's show us that radically liberatory narratives of embodiment are not able to account for the material reality that some forms of embodiment are simply not a matter of choice. Indeed, Seymour shows us that normalising ideals that are promoted in sporty or competitive models of rehabilitation can be as counter-productive to people accommodating the irreversible changes that have taken place in their embodiment. People with spinal cord injury are at once more conscious of their embodiment because their bodies no longer respond as they once did, and at the same time are more abstracted from their bodies in their experience of paralysis. And yet, Seymour's account of people's lives – their moments of refusal and acceptance – is deeply inspiring. People in wheelchairs or those permanently attached to catheters or colostomy bags *are* cyborgs: and, while many of them live full and happy lives, theirs is no liberatory ephemeral ideal.

Emily Martin similarly charts a historical trajectory of the female body and its relation to reproduction in *The Woman in the Body: A Cultural Analysis of Reproduction* (1992). Like Sarah Franklin, who was mentioned at the close of Chapter 6, Martin is an anthropologist of Western science. Unlike Franklin, one is left in no doubt that Martin has an opinion about the political impact of medical and scientific discourses to dissociate women from their own bodies. Her ethnography reveals the racism and classism inherent in mainstream medical discourse, the subjection that women feel within labour wards, and the different ways the metaphors of medical power are felt by women who are not white and middle-class. She also gives weight to women's own explanations and experiences of being embodied, the specificities of being female that are not and cannot be experienced by embodied males. And, in contrast to several of the writers in the last chapter who also write around female embodiment and reproduction, although she tracks the abstraction of women from their own embodiment, she concentrates on the moments in female reproduction in which one cannot help but know that one *is* a body not just that one *has* a body: menstruation, birth, menopause. In placing so much emphasis on assisted conception, those other writers contribute to the intensification of the abstraction of embodiment by eliding the experience of reproduction of the vast majority of women. Even though they are right that ultrasound and innumerable forms of intervention into pregnancy and labour distance women from their own bodies, they underplay the visceral 'here-ness' of vaginal birthing, something which Martin and writers like her bring to the fore.

The intensification of the abstraction of embodiment through the power of biomedical technologies becomes most obvious and most potent in the moments of human mortality. It has arisen in different ways throughout this book, in relation to both birth and death. And in turning to my conclusion, I do so with these themes firmly in mind.

Conclusion

I began this book by outlining the argument that the abstraction of embodiment is part of a wider complex of abstraction that operates at multiple levels within and across social formations. Embodiment is experienced differently across history, across social formations and across cultures. As the dominance of a social formation shifts over time, the quality and understanding of embodiment shift as well, though never evenly or uniformly. Through the close reading of the arguments of the authors dealt with in this book, we can see in their work the plotting of some of those shifts. We can also see evidence of how the body has been viewed within given cultures and how those views correspond with four types of social formation: tribal, traditional, modern and postmodern. Further, by taking a range of theorists whose personal chronologies span the twentieth century – and the shift from modernity to postmodernity – we can also discern in the ways they express their arguments and formulate their theories the effects of the social formations in which these writers are themselves immersed.

Traditional to Modern Bodies

Most of the writers of Part I deal with the body within the history of Western European culture and thereby show us how embodiment has shifted in meaning between traditional and modern social formations across a group of historically interrelated cultures. Dualism – an intensification in the abstraction of the body – is the fulcrum upon which that shift turns. To expand, as we saw in Chapter 1, Elias plots a shift in the perception and construction of embodiment over a period spanning approximately 600 years, through the evolution in social techniques of bodily control (manners). Using the writings of Erasmus as empirical evidence, Elias describes the abstraction of embodiment through behaviour and manners – outwardly stated, pedagogically purveyed rules on social management and self-control. In doing so, he shows the effects on the body of the slow and uneven movement from traditional to modern societies in Western Europe. Elias's preoccupation with manners is in some measure at least shaped by a close knowledge of the social impact of the Great War and the subsequent social unease that forced him to flee to England, which is barely implicit in his long discursion on the formalisation of ideas of culture and civilisation in his homeland.

Ariès writes of a similar period and uncovers the same shift but through a different medium of bodily understanding. He describes another process of the abstraction of embodiment, through the gradual partition of the progress through life into a series of increasingly demarcated life-stages, and in particular the invention of childhood as a separate category of embodied being. In different ways, both Elias and Ariès showed in their later work that the fundamentally embodied experience of death, and the way both individuals and societies mark it, has also become increasingly abstracted across time, from traditional to modern to late-modern societies. Foucault describes in detail the abstraction of embodiment consequent to the slow acceptance of dualism – a quintessentially 'modern' concept – and shows in detail the multiple ways in which that took effect across time and across epistemes (Chapter 2). He too looks to bodily self-control as the mechanism by which this is effected through a range of 'authorised' mechanisms – medical, judicial, religious, psychological, etc. – that cut across classes. These mechanisms of diffuse power, unlike Elias's courtesy manuals and Ariès's educational tracts, don't work through stated rules but via slow-moving, implicit acceptance of the validity of knowledge systems and the internalistion of their regimens. In this, even though what he describes so effectively is the shift to modernity, like Elias's implicit preoccupation with the rise of fascism, Foucault's approach is shaped by the effects of the late modernity of which he was a part, and the general rejection of 'the Establishment' that exploded in the academies in which he worked in the 1960s.

Tribal and Modern Bodies

Bourdieu, by contrast, does not deal with history. He writes in a present moment, even if we can now look to his work and see detailed snapshots that capture tribal and late-modern societies in all their messy 'reality'.

He describes the abstraction of embodiment through the detailed tracking of social facts and the social regulation of selves, using his theorisations of *habitus*, hexis and 'fields of play' (Chapter 3). Amongst the Kabyle he shows the complex embodied relations in a tribal community, and in his study of the residents of 1960s Paris he gives us a 'slice' of the experience of embodiment across social classes in a particular expression of modernity. In doing so, he doesn't uncover a shift, but he does give us a comparison of two social formations that elucidate different levels of embodied abstraction between the tribal and the modern.

Similarly, Mary Douglas (Chapter 4) shows how a range of tribal groups experience their bodies, their bodily fluids and their bodily habits. Further, she gives many examples that in their expression differ from Western bodily norms, and yet finds in both tribal and modern societies correspondences in the power vested in bodies that cross borders and boundaries. The bodily preoccupations of a range of tribal peoples is explicitly contrasted with experiences of the kinship groups in 1960s London (the Bog Irish), who still retain vestiges of traditional social customs even though they live in the thick of modern industrialised urban communities. We have seen that Douglas conflates the very important differences between these groups herself, but her work shows how bodily boundary-crossing can be understood as another pivotal point upon which embodied abstraction turns, whether in tribal or modern (and by extension traditional or postmodern) social formations.

Modern to Postmodern Bodies

The remaining writers I have dealt with in detail either experienced the influx of poststructuralism, or had it as their formational experience, within their academic careers. As such, we can see in their work a rejection of modernist assumptions about and stereotypes of embodiment, and an embracing of indeterminacy, plurality and difference. When we come to the writers who were the concern of Chapters 5, 6 and 7, we enter into a 'history of the present'. Each of them has learned from Foucault and each in their way is trying to explain a shift – from modernity to late- or postmodernity – from the inside. As I noted towards the end of Chapter 7, whether this is in fact an epistemic shift only the benefit of hindsight will show. However, what is clear is that in foregrounding their allegiance to, or distance from, postmodern theory, they are in fact active participants in the 'invention' of postmodern embodiment. In Chapters 5, 6 and 7 the connection between the social formation and the level of abstract theorisation is much more explicit and I spent a good deal of time detailing the poststructuralist and postmodern theorisations of embodiment therein. Consequently there is less need to rehearse the fractured and in some cases intensely abstracted postmodern embodiment that results: from the work of Butler, in her writing on performativity; from Kristeva, in her evocation of abjection; from Haraway, in her formulation of transcendent cyborgs; and, from Bordo's finely textured studies of the social construction of gender.

I have been using each of the moments of abstraction from these writers to build an idea of the history of bodily abstraction, not just in sociology and anthropology but in theory in general to the moment. I want to use that as a platform to argue that as a group they do open the way to understanding the changing nature of embodiment across time and space, that each of the theorists has something to offer, but what each of them offers us is not enough on its own. I want to conclude the book by taking a brief case study to both 'flesh out' and challenge the theories we have looked at, through the effect on embodiment of embryonic stem cell technology. It offers a complex case for future directions on understanding embodiment. I shall use these writers' work as a departure point for looking at embodiment in all its temporal and spatial complexity. I would argue that it is imperative we find ways to accommodate instead of flattening out what already exists, even if in tension: different understandings of embodiment within and across social formations.

Abstracted Embodiment in Global Context

In Chapter 6 we saw that several writers see great potential in reproductive technologies for the future of embodiment and the future of social formations. For them, it variously offers a more open notion of kinship, that escapes middle-class, heterosexist norms; a way out of being confined to ideas of womanhood that are ingrained with ideas of stereotypical associations with feminine nature and inevitable motherhood; and, a productive metaphor for re-imagining embodiment. Even if we accept the defence that this is not meant to imply a total transcendence of the limits of embodied matter – if not embodiment itself – I have already stated my reservations with regard to the cultural specificity of such arguments. I want to use the following case study to bring out how that construction of modern/postmodern embodiment takes part in a broader globalisation of that (technoscientific) understanding of embodiment, which is in active tension with and in the process of overlaying those of other social formations. Further, in the face of this intense abstraction of social relations and the technologies of human embodiment, the writings of the authors canvassed throughout this book either become empirically descriptive or are left behind. For example, Bourdieu's approach, with its emphasis on 'interest', no longer has sufficient purchase on the radical restructuring of the whole nature of bodily hexis, even if we can clearly see that some of the scientists are involved in processes of cultural capital accumulation. And while they could do so accurately, the approaches of Elias and Ariès are rendered impotent, able only to account for these processes by describing how they are yet another step in the medical rationalisation of life and death.

In the developed world, seemingly daily there is a new medical proposal that pushes these technologies past their initial application – a means to enable infertile women to conceive in an era when adoption was becoming increasingly rare – and further into the realms of 'choice'. The benign appellation 'assisted reproduction' makes claims to a benevolence and altruism that is frequently constrained (and devoid of reciprocity) in the application of these technologies. This is particularly so when feel-good terminology masks the prevention of bringing into being certain 'classes' of humans (through pre-implantation diagnostic screening), or the exploitation of certain groups of women. However, I want to take the last of the three positive claims outlined above – that reproductive technologies offer a way of reconceiving embodiment as a whole – and look a little more closely at how one reproductive technology, embryonic stem cell technology, is both affecting understandings of embodiment and how that may play out in practice beyond the cultures of the developed (Western) world.

Recent events at the United Nations in New York suggest that ethicist Donna Dickenson's (2002) concerns were well-founded, that women in undeveloped countries are in danger of exploitation as 'egg-farms' to supply therapeutic cloning research for the treatment of the diseases of the developed world. There is a strong possibility that embryonic stem cell technology will create a global and potentially lucrative market in human ova. Even without addressing either the basic ethics of the technology or the overstated claims of its prospective benefits (Cregan and James 2002), this is an unpalatable prospect. As Elias and Ariès would recognise, it entails the rationalisation and commodification of embodiment, in both the developed and the undeveloped world.

On 2 June 2004 scientists and lobbyists from around the world organised a 'conference' in New York on 'Human Cloning Issues in All Its Aspects for the United Nations' and made representations to delegates at the General Assembly defending therapeutic cloning. They did so because on 9 December 2003 the Sixth (Legal) Committee of the UN deliberated on what has become known as the 'Costa Rican Proposal'. This proposal sought to ban all forms of cloning. Further debate and voting were deferred until October 2004, when deliberations were again deferred until 18 February 2005, at which time the Committee voted to recommend a worldwide ban of both reproductive and therapeutic cloning. The vote was 71 in favour of the ban, 35 against, with 43 abstentions. The majority of the abstentions were from Muslim countries who made it clear through their spokesperson (the Turkish delegate) that they would not vote on a motion for which there was no broad consensus. This was after strong lobbying of Muslim states, at a conference in Cairo hosted by the WHO and supported by UNESCO, to endorse therapeutic cloning. A series of delegates, all of whom represented countries that have substantial research and development underway in the technology – including the UK, South Korea, China, Belgium, Singapore and Japan – rounded out the session by affirming their vote in the negative, insisting on the non-binding nature of the declaration (A/C.6/59/L.27) and stating their intention to pursue therapeutic cloning research under the guidance of the ethics bodies and laws of each of their sovereign states. They did so on the grounds of plurality: cultural, ethical and religious difference.

We can see in the statements made by the delegates the conscious deployment of arguments from cultural relativism that poststructuralist, postcolonial and postmodern theorists like Butler and Haraway (quite rightly) propound. However, there is something slightly odd in arguing from cultural relativism – a strategy usually employed to support the claims of marginalised groups – to support what is a dominant mode of production: technoscience. Our purpose here, however, is to look at the material affects of those countries' pursuit of this technology on embodiment across social formations. To that end I will first explain in some detail the issues at stake in the declaration before offering a broader analysis of the impact on embodiment. While much of the reporting of the debate has cast it in terms of an opposition between science and religion – reason and faith – I shall concentrate instead on the potential social effects that are based in a cross-cultural and social ethical critique.

This 'conference' on human cloning had been organised in an attempt to sway opinion amongst UN delegates to ban reproductive cloning but allow therapeutic cloning. To take three examples of the current practice in regard to therapeutic cloning, the UK allows therapeutic cloning under licence within their laws and under local ethical guidelines; in Australia there was a two-year moratorium after which donated 'excess' IVF embryos could be used for research; and, in the USA lucrative federal funding cannot be expended on it but private funding can be used to support it wherever state law allows. Why then should these scientists and lobbyists be so concerned about the UN's deliberations, when most of them come from countries that one would think could easily decline to abide by such a declaration? Indeed, as they formalised their dissenting votes and expressed their 'regret' at the vote against therapeutic cloning, those with the most to lose made clear that in a pluralistic world where each country should be able to pursue such research as they see fit, they would continue with their research. Certainly, had the declaration been a treaty, as originally proposed, a ban would have complicated privately funded research if the US had been a signatory – a highly likely outcome under President Bush – but then that research could simply have gone 'offshore' as much contentious research already does. The most likely answer appears (ironically) to be twinned: funding and access to eggs. A brief explanation of the processes involved helps to clarify why neither one of these answers can be taken on its own.

Undifferentiated human embryonic stem cells were successfully isolated in 1998, taking the first step in the control of life-formation. For the following two years, researchers were busily employed trying to culture significant banks of the cells and to control the restarting of the developmental process. This is part of the second step necessary for therapeutic practice: being able to control the forming of specific cell types (nerve, muscle, blood). Mary Douglas could indeed describe embryonic stem cells as boundary-crossing human matter – both sacred and dangerous – for they are the basic building blocks of the human body, which at this early stage of development have the potential to differentiate into any cell type. Some of the embryonic stem cell researchers around the world have had a measure of success in differentiating cells in *some* of their lines. However, despite repeated positive claims in the media that often conflate the outcomes of adult and embryonic stem cell research, there are many steps before this biotechnology could even possibly be applicable in practice, and many question marks over whether any of it will ever be useful in direct therapeutic applications.

Having been grown on mouse tissue, virtually all the current cell lines in the world are unsuitable for implantation. Their potential for rejection in a person's body is no different from a whole organ xenotransplant (animal-to-human transplant). This also implies the further concerns of any xenotransplant: namely, that it may introduce cross-species diseases into recipients. Further, even if embryonic stem cells are successfully mass grown on human foetal or fallopian tissue – as has been claimed to have been done in Singapore (*Far Eastern Economic Review*, 15 November 2001) – they would induce rejection, even with close tissue-typing, like any human-to-human transplant.

One possible further leap that is currently proposed as a way of overcoming that particular hurdle is therapeutic cloning. Despite the humanitarian reclassification of its name and purpose, this is human cloning, pure and simple – a fact that has led many researchers to now prefer to call the process 'somatic cell nuclear transfer' to avoid any association with cloning. However, the only difference is that it does not progress to implanting the cells into the uterus of a human female, and therefore stops short of forming a cloned foetus. Therapeutic cloning involves removing the nucleus of an egg, fusing the nucleus of a somatic (body) cell from a person requiring treatment with the enucleated egg, and restarting the resulting embryo along its developmental process. Once the cloned embryo has developed to a stage at which stem cells could be removed, embryonic stem cells would be 'harvested' from it and differentiated to form the specific tissue required: supposedly, pancreatic cells for diabetes, nerve cells for Parkinson's, heart cells for cardiac disease. The problems inherent, even in medical theory, are serious – the possibility of the implanted cells spontaneously mutating and forming tumours being just one issue – and as debate around the world has shown, the ethics are fraught. Indeed, the debates polarise around religious and utilitarian arguments, at both ends of which we can see Kristeva's notion of the abject – human matter that is revered and reviled.

To be used as a direct therapy, therapeutic cloning would require massive harvesting of human eggs, raising the question of who would be most likely to donate and why. Poor women, quite possibly from countries with less stringent (or no) legal prohibition against such exploitation, would be the most likely candidates (Dickenson 2002). As even Haraway would recognise (as she did in relation to the bottle-feeding of infants in undeveloped countries), on an immediate, pragmatic level therapeutic cloning could lead to the rank commercialisation and exploitation of women, most probably poor women from undeveloped countries, to provide the raw materials for the treatment of diseases of the developed world. It could lead to a global trade in human eggs. This was one of the strongest arguments used in favour of banning in the debates at the UN.

Indeed, these processes are already subject to international interests and globalising influences. Researchers around the world want access to American dollars from the lucrative National Institute of Health funds, and to enhance their chances of doing so, they tailor their research to the standards that the NIH has set. International research partnerships can motivate researchers to lend their support in lobbying each other's governments when regulatory legislation is proposed – or in this case the UN. There is the impetus of ensuring that research is not hindered, and (seemingly) contradictorily concerns, expressed as feigned nationalism, that if this technology is not allowed to proceed unfettered, we will somehow lose our 'competitive edge' or 'market advantage', and that research will go offshore. Complex patent licensing agreements between international research partners rule the distribution of the financial outcomes of this research far more than regional legislation. This biotechnology is thus part of a global-economic rationalising of life.

Partly in reaction to the unpalatable nature of these possibilities, and to the practical problem of 'harvesting' what would have to amount to millions of eggs to treat the most commonly invoked diseases like Parkinson's, a further possibility has been raised: fusing the nucleus of an adult cell with an enucleated undifferentiated embryonic stem cell (*The Australian*, 8 June 2002, p. 3). That is, reversing the adult cell from its stable state of development and restarting it again as a stem cell of the tissue that the client desired. This, supposedly, overcomes the ethical and practical problems of using donor eggs, and coincidentally would not be covered by any legislation banning therapeutic cloning. Here we run up against a problem that is inherent in all the possibilities we have outlined so far. Whether in an enucleated embryonic stem cell or an enucleated donor egg, not all the DNA in the cell is removed. Mitochondria, the 'energy packs' in every cell, carry DNA. Even if the DNA from the cell of the person who is ill is compatible, as has been pointed out,[1] the mitochondrial DNA of the embryonic stem cells, or the donor egg into which it is introduced, will most likely produce a rejection problem in itself. Finally, it seems that fusion technology would still be dependent at least to some degree on research into the molecular biology of therapeutic cloning to be successful.

And we know very well, with the pressure to recoup research and development funding, those in the poorer sections of the developed world and the vast majority of those in the undeveloped world will not have access to any of this technology, if it ever finds a viable application. A long history of pharmaceutical conglomerates withholding generic therapies and dumping unsafe drugs on third world markets has taught us that much.

So who were the lobbyists assembled in New York to ensure the banning of reproductive cloning and avert a worldwide ban on therapeutic cloning? The leading scientists included the creator of Dolly, Ian Wilmut of the Roslin Institute, the now disgraced Dr Woo Suk Hwang of Seoul

National University who claimed he had 'created' the first documented therapeutic clone, and Prof. Alan Trounson of Monash University, who derived one of the earliest embryonic stem cell lines with colleagues at the National University of Singapore, including Prof. Ariff Bongso. This 'conference' was co-sponsored by the UN Asian Group of Legal Experts Meeting and organised by the Genetics Policy Institute. According to their press release, the Genetics Policy Institute is

> a nonprofit organization dedicated to preventing human reproductive cloning and advocating the responsible use of therapeutic cloning research. We encourage funding and support for stem cell research and sponsor international projects and educational programs relating to the law and regulation of reproductive cloning, therapeutic cloning (SCNT) and stem cell research. GPI serves as a gateway to the public, media and key decision-makers regarding those issues. GPI is a sponsored project of the National Heritage Foundation, a federally recognized 501(c)(3) non-profit, tax-exempt organization. (www.eurekalert.org/pub_releases/2004-05/dnl-lcf051104.php).

In other words, it is a lobby group in favour of embryonic stem cell technology research. Further, this conference was 'endorsed' by medical research institutes with vested interests and well-known individuals hoping to have their personal suffering relieved by the products of such research, including the late Christopher Reeve. Not so much a 'grass-roots' initiative as Astroturf. Not surprisingly these same lobbyists, using just the kinds of publicity and marketing tactics that Bordo has shown are at work in the cultural production of body image, have been prominent in debates on embryonic stem cell research and therapeutic cloning in the UK, Australia and the USA, with variable success.

One can begin to see why the possibility of global sanctions on therapeutic cloning becomes important. Research is global. It currently flourishes in the gaps between national legislation. Any international ban that might attract sanctions would threaten that. With respect to access to eggs, even if countries decline to observe the declaration, their ability to work within those legal gaps and access the eggs from women in undeveloped countries could be severely restricted if the USA chose to use the power of its trade and aid. Which is why I say that Donna Dickenson's concerns were well-founded: this round of lobbying at the UN was at least in part motivated by a desire to leave open the possibility of researchers gaining access to women's ova across and around the world. Evidence from interviews suggests that there is a history of researchers carrying embryonic material across national borders and through customs in their suitcases. In other words, human material extracted and developed under one legal regime was being transferred to the West, where the legal restrictions were clearer. What we are seeing now is a coming out, as it were, a direct argument for globalising the movement of abstracted human body parts.

To go ahead with therapeutic cloning for direct clinical applications a massive pool of eggs would be required. Many developed countries that are inclined to ban human cloning, but leave open the possibility of therapeutic cloning, would be highly unlikely to be able to service the need for eggs from those that are surplus to IVF treatments in their own countries. Which leaves us with the question, where would the eggs come from? People already sell their eggs in the US for surrogacy or IVF. Though this may not be the means which Butler may herself favour, these are the conditions of possibility by which a rewriting of the normative nuclear family are already underway. However, these are not the eggs that scientists will want to buy, they would be far too costly for the numbers required. Therapeutic cloning, even if only to facilitate further research into 'fusion', would need a steady supply of cheap eggs. Women in developing countries well-provided with IVF clinics and trained staff – China and Romania spring to mind – seem a logical source of 'donors'. The prospective practical effects on those women would appear to be little different from those on the poor of the developing world who are drawn into selling their kidneys. There are comparable health risks, that poor people are far less likely to be able to cope with – after-effects that in a well-nourished, healthy woman are bad enough but would be massively stressful on an undernourished poor woman. It involves intrusive procedures to 'harvest' the eggs and having to be injected daily in order to hyper-ovulate for that purpose. Given that the AIDS crises in both Africa and China have shown there is little hope of ensuring the non-reuse of needles in situations of poverty, it seems inevitable that there could also be a whole raft of possible flow-on problems. Women would be likely to undergo procedures they do not need, that are of transient benefit to them at best, to satisfy the desires and diseases of the developed world.

Within this brief discussion of the potential effects of one reproductive technology that may or may not become a major therapy in time, we begin to see ways of applying each of the theories or approaches canvassed in this book. Between the postmodern medical epistemic approach to embodiment and in religious arguments against cloning from the 'sanctity of life' – a highly contentious source of opposition that informed the UN debates – we see a view of embodiment that is still informed by the vestiges of a traditional understanding of being, one informed by religious dogma that have shifted only marginally since early modern times. This is the same kind of tension we saw in Mary Douglas's work on the

Bog Irish – where the symbolic meaning of eating fish on Friday persists, even when the Church no longer insists on it. We see an extension of the kinds of power dynamics that Emily Martin found in obstetrics wards. In the whole narrative we see the practical effects at a global level of the technologies in which Donna Haraway finds such transcendent possibilities. If we look to the historical and cultural antecedents to the medico-technical approach to the human body implicit in this narrative, in the spirit of our first three authors – Elias, Ariès but most appropriately Foucault – we will see both the culmination of a long, slow series of shifts in medical theory and also a tension between understandings of embodiment informed by different social formations. In the concentration on the particularised human matter at stake, we can see a bearing out of Elias's concerns in his later work on the dying, that bodily organs are increasingly seen as capable of functioning autonomously, or at least as replaceable, interchangeable items. Foucault could give a detailed description of the institutionalised control of the discursive construction of embryonic stem cells within the rhetoric of the scientists who work upon them. I want to take things a little further, however, and set this understanding of embodiment within a global, temporal and spatial matrix of abstracted embodiment.

The process of medically abstracting the body is not a new phenomenon, and in a crucial sense it was a logical correlate of developing what we now call 'medical knowledge'. Even going back to period of Hippocrates and to the ancient Egyptians, it is possible to generalise that this involved three intersecting processes: first, recording and later systematising patterns of symptoms and responses (codifying the body); second, cutting into, dismembering and later mechanically peering into actual bodies (anatomising the body); and third, rendering images of body parts and body systems in a way that made social and technical sense of them (imaging the body). However, it was not until late modernity that the processes of codifying, anatomising and imaging the body came together as a rationalised system that completely dominated medical knowledge.

Across history it is possible to identify a number of shifts in this three-fold process. The rationalising systems of 'medical knowledge' have metamorphosed from traditional natural philosophies, into the early-modern natural sciences, into the late-modern technologies of the body. Visual perception and representation, whether trusted or reviled, have been central to each of these paradigms of enquiry. Natural philosophies prioritised philosophical heritage over the evidence of the 'fallible senses'; natural sciences reversed that balance with empirical observation and deductive reasoning taking precedence over 'disputable dogma'. With the rise of technoscience the empirical observations of the scientist are rapidly losing ground to a reliance on technological infallibility. Machines that observe more perfectly in ghostly images are replacing the 'ghost in the machine'. Technological developments in the twentieth century, beginning with the x-ray, created diagnostic images of internal structures and processes from the living body. These examples culminate and converge in the technology of cyber-surgery, bringing together our threefold and intersecting process of medical abstraction. The cyber-surgeon, trained in *codified* knowledge, sits cocooned within a video console reminiscent of a flight simulator, physically separated from the *anatomised* patient-body that is surrounded by robotic arms fed by human assistants. The surgeon armed with the *imaged* foreknowledge afforded him or her by ultrasound or MRI, concentrates on magnified digitalised representations of the patient-body relayed from a video-microscope as s/he operates by remote control. The creation of embryonic stem cells is similarly abstracted. We lose sight of the woman undergoing IVF, the repeated intrusion into her body – see Susan Bordo on the eliding of women's personhood – and also of the wider social consequences.

As technological systems become more sophisticated, physical systems become devalued and distrusted. With the increasing technologisation of medicine, doctors have been overriding the learning and honing of their powers of deduction in favour of the diagnostic capacities of machines. Take pregnancy and childbirth as an example: in the eighteenth century pregnancy 'was a period of uncertainty that would not become a fact until the woman had given birth to a child'.[2] The physical experience of 'quickening', at around five months, was the predominant marker of 'being with child'. And the possibility that neither would survive the 'grim lottery of the child-bed' was an acknowledged fact. Today, amniocentesis, ultrasound, induction, caesarian section, epidural anaesthesia, forceps delivery, episiotomy, foetal monitoring – which were until relatively recently emergency interventions – have all become, more or less, part of the 'normal' pregnancy and birthing experience in the West. Foetal paediatrics, and its partner discipline, foetal surgery, have emerged as new specialities. Drug-free or low-dose labour, midwife controlled and/or home-births are considered 'dangerous' by most doctors or, at best, lifestyle options. The natural and biological have become pathological. At its most extreme, IVF, the bulk of which is performed on and in the female body, can be proposed as the best remedy to male infertility; or the ultimate in reproductive empowerment for women.

But which women, and what does it mean for reconstituting the nature of human embodiment? Therapeutic cloning – treating human embryos as abstracted disembodied matter – is inextricable from the processes of IVF. It has arisen as a direct result of the research into assisted reproduction and it will depend on exactly the same techniques of hyper-ovulation, egg extraction and in vitro fertilisation. In this medical technology we can see the shift that Butler and Haraway argue for, a postmodern body that is capable of being re-visioned outside and beyond earlier forms of embodiment. But more importantly, in a spirit more in sympathy with Bordo, we see in its reliance on a global trade in body matter a concrete example of the inapplicability of such arguments outside the culture with the power of signification. The needs, wants and desires of postmodern social formations are satisfied: and it is the tribal, traditional or modern body that is the most likely to supply the raw materials.

In taking so much on trust in technoscience, theorists of the postmodern body like Donna Haraway may not lose sight of, but radically underestimate the social consequences and the speed of, technoscientific advances. In doing so, they may minimise the potential social effects of technologies for those who are not members of the dominant social formations who hold controlling interests in them. The cyborg has much to say that is valid in relation to dominant Western cultures, but it is a universalising creature that has the potential to embed social exclusion and intercultural exploitation. If, instead, we take what is useful from each of the writers covered throughout this book and appreciate how they deal with specific instances of what is a much greater interplay of ways of understanding embodied being, we have a way of beginning to appreciate the body in all its social complexities, across time, across space and across social formations.[3]

Notes

1 Dr Perry Bartlett, Head of Development and Neurobiology, Walter and Eliza Hall Institute of Medical Research confirmed this was most likely the case when asked by Nicolas Tonti-Filippini in question time at 'Cloning and Embryonic Stem Cell Research: Does Australia need a Moratorium?', Dean's Lecture Series, University of Melbourne, 26 July 2002.

2 Barbara Duden (1999: 16).

3 This will be the subject of my next book, to be co-authored with Paul James.

References

Ariès, Phillipe. (1962) *Centuries of Childhood: A Social History of Family Life*. Tr. Robert Baldick. New York: Alfred A. Knopf.

—— (1974) *Western Attitudes to Death from the Middle Ages to the Present*. Baltimore: Johns Hopkins University Press.

—— (1981) *The Hour of Our Death*. Tr. H. Weaver. London: Allen Lane.

—— (1985) *Images of Man and Death*. Tr. J. Lloyd. Cambridge, Mass.: Harvard University Press. *The Australian*, 8 June 2002.

Bakhtin, Mikhail. (1984) *Rabelais and His World*. Tr. Helene Iswolsky. Bloomington: Indiana University Press.

Barker, Francis. (1984) *The Tremulous Private Body: Essays on Subjection*. London: Methuen.

Bordo, Susan. (1993) *Unbearable Weight: Feminism, Western Culture and the Body*. Berkeley: University of California Press.

—— (1999) *The Male Body: A New Look at Men in Public and in Private*. New York: Farrar, Straus & Giroux.

Bourdieu, Pierre. [1972] (1977) *Outline of a Theory of Practice*. Tr. Richard Nice. Cambridge: Cambridge University Press.

—— [1979] (1984) *Distinction: A Social Critique of the Judgement of Taste*. Tr. Richard Nice. Cambridge, Mass.: Harvard University Press.

—— [1980] (1990a) *The Logic of Practice*. Tr. Richard Nice. Stanford: Stanford University Press.

—— (1990b) *In Other Words: Essays towards a Reflexive Sociology*. Tr. M. Adamson. Cambridge: Polity Press.

—— (1998) 'Is a Disinterested Act Possible?', in P. Bourdieu, *Practical Reason: On the Theory of Action*. Cambridge: Polity Press, pp. 75–91.

Branson, Jan and Miller, Don. (1995) *The Story of Betty Steel: Deaf Convict and Pioneer*. Petersham, NSW: Deafness Resources Australia.

Bray, Alan. (1982) *Homosexuality in Renaissance England*. London: Gay Men's Press.

Bryson, Anna. (1990) 'The Rhetoric of Status: Gesture Demeanour and the Image of the Gentleman in Sixteenth- and Seventeenth-Century England', in L. Gent and N. Llewellyn (eds), *Renaissance Bodies: The Human Figure in English Culture c.1540–1660*. London: Reaktion Books, pp. 136–53.

Burke, Peter. (1990) *The French Historical Revolution: The Annales School, 1929–1989*. London: Polity Press.

Butler, Judith. (1990) *Gender Trouble: Feminism and the Subversion of Identity*. New York: Routledge.

—— (1993) *Bodies that Matter: On the Discursive Limits of 'Sex'*. New York: Routledge.

Bynum, Carolyn Walker. (1991) *Fragmentation and Redemption: Essays on Gender and the Human Body in Medieval Religion*. New York: Zone Books.

Calhoun, Craig. (1993) 'Habitus, Field and Capital: The Question of Historical Specificity', in C. Calhoun, E. LiPuma and M. Postone (eds), *Bourdieu: Critical Perspectives*. London: Polity Press.

Cregan, Kate. (1999) 'Microcosmographia: Seventeenth-Century Theatres of Blood and the Construction of the Sexed Body'. PhD dissertation, Monash University, Melbourne.

—— (2004) 'Blood and Circuses', in E. T. Klaver (ed.), *Images of the Corpse: From the Renaissance to Cyberspace*. Wisconsin: Wisconsin University Press/Popular Press, pp. 39–62.

—— and James, Paul. (2002) 'Stem-Cell Alchemy: Techno-Science and the New Philosopher's Stone', *Arena Journal*, 19: 61–72.

Darnton, Robert. (1984) *The Great Cat Massacre and Other Episodes in French Cultural History*. Harmondsworth: Penguin.

Dickenson, Donna. (2002) 'Commodification of Human Tissue: Implications for Feminist and Development Ethics', *Developing World Bioethics*, 2 (1): 55–63.

Douglas, Mary. (1975) *Implicit Meanings: Essays in Anthropology*. London and Boston: Routledge and Kegan Paul.

—— [1970] (1996) *Natural Symbols: Explorations in Cosmology* (with a new Introduction). London: Routledge.

—— [1966] (2002) *Purity and Danger: An Analysis of Concept of Pollution and Taboo*. London: Routledge.

Duden, Barbara. (1991) *The Woman Beneath the Skin*. Tr. T. Dunlap. Cambridge, Mass.: Harvard University Press.

—— (1999) 'The Fetus on the "Farther Shore": Toward a History of the Unborn', in *Fetal Subject: Feminist Positions*. Philadelphia: University of Pennsylvania Press.

Elias, Norbert. (1985) *The Loneliness of the Dying*. Tr. E. Jephcott. London: Continuum.

—— (2000) *The Civilizing Process: Sociogenetic and Psychogenetic Investigations* (revised edition). Tr. E. Jephcott. Eds E. Dunning, J. Goudsblom and S. Mennell. Oxford: Blackwell Publishers.

Elias, Norbert and Scotson, John. (1965) *The Established and the Outsiders*. London: Cass & Co.

Far Eastern Economic Review, 15 November 2001.

Fardon, Richard. (1999) *Mary Douglas: An Intellectual Biography*. London: Routledge.

Featherstone, Mike, Hepworth, Mike and Turner, Bryan (eds). (1991) *The Body: Social Process and Cultural Theory*. London: Sage.

Feher, Michael (ed.). (1989) *Fragments for a History of the Human Body, Part 1–3*. New York: Zone Books.

Finkelstein, Joanne. (1991) *The Fashioned Self*. London: Polity.

Foucault, Michel. (1975) *The Birth of the Clinic: An Archaeology of Medical Perception*. Tr. A. M. Sheridan Smith. New York: Random House.

—— (1988a) *Madness and Civilization: A History of Insanity in the Age of Reason*. Tr. R. Howard. New York: Vintage Books.

—— (1988b) *Politics, Philosophy, Culture: Interviews and Other Writings, 1977–1984*, Tr. A. Sheridan and others. Ed. L. D. Kritzman. New York: Routledge.

—— (1990) *The History of Sexuality, Volume 1*. Tr. R. Hurley. Harmondsworth: Penguin.

—— (1991) *Discipline and Punish: The Birth of the Prison*. Tr. A. Sheridan. London: Penguin.

—— (1994) *The Archaeology of Knowledge*. Tr. A. M. Sheridan Smith. London: Routledge.

Franklin, Sarah. (1997) *Embodied Progress: A Cultural Account of Assisted Conception*. London: Routledge.

Gallagher, Catherine and Laqueur, Thomas (eds). (1987) *The Making of the Modern Body: Sexuality and Society in the Nineteenth Century*. Berkeley: The University of California Press.

Gatens, Moira. (1983) 'Critique of the Sex/Gender Distinction', in J. Allen and P. Patton (eds), *Interventions after Marx*. Sydney: Intervention.

Genetics Policy Institute. (2004) 'Landmark Conference for United Nations on Human Cloning and Stem Cell Research', 11 May, www.eurekalert.org/pub_releases/2004-05/dnl-lcf051104.php

Gilman, Sander. (1988) *Disease and Representation: Images of Illness from Madness to AIDS*. Ithaca: Cornell University Press.

—— (1999) *Making the Body Beautiful: A Cultural History of Aesthetic Surgery*. Princeton: Princeton University Press.

Gittings, Clare. (1984) *Death, Burial and the Individual in Early Modern England*. London: Croom Helm.

Goudsblom, Jan and Mennell, Stephen (eds). (1998) *The Norbert Elias Reader*. Oxford: Blackwell.

Greenblatt, Stephen. (1980) *Renaissance Self-Fashioning: From More to Shakespeare*. Chicago: University of Chicago Press.

Grosz, Liz. (1994) *Volatile Bodies: Toward a Corporeal Feminism*. Bloomington: Indiana University Press.

—— (1995) *Time, Space and Perversion: The Politics of Bodies*. New York: Routledge.

Hancock, P., Hughes, B., Jagger, E., Paterson, K., Russell, R., Tulle-Winton, E. and Tyler, M. (2000) *The Body, Culture and Society*. Buckingham: Open University Press.

Haraway, Donna. (1991) *Simians, Cyborgs and Women: The Reinvention of Nature*. London: Free Association Books.

—— (1997) *Modest_Witness@Second_Millennium.FemaleMan©_Meets_OncoMouse™: Feminism and Technoscience*. New York and London: Routledge.

Harding, Sandra. (1986) *The Science Question in Feminism*. Ithaca: Cornell University Press.

Highfield, Roger. (2004) 'Scientists Lobby the UN to Ban Cloning', *The Telegraph*, 31 May 2004.

James, Paul. (1996) *Nation Formation: Towards a Theory of Abstract Community*. London: Sage.

—— (2001) 'Abstracting Modes of Exchange: Gifts, Commodities and Money', *Suomen Antropologi*, 26 (2): 4–22.

—— (2005) *Globalism, Nationalism, Tribalism: Bringing Theory Back In*. London: Sage.

Jenkins, Richard. (1998) *Questions of Competence: Culture, Classification and Intellectual Disability*. Cambridge: Cambridge University Press.

Jewson, Norman. (1976) 'The Disappearance of the Sick Man from Medical Cosmologies: 1770–1870', *Sociology*, 10: 225–44.

Jordanova, Ludmilla. (1989) *Sexual Visions: Images of Gender in Science*. Madison: University of Wisconsin Press.

Kristeva, Julia. (1980) *Powers of Horror: An Essay on Abjection*, Tr. L. Roudiez. New York: Columbia University Press.

Laqueur, Thomas. (1992) *Making Sex: Body and Gender from the Greeks to Freud*. Cambridge, Mass.: Harvard University Press.

Lovell, Terry. (2000) 'Thinking Feminism with and against Bourdieu', in B. Fowler (ed.), *Reading Bourdieu on Society and Culture*. Oxford: Blackwell Publishers.

Luke, Carmen. (1989) *Pedagogy, Printing, and Protestantism: The Discourse on Childhood*. New York: State University of New York Press.

Lyotard, Jean-François. (1984) *The Postmodern Condition: A Report on Knowledge*. Tr. G. Bennington and B. Massumi. Minneapolis: University of Minnesota Press.

Martin, Emily. (1992) *The Woman in the Body: A Cultural Analysis of Reproduction*. Boston: Beacon Press.

Mauss, Marcel. (1979) *Sociology and Psychology: Essays*. Tr. B. Brewster. London: Routledge & Kegan Paul.

—— (1990) *The Gift: the Forms and Reasons for Exchange in Archaic Societies*. Tr. W. D. Halls. Foreword by Mary Douglas. New York and London: W.W. Norton and Co.

McNay, Lois. (1992) *Foucault and Feminism: Power, Gender and the Self*. Cambridge: Polity Press.

Mennell, Stephen. (1991) 'On the Civilising of Appetite', in M. Featherstone, M. Hepworth and B. Turner (eds), *The Body: Social Process and Cultural Theory*. London: Sage, pp. 126–56.

—— (1996) *All Manners of Food: Eating and Taste in England and France from the Middle Ages to the Present* (second edition). Urbana: University of Illinois Press.

Moi, Toril. (1990) 'Appropriating Bourdieu: Feminist Theory and Pierre Bourdieu's Sociology of Culture'. Reprinted in T. Moi (1999) *What Is a Woman? And Other Essays*. Oxford: Oxford University Press.

Nettleton, Sarah and Watson, Jonathan. (1998) *The Body in Everyday Life*. London: Routledge.

Oakley, Ann. (1972) *Sex, Gender and Society*. London: Temple Smith.

Orgel, Stephen. (1996) *Impersonations: the Performance of Gender in Shakespeare's England.* Cambridge: Cambridge University Press.

Parfitt, George (ed.). (1988) *Ben Jonson: The Complete Poems.* Harmondsworth: Penguin.

Robbins, Derek. (2000) *Bourdieu and Culture.* London: Sage.

Said, Edward. (1978) *Orientalism.* New York: Pantheon Books.

Scarry, Elaine. (1985) *The Body in Pain: The Making and Unmaking of the World.* Oxford: Oxford University Press.

Sennett, Richard. (1994) *Flesh and Stone: The Body and the City in Western Civilization.* New York: W.W. Norton & Co.

Seymour, Wendy. (1998) *Remaking the Body: Rehabilitation and Change.* Sydney: Allen & Unwin.

Shakespeare, Tom (ed.). (1998) *The Disability Studies Reader: Social Science Perspectives.* London: Cassell.

Shakespeare, William. (1977) *Shakespeare's Sonnets.* Stephen Booth (ed.). New Haven and London: Yale University Press.

Sharp, Geoff. (1985) 'Constitutive Abstraction and Social Practice', *Arena Journal*, 70: 48–82.

Shildrick, Margrit. (1997) *Leaky Bodies and Boundaries: Feminism, Postmodernism and (Bio)Ethics.* London: Routledge.

Shilling, Chris. (1993) *The Body and Social Theory.* London: Sage.

—— (2005) *The Body in Culture, Technology and Society.* London: Sage.

Simmel, Georg. (1950) *The Sociology of Georg Simmel.* Tr. K. H. Wolff. New York: The Free Press.

Sontag, Susan. (1991) *Illness and Metaphor/AIDS and its Metaphors.* Harmondsworth: Penguin.

Stone, Lawrence. (1979) *The Family, Sex and Marriage in England 1500–1800.* (abridged edition). London: Penguin.

Synnott, Alan. (1993) *The Body Social: Symbolism, Self and Society.* London: Routledge.

Turner, Bryan S. [1983] (1991) *Religion and Social Theory* (second edition). London: Sage.

—— [1984] (1996) *The Body and Society: Explorations in Social Theory* (second edition). London: Sage.

—— with Samson, Colin. [1987] (1995) *Medical Power and Social Knowledge* (second edition). London: Sage.

Turner, Victor. (1982) *From Ritual to Performance: The Human Seriousness of Play.* New York: Performing Arts Journal Publications.

Weeks, Jeffrey. (1991) *Sexualities and its Discontents: Meanings, Myths and Modern Sexualities.* London: Routledge.

Williams, Simon and Bendelow, Gillian. (1998) *The Lived Body: Sociological Themes, Embodied Issues.* London: Routledge.

Ziguras, Christopher. (2004) *Self-Care: Embodiment, Personal Autonomy and the Shaping of Health Consciousness.* London: Routledge.

Index

Bourdieu, Pierre *cont.*
  gender 68, 81, 84, 86–87
  habitus 64–88 *passim*, 100, 102
  hexis 68–88 *passim*, 100, 187, 189
  the individual 68–85 *passim*
  interest 84–85
  Kabyle 64–86 *passim*, 187
  The Logic of Practice 66–67, 82–83
  manners 69–70, 75–76
  mind 81, 83
  norms 74–75, 79
  objectification 69, 71, 82
  objective, objectivity, objectivism
      69–86 *passim*
  Outline of a Theory of Practice 66–67,
      75, 78, 82, 84, 86
  physicality 66–82 *passim*
  power 68, 78–79, 81, 87–88
  regulation 70–71, 79
  rites 68–69, 73–74, 84
  ritual 67–84 *passim*
  space 11, 45, 65–71 *passim*
  subjective, subjectivity 82–83
Branson, Jan 87
  deafness 87
Breughel, Pieter 34
Burke, Peter 20
Butler, Judith 12, 87–88, 111, 113–136,
      143, 145, 147–150, 152, 156,
      167–168, 170, 173–175, 188, 190,
      195, 198
  agents and agency 147
  being 117–119, 122–123, 135
  Bodies That Matter 120–131, 175
  bodily parts 122–123
  boundaries and boundary-crossing
      115–133 *passim*
  childhood 121, 123, 126
  chora 120–121
  class 116, 124–126, 128
  community 125, 134
  construct 115–131 *passim*
  control 119–120, 123, 130
  corporeality 119
  culture 125, 133–136 *passim*
  death 126–127
  deconstruction 115, 130
  difference 114–136 *passim*
  discourse 114–134 *passim*
  disembodiment 115
  drag 125, 130, 134
  epistemology 123, 135
  female and femininity 116, 120–131
      passim

Butler, Judith *cont.*
  feminism 114–132 *passim*
  gender 88, 114–136 *passim*
  gender-ambivalence 126–127
  Gender Trouble 115–120, 175
  hegemony 118, 123–126, 134
  heterosexuality 116–133 *passim*, 175
  homosexuality 117–119, 122–125, 131
  Imaginary 114, 122–125, 131, 133
  the individual, individualization and
      individuality 115, 124–125, 133–134
  language 88
  language games 115, 118–119, 135
  lesbian 114–133 *passim*
  male and masculinity 115–127 *passim*
  material 14
  metaphor 115, 120, 128, 130, 135–136
  norms 116–126 *passim*
  pain 122–123, 132–133
  performativity 88
  power 116–136 *passim*, 168
  regimes 116
  regulation 116, 119–120, 128, 147
  sex and sexuality 114–133 *passim*
  signification 118–119, 123, 126,
      129–130, 136
  Symbolic 114, 122–124, 126–128,
      132–133
  queer studies and politics 114–132
      passim
  race 116, 124–127
  radical inclusion 132
  transgressive 116–117
  universalization 115–136 *passim*

Cambridge University 19
Canguilhem, Georges 44
Castiglione 76
Cather, Willa 126–127, 134–135
children and childhood 2, 10, 39, 81,
      117, 155, 167, 171; *see also* Ariès,
      Butler, Douglas, Elias, Kristeva
civilisation 6, 20; *see also* Elias
civilising structures 29
Cixous, Hélène 114
class 1, 11, 60, 141, 143, 155, 188–189;
      see also Ariès, Bordo, Bourdieu,
      Butler, Elias, Foucault
  cloning 5, 189–198 *passim*
  Collège de France 43
  Colonial Office 93
  commodification 4, 6, 79, 189
  communication 3–6, 48, 69, 135;
      see also Douglas, Haraway